Rewind, Replay

# Rewind, Replay

## Britain and the Video Boom, 1978–92

Johnny Walker

EDINBURGH
University Press

*For Nik, Ro, Pen and Will*

Edinburgh University Press is one of the leading university presses in the UK. We publish academic books and journals in our selected subject areas across the humanities and social sciences, combining cutting-edge scholarship with high editorial and production values to produce academic works of lasting importance. For more information visit our website: edinburghuniversitypress.com

© Johnny Walker, 2022

Edinburgh University Press Ltd
The Tun – Holyrood Road
12 (2f) Jackson's Entry
Edinburgh EH8 8PJ

Typeset in Ehrhardt MT Pro by
Cheshire Typesetting Ltd, Cuddington, Cheshire,
and printed and bound by CPI Group (UK) Ltd, Croydon, CR0 4YY

A CIP record for this book is available from the British Library

ISBN 978 1 4744 5447 6 (hardback)
ISBN 978 1 4744 5448 3 (paperback)
ISBN 978 1 4744 5449 0 (webready PDF)
ISBN 978 1 4744 5450 6 (epub)

The right of Johnny Walker to be identified as author of this work has been asserted in accordance with the Copyright, Designs and Patents Act 1988 and the Copyright and Related Rights Regulations 2003 (SI No. 2498).

# Contents

| | |
|---|---|
| *List of Figures* | vi |
| *Acknowledgements* | viii |
| Introduction: Rewind, Replay | 1 |
| 1. We've Got It Taped | 17 |
| 2. Shrugging Off the Recession | 62 |
| 3. Threats and Benefits | 95 |
| 4. Regulation and Adaptation | 133 |
| 5. Independent Spirit vs Corporate Muscle | 173 |
| Conclusion: Video Legacies | 215 |
| *Select Bibliography* | 227 |
| *Select Film/TV/Videography* | 233 |
| *Select Periodicals* | 238 |
| *Index* | 240 |

# Figures

| | | |
|---|---|---|
| I.1 | The last Blockbuster in *The Last Blockbuster* | 2 |
| I.2 | Dominic Sandbrook evoking the mythology of the video nasties | 8 |
| I.3 | Enid in Prano Bailey-Bond's horror film, *Censor* | 10 |
| 1.1 | Videos for discos | 20 |
| 1.2 | Intervision's first catalogue projects diversity to prospective customers | 24 |
| 1.3 | Mountain Video advertises feature films for 'all the family' | 26 |
| 1.4 | Sex over Spielberg? | 30 |
| 1.5 | Soho's Adult Video Centre advertises video copies of uncut sex films | 35 |
| 1.6 | French Label offers its consumers a 'double guarantee' | 38 |
| 1.7 | The (initial) branding incoherence of independent distributor Hokushin | 41 |
| 1.8 | Examples of Intervision's generic, 'Family Entertainment' video sleeves | 43 |
| 1.9 | VCL offers consumers an enhanced television experience | 48 |
| 2.1 | The managing directors of Intervision, Richard Cooper and Mike Tenner | 63 |
| 2.2 | Catalogues of two of the earliest mail order video clubs, The Video Club and Video Unlimited | 67 |
| 2.3 | One of Joe Pina's stores: The Video Cassette Shop | 69 |
| 2.4 | A prince of industry: Joe Pina of Carnaby Video | 72 |
| 2.5 | Archive news footage of Dave Pan & Sweets Centre (later Pioneer Video Emporium), Leicester, c.1982 | 76 |
| 3.1 | Intervision's first ever children's catalogue | 99 |
| 3.2 | Go Video brings a children's comic to life in *Video Comic* | 101 |
| 3.3 | Copies of Channel Video's My Video Party came with supplementary activities for children | 101 |
| 3.4 | Fletcher Video plugged a gap in the market by offering consumers adaptations of fables made popular by Walt Disney Studios | 107 |

| | | |
|---|---|---|
| 3.5 | *Cannibal Holocaust* and *SS Experiment Camp*: promotional images | 109 |
| 3.6 | Merlin Video encourages dealers to stock two 'hard action' videos | 111 |
| 3.7 | Aping VIPCO's branding | 118 |
| 3.8 | Remarketed as a 'nasty': the first and second video releases of *Dark Places* | 120 |
| 4.1 | A sign of things to come: a haul of pirated cassettes | 134 |
| 4.2 | Go Video was one of many independent distributors with international connections | 141 |
| 4.3 | VCL's 'descriptive' new logo | 145 |
| 4.4 | Pushing the envelope post-VRA | 155 |
| 4.5 | The world's lowest prices | 157 |
| 5.1 | Two variations of the West Coast Video logo | 180 |
| 5.2 | The logo of Ritz Video Film Hire | 181 |
| 5.3 | The exterior and interior of a Ritz shop, c.1990 | 181 |
| 5.4 | The Video Trade Association's 'Family Code', launched in 1988. | 185 |
| 5.5 | Coming soon to a high street near you: Hollywood Nites | 193 |
| 5.6 | The Hollywood Nites symbol group permitted shopkeepers to retain their original business name | 195 |
| 5.7 | *My Beautiful Video Shop* homages *My Beautiful Laundrette* | 197 |
| 5.8 | Parkfield apes the video artwork of *My Beautiful Laundrette* | 198 |
| 5.9 | One of Blockbuster's first British stores, Clapham Junction | 201 |
| C.1 | Video Box Office membership card, c. early 2000s | 218 |
| C.2 | Choices – one of Blockbuster's British rivals | 218 |
| C.3 | 20th Century Flicks, Bristol, as it appears in *The Last Video Store* | 222 |
| C.4 | Street protest: Free Blockbuster | 223 |

# Acknowledgements

Thank you for reading this book. It's very much appreciated.

Thanks also to Gillian Leslie at Edinburgh University Press, who contracted the book after a somewhat turbulent beginning and for continuing showing faith in me and my work. I extend my gratitude to the wider EUP team (past and present), especially Eddie Clark, Emma Rees, Richard Strachan and Sam Johnson. The following people were also very supportive during the book's early stages, and I appreciate their encouragement, professionalism, and help: James Campbell (especially you, my friend), Tim Mitchell, Jelena Stanovnik, Amy Damutz and Katie Gallof.

I am lucky to work alongside terrific scholars and friends within the Department of Arts at Northumbria University: Sarah Bowman, Mark Davenport, Roger Domeneghetti, Kate Egan (who is available to talk 'video history' with me at any time), Russ Hunter, Steve Jones (whose critical feedback is second to none), Sarah Ralph-Lane, Jamie Sexton, James Leggott, Noel McLoughlin, Gabriel Moreno Esparza, Massimo Ragnedda and Clarissa Smith.

I have terrific PhD students in Maddie Culver-Goldstein, Adam Herron, Erin Wiegand; they have shown me much support and patience during the research and writing process.

Thanks also to David Gleeson, Solomon Lennox, Matthew Potter and Steve Taylor for the financial support and periods of study leave that allowed me to make real headway on the project.

The late Peter Hutchings offered me excellent advice at every turn. Rest in power, Hutch.

I can't put into words how grateful I am for the friendship of the following individuals, who I can always rely on for laughter, encouragement, and doses of straight-talking: Shelly Addison, Emma Casey, Austin Fisher, Gary Jenkins, Neil Jackson, Mary Laing, Laura Mee, Missy Molloy, Meryl Shriver-Rice, Nathan Stephens Griffin, Hunter Vaughan and Tom Watson. Legends, the bloody lot of you.

In 2019 I was fortunate enough to meet Ian Richardson, who kindly shared with me his mammoth collection of video business ephemera. I remain floored by this act of selflessness. That encounter and the many chats we've had since have improved the contents of this book no end. Thanks mate!

The following scholars and individuals offered help in the form of feedback on chapter drafts, at conferences, in general conversation, or have expressed generosity in other ways: Peter Alilunas, Mark Betz, Jilly Boyce Kaye, Matt Boyd Smith, Allan Bryce, Oliver Carter, James Chapman, Steve Chibnall, David Church, Maddie Culver-Goldstein, Kate Egan, David Gregory, Elena Gorfinkel, Stuart Hanson, Dan Herbert, Tanya Horeck, Neil Jackson, Mark Kermode, Shaun Kimber, John Mercer, Kaitlynn Mendes, Paul McDonald, Mark McKenna, Rachael Mosely, Richard Nowell, Julian Petley, Eric Schaefer, Martha Shearer, Josh Schulze, Iain Robert Smith, Justin Smith, Graeme Spurr, Jaap Verheul, Ed Vollans, Tom Watson, Helen Wheatley and Helen Wood.

Thanks to Alex Godfrey for letting me tenuously plug *Rewind, Replay* in *The Guardian*, to Tris Thompson being a genuine soul (and for sending me things in the post – please keep doing that), to Martin Brooks for sharing with me swathes of research materials and titbits of crucial information, to Jason Impey for asking me to be a talking head in *VIPCO: The Untold Story* (and to Mark McKenna for setting that up), to James Newton for interviewing me about this research on his podcast *Newton Talks*, to Darren Gordon and Tony Earnshaw for granting me permission to use hi-res scans of 'pre-cert' cover art, to Kevin Hall for sharing copies of trade periodicals I couldn't otherwise access, to Mark McKenna for all the meaningful chats over the years, and to Steve Chibnall, both for showing (before selling) me the copy of *Video Business* that inspired this research in the first place and then writing a letter in support of a project that could have resulted in a wholly different book (had the funders funded it).

Individuals working at the following places have been terrific: the British Film Institute, the British Library Boston Spa, and Northumbria University Library. I owe a lot to both ProQuest's Entertainment Industry Magazine Archive and LexisNexis, too.

Prano Bailey-Bond and Helen Jones helped me source, and granted me permission to use, a promotional still from *Censor* in the introductory chapter, and Aaron Hendy of *The Argus* granted me permission to reproduce various press photographs. Thanks all!

Many people have sold me rare video-related artefacts over the years. Of those individuals, I'd like to acknowledge the wonderful Jane (RIP) from Leicester Market and Val and Steve (RIP) from Tynemouth Market.

Conversations with the following people proved hugely significant: Joseph Brant, Steve Ellison, Barrie Gold, David Kerekes, Marc Morris, Tim Murray, Martin Myers, 'Pops' of Pioneer Video Emporium, Mike Tenner, Darren Stuart and Jake West.

Thanks to the administrators and members of the Pre-Cert forum (http://pre-cert.co.uk), and the following Facebook groups: General Pre-Cert and DPP Chat, Videorama, Horror VHS Collectors Unite, and Cult Cinema Collectors Corner.

I finished this book in Rustic Cup, Whitley Bay. Thanks to the great staff there, and also to the awesome people working at another of my favourite Whitley cafes, Kith and Kin. Oat lattes for the win.

I have delivered several papers based on research for this book at: the Media, Communication and Cultural Studies Association's annual conference (Northumbria University, 2014), Archaeologies of Media (University of Bradford, 2014), Birmingham City University (2015), the Society for Cinema and Media Studies annual conference (Atlanta, 2016), King's College London (2017), the Screen Studies annual conference (University of Glasgow, 2018), the University of Leicester (2018), and the biannual conference of the International Association for Media and History (Northumbria University, 2019). I thank those who were present at any of the aforementioned talks for their insightful questions and helpful comments, and to the following individuals for inviting me to present at their Institutions: Oliver Carter (Birmingham City), Jilly Boyce Kaye (Leicester) and Iain Robert Smith (King's College, London).

Revised parts of Chapter 1 have previously appeared in a special issue of *Post Script: Essays in Film and Humanities* ('Home Video and Media Texts', 35.3, summer 2016) and the *Routledge Companion to British Cinema History* (2020). Thank you to the editors of *Post Script*, Gerald Duchovnay and J. P. Telotte, the journal's sponsors, the Texas A&M University-Commerce and the Georgia Institute of Technology, and the editor of the special issue, Richard Nowell, for allowing me to reprint material here. The same goes for the editors of the *Routledge Companion*, I. Q. Hunter, Laraine Porter and Justin Smith, and to the volume's publisher, Taylor & Francis. Some of the material about 'kidvids' in Chapter 3 first appeared in the *Historical Journal of Film, Radio and Television* (37.4, 2017). Thanks to James Chapman and Taylor & Francis for allowing me to reprint parts of the article in this volume.

Big-league thanks go to Susan 'Granny Sooz' Chivers, whose support with childcare, cups of tea and day-to-day mockery has played a major role in the completion of this project. Thanks, pet.

Endless thanks to my parents, Jacqueline and Robert. I feel very fortunate to have been raised by such caring individuals who continue to support me and my interests and who play such an active role in mine and my partner's children's lives. Lots of love to you both.

Finally, I'd like to give the biggest thanks of all my partner, Nikki, and our wonderful children, Rowan and Penny. Nik: thank you for continuing to love me, for showing patience (sometimes) and understanding (always), and for being the best role model for the kids. We are beyond lucky to have you in our lives. Ro and Pen: cuddles, kisses and smiles from you two are the greatest gifts. I love you and your mammy so much. And who could forget Willis, the best dog in town. Love you, mate, even when you eat the kids' toast.

INTRODUCTION

# Rewind, Replay

>...the history of video in Great Britain...
would be a book unto itself.
>
> Joshua M. Greenberg, *From Betamax to Blockbuster*

Those too young to know otherwise would be forgiven for assuming that the pastime of video rental, whereby individuals went to their local video shop to rent a pre-recorded videocassette for the evening, was, like hamburgers and southern fried chicken, a US phenomenon. Until its filing for bankruptcy in 2010, the Blockbuster Video brand, owned by US conglomerate Viacom since 1994, was 'the dominant player in the [video] rental business' and the mainstream public face of video store culture throughout the globe.[1] Established in Dallas, Texas, in 1985, within three years it was North America's leading rental chain and, in the decade that followed, penetrated markets all over the world. Today, when screen entertainment is accessed largely via various streaming platforms, and when at the time of writing there is only one remaining Blockbuster store in operation (in Bend, Oregon, USA), Blockbuster's 'yellow and blue' branding remains, for many, 'iconic': a nostalgic signifier of a bygone era.[2]

In March 2021, in a somewhat ironic turn of events, the streaming service that usurped Blockbuster's empire in the mid-2000s, Netflix, released *The Last Blockbuster* (Taylor Morden, 2020), a documentary exploring Bend's quirky anachronism.[3] The film is, in part, a human drama: an introspective look at how a group of passionate individuals, led by committed store manager Sandi Harding (affectionately nicknamed 'Blockbuster Mom'), have shaped the Blockbuster store into a community space once again: a heritage site, which could, at any minute, close for good. But the film is also, to quote the Sundance Institute, an 'entertaining tribute' to the video shop era, and a film that happens to be another in a long list of documentaries and narrative features of the past few years that, in various ways,

Figure I.1 The last Blockbuster in *The Last Blockbuster*.

celebrate pop cultural touchstones of the 1980s and 1990s, of which video rental was one, and which Blockbuster, as *The Last Blockbuster* shows, continues to emblematise.[4]

From its beginnings up to its demise, Blockbuster Inc., like the McDonald's fast-food chain, denoted capitalism of an 'American' style. Its global expansion was rapid, aggressive, uncompromising.[5] Prior to the digital age when Blockbuster's fortunes started to wane, it was operating around 9,000 stores across the world in territories as vast as the US, Europe, Asia and Australia.[6] Its executives' goal to create an environment and consumer experience that was the same no matter which store you visited was, as scholars such as Joshua M. Greenberg have shown, inspired by McDonald's. Its chief marketing executive had worked for McDonald's for almost twenty years prior to joining the company. In 1988, at a video business convention in the USA, an image of Blockbuster's CEO Wayne Huizenga was projected next to a photograph of McDonald's CEO Ray Kroc – as clear as any indication of the similarities between the company visions.[7] To all intents and purposes, Blockbuster became McDonald's home video equivalent, and, like the fast-food chain, an 'icon of Americana' known the world over.[8]

Of course, Blockbuster was not the only corporate video chain (nor was it the first video chain to cite McDonald's as an influence – see Chapter 5). In the US alone it had several heavy-weight competitors throughout its history, including West Coast Video, Hollywood Video and

Movie Gallery. But there were also thousands of national chains throughout the world, including, among others, Video Flicks in Australia, Xtra-Vision in Ireland, Christianshavn Video in Denmark, Ritz Video Film Hire in the UK, and, within each country, a multitude of regional chains. None of these were 'the same'. Yet they all strived, in their own way, to create a consistent experience for their customers that Blockbuster would come to embody. Not insignificantly, the named examples above were all acquired by Blockbuster at various points between the 1990s and the mid-2000s.[9]

The narrative I have sketched here is all too familiar: a classic example of Americanisation, or to be more specific, and to ape George Ritzer's term, 'McDonaldization', whereby an American corporation bulldozes into national territories, imposing on native consumers a standardised, sanitised consumer experience.[10] What is missing from my – admittedly reductive – account of Blockbuster's expansion, however, is the contribution that the aforementioned national chains – and indeed, the thousands upon thousands of regional chains and single, independently owned video shops – made to the business that Blockbuster proceeded to dominate. These stores carved a niche, a consumer experience, a set of expectations, a culture, for Blockbuster to then exploit. The most significant of Blockbuster's acquisitions, it turns out, was the British chain, Ritz, which it took over in 1992, enabling the US company to penetrate the UK and Europe, and acquire almost 1,000 shops overnight in the process.[11] Put differently, Britain's Ritz in many ways *made* Blockbuster the international force it was. Yet Ritz and other shops like it are scarcely remembered, invoked only as statistics to attest to Blockbuster's global domination.[12]

It might seem obvious, pointless even, to reiterate such a blatant truism, that Blockbuster owed its success to a series of international acquisitions. But there is much nuance missing from this story. Whereas the prevailing image of mainstream video rental is one of a hugely successful US behemoth, it is important not to reduce its acquisitions *solely to* their status as acquisitions. Before they were Blockbusters – or smaller Blockbuster Express stores – they had identities all their own. The stores, the countries from which they stemmed, and the iterations of the 'video business' they helped shape and represented for their respective communities were integral not only to Blockbuster's attainment, but to that of the penetration of home video as a truly global phenomenon. The history of the shops and the distributors that supplied them with product are stories of bespoke nuance; stories that, for the most part, are yet to be told. This book is Britain's.

Before we proceed, some clarity is needed. By claiming that such 'stories are yet to be told', I do not mean to imply that scholars have not yet looked 'beyond' Blockbuster or, for that matter, beyond the formal distribution channels of corporate Hollywood that the chain was committed to upholding. There are several significant interventions that do precisely this, albeit usually with a focus on North America. Fredrick Wasser's *Veni, Vidi, Video: The Hollywood Empire and the VCR*, for example, while ostensibly concerned with the relationship intimated by its title also gives some detailed consideration to, for example, independent video distributors and the various socio-cultural-economic factors that explain North America's 'video revolution'.[13] Others consider video's cultural impact, such as Greenberg in *From Betamax to Blockbuster: Video Stores and the Invention of Movies on Video*, which addresses video cinephilia, 'mom and pop' video stores of the 1970s and the coming of Blockbuster in the following decade. A special issue of *Media Fields Journal* is dedicated to the history and legacies of video stores, while Daniel Herbert's *Videoland: Movie Culture at the American Video Store* explores how video stores across America 'altered people's space- and taste-based relations with movie culture', and provides numerous widely diverse case studies.[14] Michael Z. Newman's *Video Revolutions: On the History of a Medium* focuses on the changing meanings of video, from the use of magnetic tape in the television industry in the 1960s and the dawning of the VCR to the use of video 'in relation to certain other cultural practices, such as making home movies and artworks'.[15] Peter Alilunas, in *Smutty Little Movies: The Creation and Regulation of Adult Video*, explores how nascent video technology led to a boom in adult product in the US, and the impact this had on the adult film business and popular culture more broadly.[16] Other work takes interest in – broadly speaking – the *materiality* of video, as in the case of Lucas Hildebrand's *Inherent Vice: Bootleg Histories of Videotape and Copyright*,[17] and its spectatorial implications, as in Caetlin Benson-Allott's *Killer Tapes and Shattered Screens: Video Spectatorship From VHS to File Sharing*.[18] Meanwhile, work by the likes of Ramon Labato, Joshua Neves and Bhaskar Sarkar, and others, examines the experience of video beyond formal channels of access, in Africa, the Global South and elsewhere.[19] The study of video, as my brief overview attests, is broad. But where does Britain fit?

For a while, when Britain's relationship with home video was the subject of scholarly assessment at all, the focus tended to be not on industry, but rather people's usage of video hard- and software. For example, writing by Mark Levy, Ann Gray, Barrie Gunter, Marie Gillespie and Mallory Wober from the late 1980s and early 1990s is based on empirical data accrued via, for example, interviews conducted with individuals in households about their own personal usage of the VCR.[20] In all such cases, the emphasis is primarily on the practice of off-air recording (or 'time shifting'), and which members of the households under scrutiny watch what and when. Such research is hugely important. Yet the role of the pre-recorded videocassette *business* – video distribution, video shops and the retail experience – is rarely, if ever, acknowledged in such accounts.

Other scholarship investigating video in Britain tends to be anchored in some fashion or other to the 'video nasties' moral panic of the early-to-mid 1980s: the outcome of a knee-jerk response to video's boom in popularity by religious campaign groups, the media, the Conservative government and other parties, intoxicated by the notion that video, as a new industry not yet regulated, might 'deprave and corrupt' audiences through exposure to uncensored horror films.[21] The outcome of the panic saw the passing of new legislation, the Video Recordings Act 1984 (VRA), and the banning of thirty-nine video titles in all.[22] Significant work by, for example, Martin Barker and Julian Petley, has assessed the moral panic, its coverage in the press and the VRA, to counter pervasive assumptions about the media and its alleged effects on audiences.[23] Petley offers some noteworthy industry commentary, drawing from interview material with specific distributors and past Secretaries of the British Board of Film Classification, although it is fair to argue that he, like Barker, is primarily concerned with matters pertaining to press discourse and legislation, rather than the day-to-day workings of the video business itself.[24]

Work that has engaged more overtly with industrial concerns tends to do so, again, in relation to alleged 'unseemly' practices from which the video nasties panic was said to stem. Julian Upton's article on what he terms 'the rise and fall of Britain's first pre-recorded video distributors', for example, while useful in many ways (I draw from it a number of times across the book), iterates what is essentially a false dichotomy between what the author terms 'respectable' independent distributors and their catalogues of vanilla Hollywood fare, versus 'opportunistic' independent distributors trading in exploitation films and pornography.[25] Many of Upton's arguments ring true – such as his claims that the working classes gravitated more towards video at the beginning, and, indeed, that independent distributors handled greater numbers of exploitation films – but it is unfortunate that he silos distributors off from each other, given that, as the following chapters reveal, there is much that binds them.

Interventions by Kate Egan and Mark McKenna have explored the 'video nasty' sobriquet as one having taken on new meaning in popular culture since its coinage by *Sunday Times* journalist Peter Chippendale in

1982.²⁶ Egan, for example, in *Trash or Treasure? Censorship and the Changing Meanings of the Video Nasties*, offers astute analysis of the video nasty press response, how distributors marketed horror titles to the public, how such titles have become desirable among horror fan communities, and how subsequent companies have capitalised on the mythology of the video nasty by rereleasing notable titles that, in various ways, evoke their past statuses as illegal objects.²⁷ More recently, McKenna's *Nasty Business: The Marketing and Distribution of the Video Nasties* extends Egan's work into the DVD and Blu-Ray age, drawing similar conclusions, yet also calling for greater engagement with the economic context within which video nasties circulate. Noting than an overemphasis on the video nasties controversy in popular discourse (discussed below) has 'worked to limit critical discussion and obscure industrial history', McKenna seeks to explore the commercial imperatives that birthed the video nasties in the first place, to see the films as products behind which there was – and remains to this day via Blu-Ray re-releases and so on – industrial strategising.²⁸ I am sympathetic to McKenna's approach, and the present volume also foregrounds industrial (and cultural) analysis to broaden understanding of what is so often explained away as 'the video nasty era'. However, while McKenna's book is clearly an industrial history, it is an industrial history *of the video nasties* specifically: films which, while comprising a range of works from various decades, countries and economic/commercial contexts, were brought together *arbitrarily* by law enforcement officers for reasons beyond the strategic planning of their distributors. 'Video nasty' might today be, as McKenna acknowledges, a 'commercial category' that resonates internationally, but this was not always the case.²⁹ Focusing on the distribution trajectories of thirty-nine randomly collated videocassettes tells us much about the cult mythology of the video nasty and how it has grown since the 1980s – an approach Egan spearheaded with *Trash or Treasure?* – but it is little concerned about the nascent video business as a functioning whole.

McKenna is correct when he argues that, today, the term 'video nasties' functions as a 'shorthand for excess'.³⁰ This is a notion that rings true in horror- and cult film fan communities, where the embracing of cinematic 'excess' remains a central component in participants' championing of texts that are located beyond the realms of the mainstream or good taste.³¹ Such an attitude is emblematised by archetypal coffee-table volumes, emergent from the horror film fan community since the 1990s, such as *Shock! Horror! Astounding Artwork from the Video Nasty Era*, *Art of the Nasty*, *Video Nasties* and *Video Nasties 2*, which – while they reproduce video artwork from the 1980s and thus have value as historical documents – ultimately take liberties, romanticising the early video period (in an admittedly tongue-in-cheek fashion) to fit a specific agenda; one that foregrounds the illicit appeal of banned videocassettes as 'residual reminders of an authentic and meaningful' age of horror film fandom.[32] The prevailing image of the early video business in such accounts, thus, is of one where distributors and shops – 'brash and out for profit' – trade in sex, horror and nothing else.[33]

Of course, it is in the interest of cultural arbiters to keep this version of history – of the early video business as a period of outlaw antics – alive. As Egan explains, this period is routinely framed in fan discourse as a '"golden" time, an "anarchic heyday", where a previously marginalised culture of exploitation and horror films became widely available in the local corner shop much to the delight of horror fans throughout Britain'.[34] McKenna shares this view. Like Egan, he argues that the nostalgia upon which this mythologising process hinges, while problematic for the historian, is paramount for horror fan cultures; that the aforementioned coffee-table volumes, articles for the fan press and so on, revel in the illicit to 'appeal to a readership who are invested' in the pervasive image of the early video era being '*the* golden age of exploitation [films]'.[35] To dilute the rhetorical power of the video nasty in this context would render such interventions redundant and, frankly, suck the fun out of what remains a lively area of fan celebration.[36]

Evoking video nasties becomes more of an issue when done in a general sense to characterise, or more appropriately *caricature*, the entire video business in the 1980s; where the '"gee whiz", hyperemotional expostulations' historically associated with cult film fandom obfuscate historical nuance in mainstream media commentary.[37] For journalists and other cultural commentators the allure of the video nasty has proven highly attractive. Consider, for instance, the BBC's three-part documentary series from 2013, *The 80s with Dominic Sandbrook*, which affords the video boom some brief commentary in its second episode, 'Under Pressure'. There are many directions the presenter and historian, Sandbrook, could have taken here. He could, for instance, have explored how video was, for a short while at least, a recession-beater; how it exploded despite a decline in consumer spending, to become one of the UK's only growth industries at the time. Instead, however, he focused on censorship and the video nasties, drawing from the hokey caricature of a business propelled by 'slasher flicks and softcore porn', where distributors could allegedly 'get away with anything', including, he lists, 'horror, nudity, torture, rape and *even* cannibalism'. The tone of the series is comedic at times, with Sandbrook routinely providing jovial asides. Nevertheless, intended for laughs or not, the picture

**Figure I.2** Dominic Sandbrook evoking the mythology of the video nasties in *The 80s with Dominic Sandbrook*.

he paints of the British video boom is an oversimplification of the industry and its chief characteristics.

As will become apparent throughout this book, the stereotype Sandbrook evokes is precisely what the mainstream media used to condemn the video business in the 1980s and, it should come as no surprise, is what negatively impacted the businesses and lives of many of its workers. Yet versions of Sandbrook's reductive overview reappear time and time again. The discourse surrounding the release of Prano Bailey-Bond's critically revered horror film, *Censor* (2021), is a case in point. Set in the 1980s in the aftermath of the video nasties panic, the film follows Enid (Niamh Algar), a film censor responsible for cutting or banning especially horrific horror films. It encapsulates many of the debates circling around the role of the British Board of Film Censors (BBFC)[38] in the censorship process at the time to great effect, including the ostensible protection of children, and the seemingly arbitrary conclusions drawn by the censors as they navigated their own moral judgement and that of pressure groups, the government and the public. The film's thematic driver is the psychological downfall of Enid as she becomes convinced that an actor, seen in several of the films she has viewed for work, is her long-lost sister. However, despite the weight placed on Enid's malady and her emergent traumatic backstory in the narrative proper, press discourse routinely positioned the film as less a character study and more a retroactive homage to horror film culture in 1980s Britain.[39] Remarks made by the Sundance Institute, heralding the film 'a faithful, creative ode to 1980s aesthetics and a twisted, bloody love letter to the video nasties era', were typical.[40] Some of the materials used to promote *Censor* fuelled this discourse, anchoring it in various capacities to the tendency across contemporary horror (and horror-adjacent) media to draw from 1980s and 1990s popular culture, as with *Stranger Things* (2016–present), *IT: Chapter One* (Andrés Muschietti, 2017) and the *Fear Street* (various, 2021) trilogy.[41] The US poster, for example – described by the horror fan site *Bloody Disgusting*, as appearing 'Straight Out of the Video Nasty Era' – incorporates '1980s aesthetics' and thus chimes with the Sundance endorsement, its saturated colour palette of blues, greens and reds resonant of analogue television, complemented by the presence of a television set and a warning to the spectator: 'DON'T PRESS PLAY'.[42] Similarly, *Sight and Sound*, the official publication of one of *Censor*'s primary investors, the British Film Institute, featured the film as part of a 'Video Nasties' themed issue, the cover of which bears headlines such as 'THE 80s BRITISH CENSORSHIP MASSACRE' and shows a stack of televisions displaying 'nasty' iconography such as a bloodied drill and the rotten hands of zombies (*à la* banned videos *The Driller Killer* [Abel Fererra, 1979] and *Zombie Flesh Eaters* [Lucio Fulci, 1980] respectively).[43] The puff pieces that surrounded the release were just as indulgent, awash as they were with widely held assumptions about the video market in the 1980s that compound video nasties mythology, whereby the industry as a whole is reduced to sex, horror and the flagrant opportunism of wheeler-dealer distributors and shopkeepers. Thus, *Little White Lies* claims, that '[f]or a time video stores – essentially cowboy operations – could rent anything to anyone, unexpurgated and unregulated',[44] and *Games Radar* argues that 'enterprising independent labels coined it in distributing low-budget horror films using the twin draws of gruesome gore and lurid cover art'.[45]

It is of no doubt that the foregoing examples helped place *Censor* in the eyeline of audiences while also enabling media outlets to piggy-back on its hype. As with the fan periodicals discussed above, it is not necessarily in the interests of film distributors to strive for historical accuracy, when the goal is to capitalise on those elements that a specific epoch – in this case the 1980s – is best known for, however exaggerated they may be. The problem, however, is the willingness of media commentators to reinforce such a caricature, when the lawlessness and transgression associated with the video nasties is only one aspect of the British video boom's rich, and thus far uncharted, history.

**Figure I.3** Enid (Niamh Algar) in Prano Bailey-Bond's horror film, *Censor*. Credit: Maria Lax. Courtesy of Censor Productions Ltd / Silver Salt Films.

## Push play

Full disclosure: this book explores horror video, too. It also acknowledges the video nasties panic, the VRA and its impact(s) on the video industry – including the stigma faced by independent dealers. But the primary aim of *Rewind, Replay* is to add detail to what is, at present, a mere sketch of the history of the British video business during – to borrow Herbert's terminology – the medium's 'tangible phase': where 'movie culture flowed out from the theater and the living room, entered a public retail space, and became conflated with shopping and salesmanship'.[46] This means taking another look at some aspects of the business and culture that swelled around it, which, as prevailing media discourse shows, are routinely taken for granted.

I am describing what ensues as an industrial-cultural history, which, I appreciate, isn't the neatest-sounding of designations. Initially, I set out to write a strictly *industrial* history, in a manner akin to, for example, Paul McDonald's *Video and DVD Industries* or Wasser's *Veni, Vidi, Video*. But, as my research progressed, it became apparent that it would be remiss of me, in a history about the penetration of a technology that became such a central aspect of people's lives – which, to use another hokey cliché, 'democratised' entertainment – not to foreground at appropriate moments the various cultural elements upon which the success of video rested. At the risk of indulging in romanticisation myself, whereas by the early 1990s the mainstream image of 'video' consumerism in Britain was embodied by 'sanitised' retail spaces such as the likes of Ritz, Blockbuster and the Woolworths chain, the bed rock of Britain's video industry, as elsewhere in the world, was made up not of faceless corporations but of *people*: those first to take the risk, navigating an uncharted terrain as distributors, shop keepers or consumers. Video boomed in the 1980s under Prime Minister Margaret Thatcher, an era of sharp economic downturn and civil unrest in Britain. To this end, the cultural experiences of everyday individuals is of paramount importance to any history of the video business in Britain, and the cultural practices – including going to the video shop, speaking with staff, renting a video, watching it at home alone or in the company of others – it inspired. As this book reveals, video at first ran 'counter to the recession', and it did so only because the medium transcended cultural and class boundaries.

*Rewind, Replay* considers the first distributors at the outset of the industry, who took chances on all sorts of commercial entertainment including that of video nasty lore, such as horror, exploitation and so on, but also, and often with much greater emphasis, on variety and family entertainment. It considers the birth of video rental in the late 1970s, the rapidity with which it became a habitual practice, and the key players who, at the height of a recession, invested wholesale into what contemporaneous media reportage was describing as a mere 'plaything'.[47] It explores how distributors and store owners navigated various pressures, ranging from piracy and those resultant from the video nasties panic, but also the threat of market rationalisation that resulted in shakeouts across the industry, and the corporate expansion of the business in the late 1980s and into the early 1990s. Many companies and businesses came and went during this period. Yet, what follows is not strictly an account of rising and falling, but one of evolution: how the British video business began, how it navigated challenges and how it matured from its humble beginnings and associations of disrepute into a staple of high street retail.

Chapter 1, 'We've Got it Taped', considers the beginning of video distribution and how a London-based company, Intervision, created the British market for feature films on video in 1978. Today, the Intervision name remains present in home media distribution some fifty years after the company was originally founded, albeit solely as a distributor of schlocky horror films.[48] While it is true that Intervision's roster in the 1970s included numerous horror and exploitation films, its aim was never to champion 'obscure' works, but rather to capitalise on the democratising potential of the VCR and create a buoyant market that catered to everybody. Chapter 1, thus, explores how Intervision realised this aim, spearheading the nascent video industry with a catalogue of diverse titles in a variety of genres, and how this approach inspired others to write promises of variety and quality into promotional strategies.

Chapter 2, 'Shrugging Off the Recession', considers the first video clubs and shops. As suggested at the beginning of the present chapter, the prevailing image of the 'video shops' or 'video stores' is one of a retail outlet that, at the very least, brought with it and fulfilled a universal set of expectations, namely, that people could walk in, go to the appropriately labelled section, acquire a cassette for a short period of time, and then return it. Prior to landing on this model, however, there was some experimentation. The first video libraries tended not to be shops, but mail order companies operating from residential addresses in the beginning, and then warehouses as the business grew. The chapter gives some consideration to this history, arguing how entrepreneurs, embracing the free enterprise philosophy of the New Right, sought to position themselves as 'princes of industry', and help achieve the industry's status as a recession-beater. The chapter also considers the beginnings of the video business's stigmatisation, and how reports of piracy within the trade would place small dealers at the heart of such discourse.

Chapter 3, 'Threats and Benefits', explores two significant developments in the history of Britain's video boom: market rationalisation and the video nasties panic. The chapter argues that, ahead of the video nasty controversy, the main threat to the operations of distributors and shopkeepers was that, despite video's popularity, there were too many companies vying for too few consumers. Distributors therefore adopted various strategies to ride out rationalisation, which included trading more heavily in children's and family films as well as using the free press coverage of the ensuing video nasties to their own ends: trading in horror films that were in many ways redolent of films being singled out (i.e. publicised) in the media.

Chapter 4, 'Regulation and Adaptation', is concerned with the aftermath of both rationalisation and the passing of the VRA on the distribution sector. It charts the numerous shakeouts during this time, as well as several success stories that met those companies savvy and well-resourced enough to expand overseas in more buoyant markets. Consideration is also given to the development of the video retail, or 'sell-through', market, which did much to improve the image of the video business in the eyes of the media and consumers, and enabled video to boom for a second time.

Chapter 5, 'Independent Spirit vs Corporate Muscle', examines how the video shop sector responded to rationalisation and the stigma of the video nasties. It examines the various strategies adopted by independent outlets to improve the 'image' of video, before considering the emergence of corporate forces onto the market, which gave independent shops a run for their money. The chapter explores the circumstances that enabled Blockbuster, launching in the UK in 1988, to flourish and, subsequently, dominate.

It is the aim of *Rewind, Replay* to offer a new take on the beginnings of the British video business. Rewinding history and then playing it back – as it were – allows us to pause and take a closer look at a defining moment in the history of British industry and culture for which, while important for so many of us, so much remains to be said.

## Notes

1. Paul McDonald, *Video and DVD Industries* (London: BFI, 2007), 141.
2. See, for example, Tom Krazit, 'Blockbuster's last stand: inside the iconic video rental chain's only remaining store', *GeekWire* (31 March 2018), https://www.geekwire.com/2018/blockbusters-last-stand-inside-one-iconic-video-rental-chains-final-u-s-stores/; Andy Ash, 'The rise and fall of Blockbuster and how it's surviving with just one store left', *Business Insider* (12 August 2020), https://www.businessinsider.com/the-rise-and-fall-of-blockbuster-video-streaming-2020-1?r=US&IR=T; and Beatrice Verhoevan, 'How the Last Blockbuster Store Is Surviving the Pandemic: Nostalgia, Sleepovers and T-Shirt Sales', *The Wrap* (17 April 2021), https://www.thewrap.com/how-last-blockbuster-surviving-pandemic-nostalgia-sleepovers-merchandise/.
3. Damian Jones, 'Netflix is releasing a documentary on the last ever Blockbuster video store', *The NME* (9 March 2021), https://www.nme.com/news/film/netflix-is-releasing-a-documentary-on-the-last-ever-blockbuster-video-store-2897027.
4. See, for example, Jen Chacey, 'It's 2016. Why are we still obsessed with the '80s?' *Vulture* (24 October 2016), https://www.vulture.com/2016/10/2016-why-are-we-obsessed-with-the-80s.html; Sophie Goodwin, ''80s nostalgia no surprise to historians', *Auburn Plainsman* (30 December 2020), https://www.theplainsman.com/article/2020/12/80s-nostalgia-no-surprise-to-historians; and Alex Godfrey, 'Screams, slashers and Thatcher: why horror films are going back to the 80s', *The Guardian* (29 June 2021), https://www.theguardian.com/film/2021/jun/29/screams-slashers-and-thatcher-why-horror-films-are-going-back-to-the-80s.
5. Raiford Guins, *Edited Clean Version: Technology and the Culture of Control* (Minneapolis: Minnesota University Press, 2008), 100.
6. Guins, *Edited Clean Version*, 100.
7. Joshua M. Greenberg, *From Betamax to Blockbuster: Video Stores and the Invention of Movies on Video* (Cambridge, MA: MIT Press, 2007), 128.

8. Keller cited in George Ritzer, *The McDonaldization of Society: Into the Digital Age* (9th edition, Thousand Oaks: Sage, 2019), 40.
9. Guins, *Edited Clean Version*, 216–17, n.30.
10. Guins, *Edited Clean Version*, 89–124. See also Greenberg, *From Betamax to Blockbuster*, 127–9 and Daniel Herbert, *Videoland: Movie Culture at the American Video Store* (Berkeley: University of California Press, 2014), 34–5. On 'McDonaldization' see Ritzer, *The McDonaldization of Society* and, in relation to British video shops, Chapter 5 of this book.
11. See Chapter 5 of this book.
12. Guins, *Edited Clean Version*, 216–17, n.30.
13. Frederick Wasser, *Veni, Vidi, Video: The Hollywood Empire and the VCR* (Austin: University of Texas Press, 2001).
14. Jeff Scheible and Joshua Neves (eds), 'Video Stores', *Media Fields Journal* 1 (2010), available at: http://mediafieldsjournal.org/issue-1/; Herbert, *Videoland*, 5.
15. Michael Z. Newman, *Video Revolutions: On the History of a Medium* (New York: Columbia University Press, 2014), 104.
16. Peter Alilunas, *Smutty Little Movies: The Creation and Regulation of Adult Video* (Berkeley: University of California Press, 2014).
17. Lucas Hildebrand, *Inherent Vice: Bootleg Histories of Videotape and Copyright* (Durham, NC: Duke University Press, 2009).
18. Caetlin Benson-Allott, *Killer Tapes and Shattered Screens: Video Spectatorship from VHS to File Sharing* (Berkeley: University of California Press, 2013).
19. See, for example, Ramon Labato, *Shadow Economies of Cinema: Mapping Informal Film Distribution* (London: British Film Institute, 2012); and Joshua Neves and Bhaskar Sarkar (eds), *Asian Video Cultures: In the Penumbra of the Global* (Durham, NC: Duke University Press, 2017).
20. See, for example, Mark Levy and Barrie Gunter, *Home Video and the Changing Nature of the Television Audience* (London: John Libbey, 1988); Barrie Gunter and Mallory Wober, 'The uses and impact of home video in Great Britain', in Mark R. Levy (ed.), *The VCR Age: Home Video and Mass Communication* (London: Sage, 1989), 50–69; Marie Gillespie, 'Technology and tradition: audio-visual culture among South Asian families in West London', *Cultural Studies* 3.2 (1989), 226–39; and Ann Gray, *Video Playtime: The Gendering of a Leisure Technology* (London: Routledge, 1992).
21. Julian Petley, '"Are We Insane?": The "Video Nasty" Moral Panic', *Recherches sociologiques et anthropologiques* 43.1 (2012), 35–57, available at: https://doi.org/10.4000/rsa.839. This essay is also available in: Julian Petley, Chas Critcher, Jason Hughes and Amanda Rohloff (eds), *Moral Panics in the Contemporary World* (London: Bloomsbury, 2013), 73–98.
22. Herbert, *Videoland*, 3.
23. See, for example, Martin Barker (ed.), *The Video Nasties: Freedom and Censorship in the Media* (London: Polity, 1984); Martin Barker and Julian Petley (eds), *Ill Effects: The Media Violence Debate* (2nd edition, London:

Routledge, 2001); and Julian Petley, *Film and Video Censorship in Modern Britain* (Edinburgh: Edinburgh University Press, 2011).
24. Petley, *Film and Video Censorship*.
25. Julian Upton, 'Electric Blues: The Rise and Fall of Britain's First Pre-recorded Videocassette Distributors', *Journal of British Cinema and Television* 13.1 (2016), 19–41.
26. Peter Chippendale, 'How High Street Horror Is Invading the Home', *The Sunday Times* (23 May 1982).
27. Kate Egan, *Trash or Treasure? Censorship and the Changing Meanings of the Video Nasties* (Manchester: Manchester University Press, 2007).
28. Mark McKenna, *Nasty Business: The Marketing and Distribution of the Video Nasties* (Edinburgh: Edinburgh University Press, 2020), 2.
29. McKenna, *Nasty Business*, 4.
30. McKenna, *Nasty Business*, 96. See also Egan, *Trash or Treasure?* 5.
31. Jeffrey Sconce, '"Trashing" the academy: taste, excess, and an emerging politics of cinematic style', *Screen* 36.4 (1995), 371–93. See also Egan, *Trash or Treasure?* 154–81.
32. Egan, *Trash or Treasure?* 158–9. See also Johnny Walker, 'Reliability, quality and a reputation for great entertainment: the promotional strategies of Britain's early video distributors, beyond the video nasties', *Post Script* 35.3 (Summer 2017).
33. Quotation taken from the blurb on the reverse cover of Marc Morris and Nigel Wingrove's *The Art of the Nasty* (2nd edition, Godalming: FAB Press, 2009).
34. Egan, *Trash or Treasure?* 47. For a discussion about the significance of nostalgia in cult film communities in a different national context, the US, see David Church, *Grindhouse Nostalgia: Memory, Home Video and Exploitation Film Fandom* (Edinburgh: Edinburgh University Press, 2014), 3.
35. McKenna, *Nasty Business*, 3, emphasis added.
36. For example, horror fan and filmmaker Jake West who, in 2010 and 2014 shot two documentaries about the video nasties and their legacy in horror fan circles, was quoted in *The Independent* in 2014, saying: 'As much as I am opposed to censorship . . . it gave my generation of film viewers a thrilling sense of the forbidden. That thrill is gone from cinema now.' Laurence Phelan, 'Film censorship: how moral panic led to a mass ban of "video nasties"', *The Independent* (11 July 2014), https://www.independent.co.uk/arts-entertainment/films/features/film-censorship-how-moral-panic-led-mass-ban-video-nasties-9600998.html.
37. Various, 'Cult Cinema: A Critical Symposium', *Cineaste* (Winter 2008), 43–50. Quotation at 43.
38. Renamed the British Board of Film Classification in 1984.
39. I am indebted to Maddie Culver-Goldstein following a very fruitful conversation between her and myself about the press discourse surrounding *Censor*.

40. Sundance Institute quoted in Mark McKenna, 'Censor – a new film remembers a dark episode in Britain's cinematic past', *The Conversation* (19 August 2021), available from: https://theconversation.com/censor-a-new-film-remembers-a-dark-episode-in-britains-cinematic-past-166198.
41. See, for example, Alex Godfrey, 'Screams, slashers and Thatcher', available from: https://www.theguardian.com/film/2021/jun/29/screams-slashers-and-thatcher-why-horror-films-are-going-back-to-the-80s.
42. Brad Miska, 'Censor' Gets an Alternate Poster That Looks Straight Out of the Video Nasty Era!', *Bloody Disgusting* (10 June 2021), https://bloody-disgusting.com/movie/3668911/censor-gets-alternate-poster-looks-straight-video-nasty-era-exclusive/.
43. *Sight and Sound* 31.5 (June 2021).
44. Anton Bitel, Anna Bogutskaya, David Jenkins, Leila Latif, Hannah Strong and Adam Woodward, 'Every Video Nasty ranked from worst to best', *Little White Lies* (undated), available at: https://lwlies.com/articles/video-nasties-ranked-from-worst-to-best/.
45. Ian Berriman, 'Censor: the return of the video nasty', *Games Radar* (13 August 2021), available at: https://www.gamesradar.com/uk/censor-movie-interview-prano-bailey-bond-video-nasty/.
46. Herbert, *Videoland*, 3.
47. Journalist Gerry Gable speaking on *The London Programme*, 'Video Crime', London Weekend Television (13 December 1979), available at: https://lolaclips.com/footage-archive/itv_archive/ITV-01-0722/screener_the_london_programme_video_crime.
48. Anon., 'Severin to handle production for DVD label Intervision', Severin Films, available at: https://severin-films.com/severin-to-handle-productionmarketing-for-dvd-label-intervision/.

CHAPTER 1

# We've Got It Taped

The story of the British video boom begins in earnest in 1978, when the first distributors of pre-recorded video entertainment emerged, selling their wares via mail order at first, and then through many thousands of shops and membership clubs throughout the country in the years that followed. The next chapter considers the rise of video shops and clubs and how the proprietors of such navigated video's explosion in popularity. The present chapter is concerned with the early history of the distributors that supplied them and the product they offered.

The months spanning late 1978 to mid-1982 constitute the 'gold rush' phase of the British video business.[1] As industry commentator Graham Wade explained in 1985, the numbers of homeowners with a videocassette recorder 'rocketed from virtually zero to about 50%' during this period.[2] In 1979, around 165,000 machines were imported to Britain for domestic use. By the end of 1981 the figure had risen to 1 million.[3] Six months into 1982, it was clear to industry analysts that the popularity of video in the UK far exceeded that of the US, surpassed only by Japan. The trade paper *Variety* put it in the simplest of terms: 'The UK has become the strongest and fastest growing market in the world.'[4]

Britons' interest in home video led to the establishment of upwards of eighty pre-recorded videocassette distributors, covering the breadth of entertainment, from DIY programmes to music shows to travelogues to magazine-style programmes to pornography to cartoons to feature films. Companies included a plethora of independent outfits, as well as subsidiaries of major American and British film and communications companies. The present chapter considers the rise of these companies, and the strategies they adopted when attempting to communicate the excitement of video to the medium's new consumers.

The chapter begins by assessing the backgrounds of the earliest distributors and how their past experiences in adjacent industries fed into the founding of the nascent market for pre-recorded videocassettes. In the beginning it was not clear what uses video would have: what did the video-viewing public want to see? Did they want learn things from video? Did they hope to be entertained? Within a short period of time, it would become clear that entertainment, and specifically that offered by feature films, was to be the industry's primary driver. Having examined the key players, discussion proceeds to how video companies moved to appeal to a broad range of demographics; and to make as big a splash as possible with a technology whose potential was not yet known. Projecting 'variety', of offering entertainment for all, was the tack adopted by many companies, and spoke broadly to the newness of the business, and the uncertainly it brought to its figureheads. Of course, feelings of uncertainty were not restricted to those working in this business. As with all new technological developments, people began questioning its appeal and primary uses, and video sharply became associated with disreputable interests such as pornography. In part, this was due to the reliance independent distributors had on theatrical distribution companies based in London's East End that were long associated with sex work and organised crime. Video companies were forced to distance themselves from this pervasive image by stressing quality and reputability, in a manner akin to the subsidiaries of major companies commanding larger market shares. Other strategies saw companies use the newness of video as a way of promising to enhance consumers' lives through time flexibility, enabling individuals to construct their own television schedules at a time when television networks ceased broadcasting in the evening, when one of the main networks was striking, and when discussions abounded between various parties about the launch of a fourth television channel. Video distributors were well positioned to plug the gap ahead of the new channel's arrival.[5] As this chapter reveals, they did just that, establishing a foundation upon which an entire industry would build.

## 'The next exciting visual thing'

The first of Britain's video distributors emerged in the late 1970s from a mixture of backgrounds. Some had worked with video technology in various contexts for a number of years, while others already had established reputations in the home entertainment sector as distributors of film reels. Others had backgrounds in theatrical distribution. Some had no business experience at all.

Many were born of pre-existing audio-visual firms: for example, companies specialising in film projection and early forms of home cinema such as Super 8 and 16mm, film processing and the conversion of film to video formats for archival purposes, as well as closed circuit television security systems. And while pre-recorded video did not take off in any true sense in Britain until the market diffusion of Betamax and VHS in 1978, the practice of watching video images for the purposes of entertainment extended back several years, albeit in contexts different to that which eventually made the technology's name.⁶

Since the early 1970s, video technology was utilised in the public sphere in several ways. These include the screening of corporate or educational programmes in non-commercial contexts such as factories and schools, and the projecting of pop promos, concert footage and specially edited sequences on to large screens in British nightclubs. In all such instances, both cassettes and hardware (i.e. video recorders and projectors) were licensed from Britain's numerous AV companies.⁷ In the latter context, video was regarded as 'the next exciting visual thing', following other recent fads such as liquid lights and strobes, though a handful of companies recognised video's potential beyond these environments.⁸ Indeed, aware of the waves being made in the US by pre-recorded distributors such as Magnetic – which had been trading in feature film videotapes since 1976 – a few saw potential in licensing feature films on video for a general public.⁹

London-based Intervision was a pioneer in this regard, and would, over the course of the early 1980s, become the leading independent distributor. Headed by managing directors Mike Tenner and Richard Cooper, the company was established in 1974, rising from the ashes of Tenner's nightclub lighting supply company Exciting Lighting, to produce music videocassettes for discotheques.¹⁰ By 1975, the company was distributing its product to nightclubs throughout Europe, and later that year began penetrating the North American disco scene with its 'Disco Live' branded audio/projection technology.¹¹ By 1978 Cooper and Tenner had foreseen the potential of video as a narrative entertainment medium, encouraged by the penetration of VCRs in the UK – which, at the time, stood at 25,000 – and the success of the Magnetic label in the US.¹² The pair began acquiring the rights to sporting titles, children's cartoons and movies, advertising VCR and U-matic entertainment in London newspapers and AV consumer magazines, before launching the UK's first 'national video cassette library' in December.¹³

The inclusion of feature films and other non-music titles in Intervision's first catalogue – published late 1978 or early 1979 – was initially, according to Tenner, a gamble taken on a whim following several enquiries from owners of Sony U-Matic and Philips N1500 machines.¹⁴ These machines, used mostly in industrial and educational settings, were rarely bought for personal use. The N1500, for example, while able to record television

**Figure 1.1** Videos for discos: Intervision distributed its 'Disco Live' pop music videos to discotheques throughout North America. Credit: Popular Film and Television Collection.

programmes, used tapes costing around £25 per hour, making the technology prohibitively expensive for the general consumer.[15] However, following the introduction of the more affordable VHS and Betamax machines to the UK in March and April respectively, Intervision found itself as the only AV company with experience in handling films for general sale, and thus the only video distributor to predict that the future of home video was in narrative cinema.[16] Elsewhere, consumer advertising for both systems remained focused on the hardware's ability to 'time-shift'. The outcome of the famous legal battle between Universal Studios and Sony, whereby the former claimed that off-air recording using Betamax machines infringed copyright, would not be known until 1984 (with Sony emerging victorious).[17] To this end, British consumer ads, like their American counterparts, were promoting the ability to record one programme while watching another, with one memorable example depicting copies of leading television listings magazines *Radio Times* and *TV Times* engaging in a fencing battle betwixt the legend: 'When Programmes Clash! Watch them both with the Sanyo Video Recorder.'[18] Within this context Tenner and Cooper had to find a means of entering Intervision into the discourse of 'choice', which was so integral to the advertising speak of hardware manufacturers.[19] The question remained, how?

At first, there were no systems in place to monitor the taste preferences of VCR owners.[20] As sociologists Barrie Gunter and Mallory Wober argued in 1989,

> The growth in possession of VCRs happened so quickly that it caught television audience measurement contractors napping. In the UK, video was having an impact on conventional television viewing and the existing audience measurement technique was not equipped to monitor its usage.[21]

Consequently, as *Variety* reported in January 1980, while 'UK distributors . . . dip[ped] their toes in the water, they share[d] an inevitable sense of uncertainty as to what kind of swim they're getting into'.[22] Given the emphasis placed on time shifting by hardware and software manufacturers, Intervision and its subsequent competitors had to gamble on various film genres to assess what types of pre-recorded material VCR adopters might be interested in renting or purchasing outright. To turn people on to the technology, distributors had to aim for broad appeal. A means of achieving this was to carry as wide a range of titles in as a wide a range of genres as possible, in the hope of convincing consumers that pre-recorded video was worthy of their time and money.

### 'We've got the movie for you'

This approach is indicative throughout Intervision's first catalogue that features approximately 170 individual titles, around 120 of which are feature-length movies in different genres. 'Whatever your taste in entertainment', an early print advert for the catalogue confidently proclaims, 'we've got the movie for you'.[23] To an extent, such hyperbole was justified. As mentioned above, Intervision's range of cassettes was unrivalled at this time; the six or seven other distributors in operation specialised in non-fiction titles aimed at niche audiences with discrete tastes. For example, its main rival, the former-discotheque supplier VCL, offered a catalogue of merely twenty titles which, while featuring a couple of movies and sports programmes, mostly comprised music programming in keeping with its company origins.[24] The catalogues of other firms such as BBC Enterprises Film Sales, Audio and Visual Ltd, Michael Barratt Ltd, Normak Holdings, Something Special, and the International Publishing Corporation (IPC), comprised previously televised music programmes, documentaries and sports titles, while another company, Istead Audio Visual, dealt exclusively in films about space exploration from the NASA archives.[25]

The kinds of material that the majority of Intervision's competitors traded in reflects what was, for a short time, a commonly held belief that pre-recorded video was destined to be a non-fictional medium that bore little if any similarity to, say, the experience of viewing a film in a theatre. That is to say, the potential of video was seen by some in the AV industry as *functional*; as examples of what Salomé Aguilera Skvirsky has subsequently theorised as 'the process genre', or 'the sequentially ordered representation of someone making or doing something'.[26] Videocassettes as demonstrations of banal processes could be accessed as and when, referred to 'again and again', just as one would pick up a cookery book, car manual or other such reference work.[27] If the notion of 'entertainment' came into the equation at all, as in the case of VCL's music releases for instance, it was considered of a sort different to that encountered on trips to the cinema. There are a couple of reasons why companies adopted this point of view.

The first is the simple issue of rights ownership, and the financial benefits to be had from trading in programmes that were already in distributors' legal possession. The likes of the BBC, for example, already had a library of archived material it could draw from, and it is conceivable that Istead's handling of the NASA films, for example, extended back to its days as an AV firm with connections to the education sector.[28] This was certainly the position VCL was in when repurposing its various music programmes for home media. Viewed in this way, it is conceivable that the first video distributors were hesitant about paying rights for *new* materials when the buoyancy of the market was so uncertain, and when they already had a bank of programmes primed for remediation.

Second, cinema-going and the viewing of films on television were well-established and widely popular practices that need not have resonated with video distributors as experiences to replicate or complement at the dawn of the video age. In Britain in late 1978 and early 1979 cinema-going was at its most popular since the decade began,[29] while feature films were shown on television on a nightly basis.[30] Based on these facts alone, attempting to play video off against two buoyant markets was assumed a fruitless endeavour. This was the view of Michael Barratt, a former TV presenter who turned his attention to producing non-fiction instructional videos such as *New Life in the Garden* (Nigel Houghton, 1979) and *What Shall We Give Them to Eat?* (Jan Martin, 1980) in the late 1970s. As he explained at the time to the consumer magazine *Video World*: 'home video needs a different presentation, pace and style [from television and films]'.[31]

Intervision, by foregrounding narrative films, was advancing a different philosophy, realising that video's potential lay in its ability to offer consumers a presentation, pace and style that they were already predisposed to through film and TV. As Heikki Hellman and Martti Soramäki argued in 1985:

> although it is a junior medium, video software is not a new product. Rather, as the bulk of program supply consists of movies already released theatrically, video is generally no more than a new channel of dissemination and marketing of theatrical films.[32]

Intervision realised that cinema-going and watching films on television were not mutually exclusive practices, but rather two that could converge through video. The company's range of cassettes placed it in prime position to use the technology to exploit this want for movies; to offer, in a domestic setting, more of what people were *known* to enjoy.

Intervision's first catalogue became of note to the consumer press primarily for this reason, with one journalist encouraging consumers 'to ponder [it] with anticipation if not with awe', due to its manifold selection.[33] The company projected diversity to its prospective customers through the catalogue's design and layout. The inclusion on the cover of a pirate, a martial artist and futuristic superhero, alongside an image of a rock singer resembling Mick Jagger and two faces resembling Orson Welles and Peter Cushing respectively, hint at the generic diversity of the catalogue's content and, by extension, its chances of attracting numerous demographics.[34] The rhetoric employed in the introductory section reinforces the eclecticism intimated by the cover image. 'Now for the first time in Britain', the opening sentence reads, 'owners of video cassette recorders have a library of exciting films to choose from'.[35] '[E]verything' is promised, from 'sensational Concerts to Chess and Fishing' to 'Classical films. Horror films. Rock films. Children's films', as well as 'Westerns' and 'adult films'.[36] Several noteworthy titles are singled out to give a further flavour of the range and quality on offer, including, for example, the art-house film *Blow Out* (Marco Ferreri, 1973), the action-adventure film *Sunday in the Country* (John Trent, 1974), Orson Welles' adaptation of *Macbeth* (1948), and the science fiction film *The Day the Earth Caught Fire* (Val Guest, 1961), which are collectively labelled as 'great movies'.[37] The remainder of the catalogue is subdivided by genre. Each section includes short plot summaries occasionally accompanied by illustrations employed to evoke the content and tone of the film in question, by representing particularly dynamic and thrilling scenes. Examples include the listing for the action/adventure film *They Paid with Bullets* (Julio Diamante, 1969),

**Figure 1.2** Intervision's first catalogue projects diversity to prospective customers. Credit: Popular Film and Television Collection.

which shows a gun-toting gangster; the listing for the adult drama *Wonder Wall* (Joe Massot, 1968) shows a man and woman in a sexual embrace; and the listing for *Alaska Wilderness Adventure* (Fred Meader, 1978) shows a family aboard a canoe dressed in winter furs, their faces expressing delight. Knowingly comprehensive – 'you've several hundred quality movies to choose from' – the catalogue emphasises a range of entertainment crafted to appeal, as its front matter declares, to '*people of all ages*, of different tastes and interests'.[38] This includes films and programmes that appeal to individual tastes (such as those with a fondness for chess and fishing) and specific age groups (as the 'adults only' section attests), but also, and perhaps most significantly, material included to 'capture the *entire family's* imagination'.[39]

Intervision's approach paid off. By May 1979, having reportedly sold 2,000 cassettes and rented an average of 300 each month to members of its video club since its launch, the company's 'booming' success triggered an upsurge in competitors specialising in feature-length movies over the next two years.[40] These include World Video Incorporated (later World of Video 2000), a consortium established by the UK's Video Warehouse International and North America's Pleasure Tapes USA, which launched in June 1979 with thirty titles in a variety of genres.[41] In July, Nova Home Video Entertainment, an independent based in Oxford, began advertising a single release: *Who Killed Doc Robin?* (Bernard Carr, 1948).[42] In August, the first major studio-owned label, Magnetic (a subsidiary of Twentieth Century Fox), emerged onto the market with twenty-seven titles.[43] Several others emerged as the year-end approached, including a company with origins in the importation of AV hardware from Japan and Germany, Hokushin (with a number of sexploitation films);[44] the video arm of the film processor, distributor and production company, Rank Audio Visual (with twenty titles in a variety of genres);[45] and the 'Videorama' label of film-reel distributors, Iver Film Services (with some adult, horror and family films).[46]

The following year saw the emergence of yet more companies. Mountain Video and Derann Audio Visual, originally distributors of Super 8 and 16mm films, launched their video lines in January and April respectively.[47] Woodstock Video, a company specialising in video double-bills (two features on one cassette) began advertising to the consumer press in March.[48] The first adverts for Video Instant Picture Company (VIPCO) and Inter-Ocean Video, offering a range of exploitation films between them, first appeared in April.[49] In May, Art Features promoted a range of avant-garde feature films, and Carnaby promoted a video showcasing highlights from the 1978 world cup.[50] In July Vision on Video first promoted its range of thrillers and children's films, while Home Video Supplies (HVS), originally established to distribute movies on video as early as 1978, began advertising its range of 500 films to the consumer market nationally, and Taboo Films International and Dapon Film Services began promoting a range of adult videos.[51] September saw the launch of the video arm of theatrical distributor Brent Walker,[52] October saw the launched of Guild Home Video and the first adverts appear for Videomedia's range of horror films,[53] while November saw VCL premiere its new budget label, 21st Century Video,[54] and the arrival of the second major to enter the market, WCI Home Video (Warner Bros).[55] Around the same time, Tele-Cine X (TCX) launched with a range of adult videos, as did Probe Video and Intercity Video,[56] while December saw TCR Video first promote its range of music programmes and feature films,[57] along with Hikon Video promoting *Mean Streets* (Martin Scorsese, 1973),[58] the launch of Intercontinental Video with a range of kung-fu films[59] and the arrival of another major player, Paramount and Universal's UK distributor, Cinema International Corporation (CIC), with twenty 'Hollywood movie greats'.[60]

The inclusive mode of address pioneered by Intervision as a company catering for *everyone* extended across the spectrum of new video distributors. Families were targeted to help the companies reach a diverse range

Figure 1.3 Mountain Video advertises feature films for 'all the family'.
Credit: Joseph Brant/Popular Film and Television Collection.

of ages and interests. For example, Mountain promoted a range of genres, including science fiction, adult, westerns and comedies, to 'keep all the family entertained',[61] and Derann offered 'a superb range of video entertainment' including 'many movies you will want to own, to enjoy with your family and friends'.[62] 21st Century promoted a host of westerns, action films, dramas, 'spy thrillers', crime movies, comedies, musicals, films about 'wildlife', war movies and horror films, under the pretence that 'these movies have been carefully selected with all the family in mind'.[63] Vision On Video promised to cater to 'ALL THE FAMILY' with titles as broad as *Snow White* (Eric Kobler, 1955) and *Someone Behind the Door* (Nicolas Gessner, 1971), and Hokushin offered 'the choosey ... more choice', in a catalogue claiming to contain 'something for everyone'.[64] This approach to selling videos spoke broadly to the uncertainty of those working in the business at this time. It indicated the extent to which variety and, specifically, feature films were imperative factors to embrace for companies looking to identify their core demographics.

## Smut, stigma and the 'porn ghetto'

The foregoing examples show how companies attempted to attract a broad audience. However, as more consumers bought VCRs and more distributors joined the fray, the watchful eyes of journalists and other case-makers fell on the 'quality' of the material being traded.

As was the case elsewhere in the world, independent companies considerably outnumbered majors.[65] Because concerns over video piracy were heightened in the US, and big American film studios were usually unwilling to license films to video firms, smaller British companies looking to diversify their catalogues typically had to negotiate deals with independent theatrical distributors, which for the most part handled the rights to low-budget 'exploitation' films.[66] As is documented elsewhere, films of this nature tended to lack the critical cachet of mainstream films on account of their low budgets, lack of A-list actors and association with run-down inner-city cinemas.[67] As far as video distributors were concerned, however, it made business sense to trade in this material. While the films in most instances were lacking the gloss of top Hollywood product, many were proven profit generators, having played to big crowds in cinemas as A or B features. Intervision's release of the violent action film *The Exterminator* (James Glickenhaus, 1980) is a case in point. Having enjoyed successful theatrical runs in the UK and the US, the film was released onto video within weeks of it topping the London box office charts.[68] Similarly, Hokushin released the sex comedy *Come Play With Me* (George Harrison

Marks, 1977) when the film was still popular in cinemas countrywide.[69] That many other video companies adopted the same tack – from kung-fu to horror to action to sex – speaks to the pervasiveness of the belief that the visibility of exploitation films in cinemas was projected to translate into profits when the films were released onto videocassette.[70]

However, whereas trading in exploitation proved a profitable endeavour about which many video companies would subsequently boast, the video business sharply became stigmatised due to the negative associations that the films, and their licence holders, carried.[71] Many of the theatrical distributors licensing films to video companies in the early days were based in Soho, an area of London long associated with the sex trade and known the world over as one of the City's most 'notorious neighbourhoods'.[72] Soho was also, conversely, the home to the offices of several major film companies with upstanding reputations. But, as Leon Hunt notes in his ground-breaking study *British Low Culture*, the latter half of the 1970s saw 'an aggressive expansion of the porn industries' in the area.[73] Between 1976 and 1982, there were '54 sex shops; 39 sex cinemas and cinema clubs; 16 strip and peep shows; 11 sex-oriented clubs; and 12 licensed massage parlours'.[74] The permeation of what Hunt characterises as the 'permissive populism' of the 1970s anticipates the early growth of video in Soho in particular, with at least nine sex film specialists establishing outfits there. These were in addition to several others that, while not strictly 'adult' specialists, advertised adult-themed exploitation films – sex comedies and the like – in their catalogues (see Table 1.1). The associations of distributors with 'Soho's porn ghetto' and exploitation film, regardless of how broad some of their catalogues were, helped reinforce in the minds of journalists caricatures of Soho as a neighbourhood where vice ran rampant, and helped characterise the new medium of video as one for which the primary driver was pornography.[75]

One consumer magazine, *Television & Home Video*, spoke to the apparent ubiquity of adult videos on the cover of its July 1980 issue. The cover shows an illustration of a cinema stewardess offering the reader, from an ice cream tray, a VHS copy of Just Jaekin's erotic classic *Emmanuelle* (1974). The mainstream Hollywood fare she stocks – which includes copies of the James Bond film *Live and Let Die* (Guy Hamilton, 1973) and the family sci-fi *Close Encounters of the Third Kind* (Steven Spielberg, 1977) – remains untouched. The implication of the cover image is clear: video consumers are more likely to be interested in continental sex films than Bond or Spielberg.

It is crucial to note, however, that the extent of the demand for adult videos was cause for argument among those in the sex industry. The editors of the top-shelf publications *Men Only* and *Club International*

Table 1.1 Soho-based independent video distributors in 1981. Data compiled from *Video Index*, *Video News*, *Video Review* and *Late Night Video*

| Distributor | Specialism | Address |
| --- | --- | --- |
| Active Video | Adult | Old Compton Street |
| Adult Video Centre | Adult | Charing Cross Road |
| Carnaby | General | Carnaby Street |
| Chequerboard XXX (distributed by World of Video 2000) | Adult | Lexington Street |
| Facelift | Adult | Wardour Street |
| Go Video | General | Wardour Street |
| Inter-Continental Video | General | Wardour Street |
| Inter Ocean | General | Great Pulteney Street |
| Kingston Video | General | Great Windmill Street |
| Rippledale Ltd/The Video Company | Adult | Old Compton Street |
| Video for Pleasure (label operated by Carnaby Video) | Adult | Carnaby Street |
| Taboo Films | Adult | Berwick Street |
| Videomedia | General | Wardour Street |
| Video Blue | Adult | Ganton Street |
| Video View | Adult | Wardour Street |

concurred that adult videos were very popular, believing demand to be so high that in late 1980 they devised 'the first men's magazine on video', *Electric Blue*, a new 'issue' of which was 'published' quarterly.[76] Others, including the owner of the Ann Summers sex shop chain, Ronald Coleman, claimed that adult videos were, in fact, very difficult to sell.[77] While concrete data are elusive, what certainly *is* quantifiable is the process of stigmatisation faced by the video business, and the efforts that distributors made to evade it. Of course, it is true that many companies adopted bold and expectedly sexual advertising when promoting adult films, but few wanted to openly attract controversy and negatively impact their businesses, especially when they were otherwise courting legitimacy.[78] This was as true for generalists as it was for adult specialists. In the case of the former, adult films tended to be framed as one example of a vast range of material on offer, with sex films consigned to specific sections of catalogues (oftentimes at the back) or having catalogues all their own.[79] In this way, adult material constituted one component of wider offerings, thereby reinforcing projected narratives of the companies catering 'for all'. The strategy also sought to generate a sense of distance

**Figure 1.4** Sex over Spielberg? A cinema stewardess offers the readers of *Television & Home Video* magazine a VHS copy of the recent erotic hit, *Emmanuelle*.
Credit: Popular Film and Television Collection.

between 'adult' and 'family' entertainment, so as not to taint the latter with the former. This was paramount to the companies' corporate images. By trading in – as Intervision's first catalogue phrases it – '*some* adult titles',[80] and thereby not wholly aligning with the sex industry proper as the Soho-based adult labels were doing, distributors were able to remain credible in the eyes of the 'highly respectable' high-street retailers they wished to attract as stockists.[81] By the same token, it was equally as paramount for some adult specialists to appear legitimate in the eyes of their audience and the public. Like all lawful businesses, distributors across the spectrum wanted to convey a sense of quality, professionalism and reliability: an approach that was starkly at odds with their negative media image as illicit firms trading in 'badly made' sex films.[82]

There were numerous strategies adopted by companies to counter the negative media coverage and assure would-be video consumers of their legitimacy. First, some would repeatedly stress an affinity with major film studios. Often this was done by drawing upon their company's historic legacy or high standing within the media industries. Second, distributors would mobilise in their promotional materials the presence of 'star' performers or frame such releases as 'major' events. Whereas much of independents' catalogues consisted of material that was likely unfamiliar to most people, they also traded in films featuring early roles from contemporaneous Hollywood actors before they had made their name. As for the 'major' status of films, distributors took the liberty of embellishing the truth to generate consumer interest. Lastly, the flexibility of video, and the 'exclusive' pleasures it could afford, was endorsed as one of the technology's chief attractions. Videos were promoted on the grounds that they could be watched by anyone at any time and that many of the material available on videocassette was likely never to be shown on television or in cinemas. All of the strategies evidence independent distributors striving for legitimacy, by presenting the new medium of video as one of quality that could cater for all.

## 'Renowned in the film industry'

Because many of the bigger North American firms such as Twentieth Century Fox and Warner Bros had longstanding reputations in the film and television industries, advertisements and news articles would draw on their distinguished histories to evoke an air of quality and prestige around their video products. For example, *Screen International* framed Magnetic's launch onto the market in August 1979 as 'the first full-scale launch . . . of major feature films on pre-recorded video cassettes', and, in echo of Magnetic's first consumer ads, drew attention to its range of 'blockbusters' including *The Sound of Music* (Robert Wise, 1965), *The French Connection* (William Friedkin, 1971) and *M\*A\*S\*H* (Robert Altman, 1970).[83] Similarly, the first print advertisement for Warner Communication's video label promised to bestow the grandeur of the Hollywood blockbuster upon Britons' living rooms by 'giv[ing] the small screen the big treatment' with box office hits such as *Dirty Harry* (Don Siegel, 1971), *Deliverance* (John Boorman, 1972), *Enter the Dragon* (Robert Clouse, 1973), *Blazing Saddles* (Mel Brooks, 1974), and *The Exorcist* (William Friedkin, 1974).[84]

Most independents could not make claims of this magnitude. Many were simply too new and thus had no relevant 'history' to boast of. This was certainly true of the majority of companies discussed in this chapter so far, as it was for the many emerging onto the market throughout 1981.[85] In other cases, independent distributors had names synonymous with industries that lacked the allure of major competitors (disco, telesales, etc.). However, amid the wilderness, several independent operations did have histories worth exploiting and, as such, ensured their legacies were centralised in their promotional campaigns.

Derann and Walton Video had several decades' experience between them, both having distributed feature films on Super 8 and 16mm since the 1960s. Both had relationships with major industry players including several Hollywood studios, as well as pre-established distribution arrangements with leading high street retailers. Derann was certainly keen to boast of its company history on its move into video in 1980. Its first consumer advert, published in the consumer magazine *Video World*, claims the company's move into video as 'natural' on account of the fact that it has been 'leaders [sic] in Super-8 home movie distribution for many years'.[86] Its first video catalogue, published in 1981, also drew on its legacy, proudly announcing: 'Derann now [brings] to your television screen that same reliability, quality and reputation for great entertainment value that they have been bringing to your home movie screen for 18 years.'[87] Such claims were not unfounded. As Derek Simmonds, the company's managing director, later explained to the trade paper *Television & Video Retailer*, his company remained the exclusive UK agents of Universal, Paramount and United Artists for Super 8 releases, having handled highly profitable titles such as *Star Wars* (George Lucas, 1977).[88] Being 'renowned in the film industry' prior to the video boom gave Derann extra visibility compared to its newer competitors as well as an impression of gravitas at a time when many other independents were still trying to find their voices.[89] Moreover, its company slogan, 'the friendly giant from the midlands', spoke of a large business operation, comparable perhaps to a Hollywood conglomerate, that was also affable, approachable and in possession of *local* business knowledge: mobilised here to offer something the likes of Magnetic and Warner Bros could not legitimately claim.[90]

Originally established in the 1950s to trade in photographic slides, Walton Video had been in the home entertainment business longer than Derann.[91] This factor, coupled with its move into Super 8 film distribution in the 1960s, made Walton a standout operation at the dawn of the video boom. A supplemental booklet issued with the trade paper *Video Business* boasts of how, not unlike Derann, Walton's industry experience set it apart from the 'many companies that have simply jumped on the accelerating video bandwagon':[92] companies that, according to the booklet, 'spring up overnight only to disappear just as quickly'.[93] Here, as with Derann, Walton's historical success and proven passion for home entertainment is used as a legitimising factor in its foreseen longevity, while its smaller competitors are discounted on account of their opportunism and inevitable transience; they are not likely to survive, the booklet suggests, because they lack Walton's defining qualities, the most important of which are its history and longstanding industry pedigree. 'When the video industry started', the company's managing director (and former film producer and director) Hamish Gibson claims, Walton was 'already well established in the home movie business'.[94] The company's existing business relationships with high street retailers such as the electronics giant Dixons – which stocked its 8mm reels – is said to have contributed significantly to the company's situating itself as a 'major' force in home video, because, according to Gibson, such marriages 'gave [Walton] instant credibility' in the new video market.[95] Walton's history as a 'leading' market player is also used to validate further claims that the firm is reliable and that it is dealing in quality material. As with Derann and, by extension, Magnetic and Warner Bros, Walton's legacy is capitalised on to distinguish it from the many other newer and less experienced independent competitors; companies that Walton characterises as merely entering the business 'for a quick and easy buck'.[96]

The promotional practices adopted by Derann and Walton were relatively commonplace within the adult video sector, too, with various specialist distributors pushing historic company/filmic legacies and/or reputability in their marketing, to quell media assertions of low standards and cowboy operations. One such distributor showing awareness of these concerns was Probe Publications, a company distributing films licensed from 'one of the primary producers of "prestige" adult films': the American firm, Cal Vista International.[97] Peter Alilunas, writing in the US context, explains how Cal Vista moved into video in the late 1970s from production and theatrical distribution, offsetting video's well-documented inferior quality to celluloid film by bolstering the company's associations with the so-called 'Golden Age' of US pornography; a period during the 1970s where hardcore film crossed over into the mainstream, broke box office records and received favourable reviews in leading press outlets.[98] This brief period is often said to have ended following the mass uptake of the VCR, which was met with a rise in poorer-quality, shot-on-video adult films.[99] Alilunas explains how, upon entering the American video market in the 1970s, the owners of Cal Vista were aware of the stigma attached to video's inferior quality, and therefore bolstered its pre-video legacy and its associations with film in its catalogues and advertising: 'Despite the video format, Cal Vista was selling the same "quality" image associated with celluloid productions.'[100]

Cal Vista's marketing in Britain took a similar tack, with print advertising routinely stressing its legacy and associations with 'quality' adult films. Indeed, its decade-long reputation as a producer of 'major adult movies' and its self-proclaimed status as 'the Rolls Royce of the Adult motion picture industry', is promoted with regularity in British consumer publications during and beyond the early 1980s.[101] Yet the context the company was entering into when launching in Britain in 1980 was starkly different to that of the US. Britain did not experience a comparable 'golden age' of hardcore pornography. While softcore sexploitation films were widely seen in cinemas throughout Britain, the Obscene Publications Act 1959 (OPA) prohibited the legal distribution of hardcore material and, consequently, quashed any hopes of Golden Age tent-poles such as *Deep Throat* (Gerard Damiano, 1972), *The Devil in Miss Jones* (Gerard Damiano, 1973) or *The Opening of Misty Beethoven* (Radley Metzger, 1976), securing formal circulation. Such films were, of course, experienced by British audiences through various means: soft photosets reproduced in magazines such as *Continental Film Review*, *Cinema X* and *Cinema Blue*, covert hardcore screenings in London sex cinema clubs, illicit 8/16mm film reels or, following the video boom, illegal cassettes distributed by companies such as the Adult Video Company, Rippledale and the Adult Tape Centre.[102] But it was not the case in Britain, as it is so often claimed about the US, that video 'ruined' the golden age of porn.[103] On the contrary, for many Britons, video opened the door to it.

Several distributors handling softcore product at this time therefore positioned their product against the pervasive media image of adult video, all the while remaining within the parameters of the law and satisfying their consumer base. This was as true of Cal Vista as it was of other adult companies such as TCX (a British company handling censored Golden

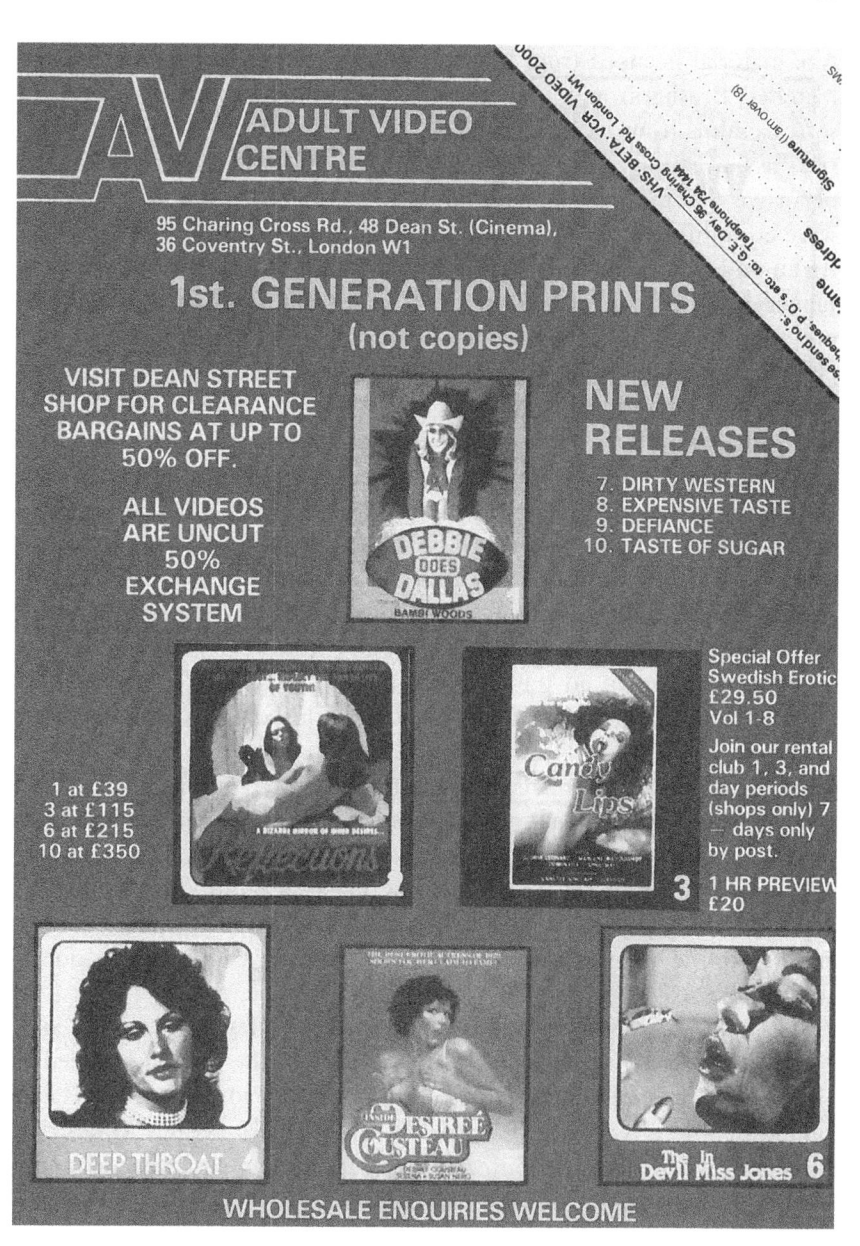

**Figure 1.5** Soho's Adult Video Centre advertises video copies of uncut sex films from America's 'Golden Age' of pornography. Credit: Popular Film and Television Collection.

Age material licensed from known US hardcore producers such as the Mitchell Brothers) and French Label (a company offering a range of softcore films from Europe and the US). Aware that more explicit material was covertly available, the company image of these firms rested on the pervasive view that videos acquired from sex shops in Soho and elsewhere were both difficult to obtain and rarely delivered what they promised.[104] As an editorial penned by journalist John Gill in *Music & Video* from January 1981 explains: 'Hard-core ... is a distant Shangri-La ... [M]ore often than not it is used as a marketing gambit (similar, almost, to a "New! Improved!" soap powder) to persuade the gullible to pay through the nose for a middling sex video.'[105] Gill warns that 'private sources, classified ads', or one's 'nearest equivalent to Soho', where one is promised to find 'something a little harder', are very risky: 'Unless you approach your purchases with the ruthlessness of a JR, you're just asking to be ripped off.'[106] Cal Vista, TCX and French Label were in many ways the antithesis to such media caricatures: adult distributors that were consumer-facing, quality-driven and committed to investing capital into distributing well-made 'adult' fare.

For example, an ad published in *Popular Video* in December 1981 echoes Cal Vista's US advertising, boasting of the company's capital assets as a symbol of its commitment to quality products and respect for its clientele. The ad, in a manner distinct from other companies' handling softcore sex films – which typically promoted their wares as 'explicit' and/or 'cheap'[107] – comparatively boasts that Cal Vista is 'The Company that Spends Big to Bring You The Biggest and Best in Adult Video Entertainment'.[108] By declaring its 'big' outlay, Cal Vista implicitly distinguishes itself from the other companies thought to reinforce adult video's downmarket image.

TCX did not possess a comparable legacy to that of Cal Vista and, consequently, was reliant upon the historicity of the films it handled as products of the Golden Age. The company's initial ad-mats are therefore telling of where its managing director, Tony Peters, wishes to position his company in the burgeoning adult market. The advertisements are simple in their design, favouring minimal text, white space and forgoing the power-selling rhetoric of other independent distributors. The ads aim to sell videos on three criteria: the title of the film/s in question and the people/company producing it (and, one assumes, their known status among cinephiles); its/their critical reception; and TCX's high standards of reproduction. Thus, the advert for TCX's first release, the well-known Golden Age title *Babyface* (Alex de Renzy, 1977), is decorated in praise from the critics, with *High Society* calling the film

'BREATHTAKING', *Hustler* describing it as 'INSPIRED EROTICA' and another claiming that the film is the 'slickest, glossiest, most expensive and most erotic hardcore film made to date'. The ad draws attention the film's multi-awarding winning status, including an award for 'BEST DIRECTOR', in the process positioning it as an erotic work of art, which, unlike much adult material available in Britain at the time, is validated by mainstream critics.[109] These advertisements work to separate TCX's releases from the adult films discussed in negative terms in the press. Indeed, as is the case across TCX's early promotional materials, quality takes precedence over the film's sexual content. These are not merely adult films, these are 'the *finest* adult movies' with a global reputation from a reputable production house, presented in 'THE BEST IN AUDIOVISUAL QUALITY'.[110]

French Label operated in a similar fashion to TCX, drawing on the historicity and associated quality of its European and American softcore films. It achieved this by offering films such as *Sins within the Family* (Bruno Gaburro, 1975) and *Sex at 7000ft* (F. J. Gottlieb, 1977) as alternatives to illegal hardcore material. This is seen most effectively in an advert that appears across two pages of the consumer magazine *Video Review* in August 1981, reading:

> Until now you were never sure what kind of films you were getting when you bought X category material.
> But now, French Label has brought a new, high standard to video.
> Here is a superb, hand-picked and guaranteed collection of the best X category films available.[111]

In the absence of a well-known brand (French Label was a new company), the advert situates several videos amid bottles of French champagne.[112] The implication, of course, is that the films are comparable in quality and status to the legendary drink. They are, in other words, of good vintage, possessing both grandeur and class. The company also offers the customer a 'double guarantee' regarding both the quality of the films on offer and their legal status. First, the films are commended for their 'storyline[s]', 'film quality' and 'exquisite photography'. Second, the advert declares that 'each film carries a British Board of Film Censor's [*sic*] Certificate . . ., the guarantee of the [film] industry's governing body'. In other words, films on French Label are not simply good examples of narrative erotica, they are the *best*, hand-chosen by experts on behalf of the discerning cinephile. And, while meeting the approval of the censor and thereby eschewing concerns that tapes might be illegal/ obscene articles, they retain the foreign allure and edginess of hardcore

Figure 1.6 French Label offers its consumers a 'double guarantee', ensuring customers quality entertainment and legal assurances.
Credit: Popular Film and Television Collection.

sex films imported from overseas.[113] In this context, as in that of Cal Vista and TCX, the artistry of the films and their compliance with the law are deemed more important – or, indeed, as potentially more appealing to consumers – than hardcore sex. According to the promotional narratives of these companies, buying legal material ensures quality and value for money, while the transparency of the companies enables them to maintain their reputation among their customer base and the law, by negating the stereotype of the sex film industry as one of murkiness, corruption and risk.

### 'Bring the stars into your home'

Demand for Cal Vista, TCX and French Label product remained consistent well into the 1980s. As niche labels with a defined demographic, their fate was secure. For other companies with wider demographics, things were not as straightforward. The legacies and historic business agreements of companies such as Derann and Walton did not protect them from what was perhaps the foremost disadvantage faced by the majority of independent distributors: namely an inability to obtain the video rights to the most desirable movies. While, as noted above, Derann owned the rights to some popular titles from major companies on Super 8, these rights rarely extended to video. Therefore, as Derann continued to trade in the Super 8 version of *Star Wars* in the early 1980s (which, as was often the case with such releases, constituted eighteen minutes of 'highlights' from the film), Fox released the full feature onto video in July 1982, to far greater success.[114] One exception to the rule is Intervision, which managed to secure a deal with United Artists in 1980, allowing the video distributor to handle twenty of the Studio's films.[115] However, as Julian Upton explains, the deal was 'trampled' within twelve months, following an arrangement that saw Warner Communications secure 'the foreign home video rights (including the UK) to more than 500 United Artists films, including all 20 that were in the Intervision package'.[116] This meant that, while Intervision was able to continue to trade in its UA titles, 'ostensibly until the end of its agreement with the studio', the robust agreement with the Warner Home Video (WHV) label prevented the independent from tapping what had been a very prestigious and lucrative income stream.[117] With more majors present on the market, independent companies had to become more creative in their marketing to present themselves as credible rivals.

Increasingly aware of the majors' prominence, independents looked to imbue their video releases with an analogous sense of iconicity and prestige. Key to this was the adoption of rhetoric in promotional copy akin to that used by majors when advertising their big releases. Smaller firms would frequently repackage older films as 'star vehicles' if they happened to feature early/later-career performances by known actors, or to market lesser-known films of varying ages and budgets as 'blockbusters' or 'major' films. For example, Mountain promised to 'bring the stars into your home' when promoting among other titles the Jack Nicholson classic *The Rebel Rousers* (Martin B. Cohen 1970),[118] while Hokushin encouraged its customers to rent, among its other videos, *No Place to Hide* (Robert Allen Schnitzer, 1973) starring 'Sylvester "ROCKY" Stallone', to ensure that 'the dark evenings' of the British winter 'have stars'.[119] In early 1982 PMA Video announced the release of four 'BIG SCREEN RELEASES!', of which only one, *Knut Hamsun's Mysteries* (de Lussanet 1978), had been exhibited theatrically, while the other three – *Dracula* (Curtis 1973), *When Every Day was the Fourth of July* (Dan Curtis, 1978), and *The Long Days of Summer* (Curtis, 1980) – were TV movies.[120] Likewise, Starcurve launched an entire range of what its promotional ephemera terms 'Video Blockbusters' comprising twenty obscure films in a host of popular genres including action-adventure titles such as *Mutiny in the Southseas* (Wolfgang Becker, 1965), *White Cargo from Hong Kong* (Stegani and Ashley, 1964), and *The Pirates of the Mississippi* (Jürgen Roland, 1963).[121] These examples evidence an old industry trick in action, where, by bending the truth, frugal wares are made to appear more opulent and enticing. The appeal of such films hinges on the success of their advertising to instil in prospective audiences the idea that, as with Hollywood blockbusters, 'consuming such films' will be 'both easy and pleasurable'.[122] The adoption of industry parlance typically associated with Hollywood releases feeds into what Barbara Klinger once described as a film's 'consumable identity'; that which 'enters into the arena in which the film is encountered'.[123] The consumable identity of the aforementioned examples is one of assumed similarity to better-known films, and the notion that, while such films are for the most part unknown, their being promoted as major releases suggests they are, as Julian Stringer argues of movie blockbusters, 'in some sense bigger – or of more noteworthy size – than the rest'.[124] Promoting films in this way enabled independent companies to cultivate a consumable identity of 'bigness' that in actuality belied the comparatively 'small' size of their businesses.

Alignment with major film studios extended beyond the incorporation of Hollywood marketing speak. When the Magnetic and WHV labels emerged onto the video market in 1979 and 1980 respectively, the artwork for their releases, not just the films they carried, was distinguishable from their competitors. As subsidiaries of major American film studios and thus allied with two of the US's most 'potent corporate trademarks', both were well attuned to the significance of branding in corporate image.[125] Across their respective video ranges, thus, was *brand uniformity* – a relatively alien concept to independents – which had been tried and tested in the US for at least twelve months prior to the establishment of their British divisions.[126] The packaging for both companies was slick, professional and consistent, the front covers composing a border displaying the company logo and/or name, and a film still or cropped theatrical poster in their centre. The spines were also uniform, displaying the film title, logo and other paratextual information, and back covers comprising, in the case of Magnetic, a list of other titles available, and, in the case of WHV, a plot synopsis and several film stills. Each of the brands bore distinctive colour combinations that were maintained across every title released: white, black, yellow and brown for Magnetic, and black, white and blue for WHV. Brand coherence was of paramount importance to these companies, as is evident from their first print advertisements, both of which feature photographs of video boxes stacked upon, or lined up against, one another, with one of the boxes front-facing. The desired effect was to reinforce the notion that these are well-known films from the leading film studios by the unifying consistency of the video packaging. Coherent branding here acts as a seal of quality, whereby each video, bearing the

Figure 1.7 The (initial) branding incoherence of independent distributor Hokushin. Credit: Popular Film and Television Collection.

recognisable hallmarks of notable film and media companies, is as worthy of consumer interest as the next.

The branding of video releases from independent distributors was less cohesive, at times varying from title to title. For example, while Hokushin's Video Movies range of cassettes denote elements of consistency, such as a maroon border surrounding an image/poster from the respective film, only some of the video boxes prominently featured the company name and/or the Video Movies moniker.[127] And even in cases where, as McKenna argues in *Nasty Business*, there were flashes of 'strategic communication', brand inconsistency was nevertheless pervasive until around mid-1981.[128] By the time Magnetic launched its UK division, only eleven out of Intervision's 200 titles had bespoke artwork bearing uniform branding.[129] Otherwise cassettes were sold in one of several generic slip-cases identifying the genre of the film in question ('Action Adventure', 'Horror', 'Family Entertainment', etc), bearing a corresponding illustration and a hand-affixed sticker signifying the title. In this scenario, regardless of whether one rented or purchased, for example, films from the 'Family Entertainment' range such as *Aladdin's Lamp* (Will Winton, 1979), *The Kingdom in the Clouds* (Elizabeta Bostan, 1968), *Men of Sherwood Forest* (Val Guest, 1954), *Dogs to the Rescue* (Paul

Fritz-Nemeth, 1972), or *Rip Van Winkle* (Will Vinton, 1978), the artwork would be the same: a painted montage featuring Robin Hood, a Middle-Eastern princess, a pirate and a young boy.[130] Branding experts Chris Lightfoot and Richard Gerstman argue that packaging is a key means through which a brand can achieve 'clearer and more appealing brand personality than any another brand in its sector'.[131] The no-frills covers of Intervision, as the launch of Magnetic exposed, did not achieve this. The disparity between the independent and that of the world's 'leading distributor of videocassettes' was evident and signalled to smaller companies that something needed to change.[132]

Intervision's subsequent decision to use bespoke box artwork for all its subsequent releases – film-specific images, uniform logo positioning and a consistent white/blue/black colour scheme – is but one indication of the ripple effect that the presence of Magnetic's brand prompted.[133] Gradually, throughout 1980 and, following the launch of WHV, into 1981, the majority of independents began prioritising catalogue-wide uniformity. Advertisements would thus regularly show a selection of cassettes stacked together like those of Magnetic and WHV, or a pageful of cover images sporting coherent branding.[134] A number of distributors also adopted the basic 'image-in-a-frame' layout of the majors, creating in the process cross-company continuity.[135] However, conveying 'quality' through brand uniformity proved tricky, given the obscure films that were being traded in by the majority of distributors.

Iver Film Services (IFS) adopted one of the most ambitious strategies. The branding of IFS cassettes not only looked like the majors but was also designed to evoke a comparable sense of history, professionalism and market positioning to those companies with a more distinguished heritage. The artworks of IFS's 1981 releases, for instance, all shared the same basic design: a film still housed in a black/white 'frame', plus the film's title, along with company information, its slogan – 'The Professionals at Pinewood' – and its logo: an illustration of an Oscar-style award displaying 'IFS' on its base.[136] The design, slogan and logo were equally paramount to IFS's company image and directly echoed that of the major companies, specifically WHV, to which the IFS design appeared to owe most. By echoing the WHV style, IFS could convey a comparable sense of consistency.[137] Moreover, the company slogan and logo suggested, echoing IFS's major rivals, that it was a firm invested in quality, award-winning films.[138] Yet while company founder George Davis had a background in film production and the IFS's offices were based at Pinewood Studios, no film in the company's 1981 range was shot at Pinewood, by IFS, and nor had any of them won an Academy

Figure 1.8 Examples of Intervision's generic 'Family Entertainment' video sleeves. Credit: Ian Richardson.

Award.[139] Rather, its catalogue comprised the kinds of independently produced film available from other independents, such as the horror film *Knife for the Ladies* (Larry G. Spangler, 1972), the action film *Honey Baby* (Michael Schultz, 1974), the family film *Elmer* (Christopher Cain, 1976), and the sexploitation film *Love Camp* (Jess Franco, 1977). Nevertheless, by directly recalling historic institutions of popular cinema in its branding, IFS projected a major image onto not-so-major productions, adding a superficial veneer of gloss to little-known films. It also served to create the illusion of creative ownership in a manner comparable to US film studios of the 1960s and 1970s, when majors began acquiring third-party films for distribution and then, through logo placement in credit sequences and on posters, 'branding independent productions as their own'.[140] Projecting an easily recognisable brand that spoke of quality, history and corporate muscle was yet another strategy employed to help an independent company appear as worthy of consumers' money as those with greater resources and reputations.

Through capitalising on the presence of 'stars' and promoting independent movies as 'major' releases, independents mobilised a sense of currency and value at a time when more recent and better-known films – on occasion featuring the same actors – were getting wide exposure from the majors. Indeed, as *Video Retailer* reported, due to the 'pulling power of a leading actor/actress in the marketing of a title', videos could sell 'merely by [the actor/actress's] presence'.[141] It is therefore of some significance that Moutain's release of *The Rebel Rousers* is promoted around the same time as Thorn EMI's release of the more recent Jack Nicholson film *One Flew over the Cuckoo's Nest* (Miloš Forman, 1975), that *No Place to Hide* is released following Intervision/United Artists' releases of Stallone's career-defining works of the day, *Rocky* (Sylvester Stallone, 1976) and *Rocky II* (Stallone, 1979), and that Intervision, in the wake of CIC's release of *Jaws* (Steven Spielberg, 1975), promotes the '*Jaws*ploitation' film *Alligator* (Lewis Teague, 1980).[142] These approaches give grandeur to older and/or lesser-known films, and help contribute to the construction of many independents' desired business images as worthy competitors to the majors, trading in films of comparable quality.

## The Fourth Channel?

By late 1981, given how well consumers were taking to video releases from major companies, almost all non-specialist distributors were prioritising the sale and/or rental of feature films.[143] Video was doing very big business, with the entire industry projected to be worth £200 million by the end of 1982.[144] New companies, from distributors to wholesalers to cassette manufacturers, continued to 'sprout overnight as quickly as mushrooms',[145] while video, at first a novel 'plaything',[146] was quickly becoming 'a standard component in ensembles of consumer electronics'.[147] With the market saturated by companies and products, the video business entered its first period of rationalisation in the spring of 1982.[148]

Up until this point, however, distributors and hardware manufacturers were continuing to get mileage out of the idea that video was a new and exciting technology, the potential of which was yet to be realised. The promise that video would enhance the life of consumers by offering a 'combination of product choice and time flexibility' remained central to sales rhetoric.[149] To bring together choice and time flexibility, independent British distributors, wholesalers and the consumer press at times hyped a narrative of *format exclusivity*. Writing in the US context, media historian Michael Z. Newman argues that, in the early-to-mid 1980s, 'video's meanings adjusted to the medium's newfound uses'.[150] One such use, he explains, sees video 'defined in a relationship of complementarity to movies and mainstream film culture', signified by, for example, families eating popcorn and dimming their living room lights 'to recreate movie theater sensations and some of the special quality of cinemagoing in distinction to more quotidian television viewing'.[151] In this way, video enabled families to replicate a familiar experience by at once improving the function of television as a new 'rival and substitute for the cinema', while also reducing cinema 'to the size of the home and the television set'.[152] Some films released to video in Britain, as discussed above, had been seen in cinemas and were therefore familiar to consumers. A great deal more, however, were not. There were, therefore, advantages to promoting lesser-known films and programmes yet to be seen on television or in cinemas, as exclusive to the video medium, and in the process present the technology as means through which consumers could enjoy filmic entertainment that could not be seen elsewhere. A number of distributors including Mountain, VIPCO and Fletcher thus advertised films as 'pre-cinema' releases, projecting to consumers that video was circumventing traditional release windows, and had become the primary exhibition mode for feature films.[153] Others, including Hokushin, encouraged customers who are 'tired of repeats' to 'Try a good movie that's not been on TV'.[154] Similarly, an ad for VCL's Cinema Features label invited its prospective customers to 'Discover', using its catalogue as a guide, 'the films the critics loved and most cinema's missed'.[155] Beneath the text is an image of a cinema ticket machine from which video covers of the company's newest releases are being dispensed: *Patrick* (Richard Franklin, 1978), followed by *Madron* (Jerry Hopper, 1970), *The Tomorrow Man* (Tibor Takacs, 1979) and, lastly, *Metal Messiah* (Tibor Takacs, 1978). The clear aim is to present Cinema Features as a gatekeeper of hidden gems. Certainly, most consumers would have been unfamiliar with the films it was advertising: *Patrick* was an obscure Australian exploitation film, *Madron* an equally obscure western, while both *The Tomorrow Man* and *Metal Messiah* were Canadian TV movies. Yet the Cinema Features ad implied, as did its company name, that, in spite of these films being relatively unknown, they are still 'great movies' that are surely worthy of a cinema release: fortunately for the consumer they remained exclusive to a video label. At the time, the consumer and trade press mooted that video could signal the death of cinema.[156] Campaigns by VCL and others showed that video, a medium so often dismissed as secondary to the theatrical experience, could in fact be a primary distribution outlet for new, exciting, quality films.

The preceding examples speak to the significance of promoting video as an uncharted cave of wonders, but they also draw attention to the central role that 'the cinema' plays in promotional discourse. Barbara Klinger has argued, that, for taste-makers, when it comes to distinguishing between a film and its video release,

> The big-screen performance is marked as authentic, as representing *bona fide* cinema. By contrast, video is characterized not only as inauthentic and ersatz but also as a regrettable triumph of convenience over art that disturbs the communion between viewer and film and interferes with judgments of quality.[157]

It is telling, thus, that the discourse of cinema remained pervasive throughout much video advertising in the 1980s, such as in an advert for Thorn EMI Home Video, which shows a cinema marquee atop a suburban home, the headline blaring: 'EIGHT GREAT FILMS ON THORN EMI VIDEO. NOW SHOWING ON A SCREEN NEAR YOU.'[158] The ad suggests that, while video is the medium, the experience is cinematic.

Yet 'television' and discourse of a *televisual experience* were not overlooked by distributors. Promoting the flexibility of video – of a format offering consumers choice *and* quality – relied heavily on what Newman terms the 'utopian fantasy' of video, within which TV played an integral role. 'Television's audience, long held captive by the networks' Newman writes, would, at the dawn of the video age, 'be free to exercise choice and to be entertained or edified at his or her convenience.'[159] Foregrounding flexibility was thus a strategic means of instilling *value* in pre-recorded video technology, as reliant on television to function, to draw consumers towards it. An early example of this practice is an advert placed by the London-based video club, Carnaby, in the pages of *Video World* in January 1980. The advert carries an image of a television set, the screen of which adorns the legend 'TODAY'S PROGRAMMES', along with the following 'schedule' beneath it:

15.30 – THE SOUND OF MUSIC
18.20 – THE RAILWAY CHILDREN
20.00 – TINA TURNER LIVE
20.30 – THE BITCH
22.00 – PLAYBIRDS
23.20 – THE HAPPY HOOKER
01.00 – TEXAS CHAINSAW MASSACRE
02.30 – CLOSE.[160]

Using an illustration of a television set, the ad signals video's utopian potential, showcasing the technology's flexibility and the autonomy it grants the consumer. On account of its ability to democratise entertainment, video could (indeed *would*) improve the televisual experience and, as a consequence, the life, of the consumer. Showcasing a range of films in various generic categories – from family musicals to horror to adult-themed drama and sex films – the ad conveyed that television scheduling could be personalised to reflect one's domestic situation: in this specific case with family films initiating the evening's entertainment, followed by a concert of one of the 1980s' biggest music performers, then a recent theatrical hit at 20.30, and more adult-themed sex and horror films (of a sort never likely to be broadcast on the traditional terrestrial networks) rounding things off.

Yet it was not simply the promise of flexible, self-managed television scheduling that video companies were able to present as an advantage to audiences. The flexibility of video intimated by the Carnaby advert came to fruition in Britain because of a perceived lack of commercial television. There were three TV networks in Britain at the time: two publicly subsidised BBC channels (BBC1 and BBC2) and the UK's only commercial station, ITV. When video boomed, ITV was home to three widely successful, and then unrivalled soap operas, *Coronation Street* (1960–present), *Crossroads* (1964–88) and *Emmerdale Farm* (1972–present), each of which boasted millions of viewers. However, in 1979, ITV's programming was suspended for a period of eleven weeks between August and October, as technicians took strike action over a pay dispute.[161] The trade paper *Broadcast* pondered at the time whether 'ITV's loss' would be 'video's gain'. Indeed, while the BBC channels saw an expected increase in ratings at this time, it was widely believed that the BBC's response to the strike was a missed opportunity to 'capitalise on its temporarily-restored monopoly'. Some argued that, in the absence of any real competition, 'the only other alternative' was video.[162]

The strike's benefit to the first video companies was insurmountable. Some inferred that it granted people an opportunity to become 'their own programme planners', as sales swung immediately from niche-interest adult titles, to 'family-type' films. By the time that ITV resumed broadcasting, Intervision (to quote one example) was claiming between 8,000 and 10,000 members and a dealer network of 200 retailers, with Mike Tenner attributing success to the temporary unavailability of the period's most popular television programmes.[163] Formative video distributors such as Intervision seized the opportunity to entice consumers to explore the medium's potential and plug several holes in their TV schedule.

Another factor pertaining to television that video companies were able to play to their advantage was the ongoing discussion initiated in the 1960s between television executives, the government and others about the hypothetical launch of a fourth terrestrial channel. Journalist Maggie Brown recalls how, for decades, television sets were manufactured with four buttons, despite only three of them having a function: 'It was known as the empty channel, and became a growing source of vexation.'[164] Conversations about a latent fourth channel emerged as the consequence of numerous factors, including a perceived need for diversification in television broadcasting, 'to attract new audiences and give an opportunity for new voices to be heard'.[165] Discussions about the channel, including the creative direction it could take, who its owners should be and who should regulate it, persisted for two decades, as 'interested groups argued, cajoled, petitioned and debated the form of the new channel and its proposed parentage'.[166] Eventually, the eponymous Channel 4 would launch to much fanfare as a subsidiary of the Independent Broadcasting Authority (IBA) on 2 November 1982.[167] In the years leading to channel's launch, however, video distributors and hardware suppliers were able to use television's extant limitations to their own ends. Oftentimes this meant selling video *as* the fourth channel: actualising the 'additional service' that the blank fourth button had for so long anticipated.[168]

This approach is ubiquitous across print media. For example, in March 1979, an advert appearing in *Television & Home Video* shows a television set displaying four channels, the first three of which are labelled BBC1, BBC2 and ITV respectively. The fourth, significantly, is *not* blank. Rather,

Figure 1.9 VCL offers consumers an enhanced television experience.
Credit: Popular Film and Television Collection.

and indicative of the video company the advert promotes, it is labelled 'VCL'. The words 'MUSIC, SPORTS, FEATURE FILMS' sit beneath the headline 'TUNE IN TO VCL', indicating the breadth of entertainment available from the company, and thus the potential for video to open the doors to an enhanced televisual experience. Electric Blue adopts a comparable tactic when telling consumers to 'ADD CHANNEL "X" TO YOUR TV' by purchasing the company's adult videos,[169] while IPC and Mountain promote their respective range of cassettes as 'exciting' alternatives to 'the same old' television programmes.[170] Arguably the most effective advert to signal video's potential to affect consumers' experience of TV, however, is one that appears in the consumer press in late 1980. The advert displays the iconic BBC 'Test Card F' that was aired when BBC1 and BBC2 ceased broadcasting for the evening: an image of a young girl, sitting next to a toy clown, playing a game of 'noughts and crosses' on a chalk board.[171] In the advertisement, the Test Card sits beneath the headline, 'TAKE A GOOD LOOK. YOU MAY NEVER SEE HER AGAIN', below which the arrival of '24-hour television' is heralded.[172] The significance of the image is two-fold. In one respect, the advert suggests that, thanks to the video, televisual entertainment is able to continue infinitely, in spite of – and beyond – the closure of the terrestrial networks. Second, it projects the demise of the foremost television company as a consequence of video's growing popularity, and thus the emergence of video as a new channel of which you, the consumer, have control.

As the previous examples attest, video was presented as an enhanced viewing experience for consumers, offering flexibility and exclusivity, a cinematic experience and a televisual one. The aforementioned ads – and countless others like them – reflect a central driver of the early video distributors: with video now widely available, broadcast television (and the rigidity with which it was associated) could, in fact, be avoided altogether.

In 1978, Intervision was a new video distributor claiming to have 'the future in view'.[173] This chapter has shown how Mike Tenner and Richard Cooper were proven right. What began as a hunch about an unknown industry, the idea that Britons would want to stay home to watch feature films on pre-recorded video cassettes, turned into a multi-million-pound industry within a couple of years. And, for a while at least, Intervision's future was bright. By 1982 the company had an annual turnover of £3.3 million, and, in 1983, was the first independent distributor to enter the stock market.[174]

However, the initial success met by Intervision and its many competitors provided little security when faced with market-wide rationalisation.

Several factors – including a greater number of corporations moving into video, the release of too many titles to meet demand, and an increase in negative press for the industry regarding the alleged pervasiveness of graphically violent films – proved for many working in the industry at best tumultuous and at worst fatal. From mid-1982, things changed drastically for the business, and much blood was spilt in years that followed.

Before we get there, however, we need to rewind slightly, and take stock of the backbone of the video business in the early days: the retailer sector. The video business emerged during one of the most fraught economic periods in modern British history and owes its initial success to those business owners who, in a similar manner to the first distributors, took a gamble by investing in the technology. With one in ten out of work between 1979 and 1981, and sales of consumer goods in decline across the piece, the new video business appeared to run counter to economic reality. As one of the only growth industries during this period, many people, from all walks of life, bought into the industry, changing their lives and those of the British consumer in the process.

## Notes

1. I am using the term 'gold rush' in a similar manner to how Joshua M. Greenberg uses it in his history of home video in the US, *From Betamax to Blockbuster: Video Stores and the Invention of Movies on Video* (Massachusetts: MIT Press, 2007), 72–7. Greenberg anchors the term to the boom in video stores c.1980, when, according to one storeowner he quotes, 'People who had no idea what they were getting into' moved into video retail (72). For the purposes of this chapter, I am using the term in relation to video *distribution*. I consider the same period from the perspective of retail in the following chapter.
2. Graham Wade, *Film, Video and Television: Market Forces, Fragmentation and Technological Advance* (London: Comedia, 1985), 22–3.
3. Wade, *Film, Video and Television*, 22–3.
4. Anon., 'UK Fastest-Growing VCR Mart', *Variety* 309.1 (3 November 1982), 34.
5. Dorothy Hobson, *Channel 4: The Early Years and the Jeremy Isaacs Legacy* (London: I. B. Tauris, 2007), 1.
6. Wade, *Film, Video and Television*, 22.
7. From December 1974 to January 1975, the trade periodical *Cinema TV* (which eventually became *Screen International*) published the UK's first 'audio-visual directory', in four parts. I cite them all in what follows.
8. Interview between author and Mike Tenner (Intervision managing director), 24 June 2016.

9. On the history of Magnetic video see Greenberg, *From Betamax to Blockbuster*, 52–6. See also Frederick Wasser, *Veni, Vidi, Video: The Hollywood Empire and the VCR* (Austin: University of Texas Press, 2001), 95–8.
10. Anon., 'The Tape Men', *Late Night Video* 2.6 (1982), 46–9, information about Exciting Lighting at 46.
11. Stephen Traiman, 'New Video Software On Way from UK', *Billboard* (26 June 1976), 49. At this time the company traded as both Intervision and Disco Scene. Trade adverts of the period encapsulate the novel qualities of the company's pioneering technology: 'DISCO SCENE merges video tape, color [*sic*] video projectors, and advanced, highly sophisticated sound into a disco wonderland.' Intervision (Disco Scene), untitled trade advertisement, *Billboard* (2 October 1976), 48.
12. Anon., 'Intervision Video launches new national videocassette library', *Broadcast* 989 (15 January 1979), 13.
13. Anon., 'Intervision Video launches new national videocassette library', 13. For an early example of a consumer advert, see Intervision, untitled consumer advertisement, *Video & Audio Visual Review* (May 1978), 21. Tenner and Cooper typically acquired film rights from Soho's independent theatrical distributors for upfront fees. As Tenner recalls, he and Richard Cooper would '[walk] up and down Wardour Street [where many of the independent theatrical distributors were based], knocking on doors'. Film rights could allegedly be obtained from anywhere between £200 and £10,000. Interview between author and Mike Tenner (Intervision managing director), 24 June 2016. See also, Anon., 'The Tape Men', 46.
14. Interview between author and Mike Tenner (Intervision managing director), 24 June 2016.
15. Barry Fox, 'Everything you ever wanted to know about video but were afraid to ask', *Broadcast* 1179 (11 October 1982; Vidcom 82 Supplement), 15–17. Citation at 16. Sony's U-matic machines were launched in 1971; the Philips N1500 was launched in 1974. Along with Cartrivision they represent the first concerted efforts to target the consumer market with video hardware. Having failed to make a splash in the market, U-matic machines eventually found their natural home in the media industries. For more information see Paul McDonald, *Video and DVD Industries* (London: BFI, 2007), 29–32.
16. On the launch of VHS and Betamax in the UK see Anon., 'JVC launches VHS in UK', *Broadcast* 954 (20 March 1978), 13; and Anon., 'Sony launches PAL Betamax in Britain', *Broadcast* 957 (10 April 1978), 10. On the accessibility of video to consumers see Julian Upton, 'Electric blues: the rise and fall of Britain's first pre-recorded videocassette distributors', *Journal of British Cinema and Television* 13.1 (2016), 19–41. Citation at 36–7. See also Chapter 2 of this book.
17. Wasser, *Veni, Vidi, Video*, 82–5.
18. Sanyo Betacord, untitled consumer advertisement, *Video World* 1.2 (June 1979), 38.

19. Anon., 'Intervision UK video library "selling"', *Billboard* 90.48 (2 December 1978), 62.
20. Wade, *Film, Video and Television*, 24.
21. Barrie Gunter and Malorie Wober, 'The uses and impact of home video in Great Britain', in Mark R. Levy (ed.), *The VCR Age: Home Video and Mass Communication* (London: Sage, 1989), 50–69. Quotation at 50.
22. Anon., 'Brit. Home Video Distribs', *Variety* 297.10 (9 January 1980), 180, 186. Quotation at 180.
23. Intervision, untitled consumer advertisement, *Video World* 1.2 (1979), 5.
24. On TVL Ltd – the company from which VCL grew – see Brenda Barton, 'Who's doing what in video cassettes (Part 4 of 4)', *Cinema TV Today* 10115 (4 January 1974), 12; on VCL's early history see Upton, 'Electric Blues', 22.
25. John Sanders, 'Recorded programmes', *Video World* 1.1 (May 1979), 20–1, 53. Quotation at 53. See also Normak Holdings, untitled consumer advertisement, *Video World* 1.5 (September 1979), 44; Anon., 'Special Something', *Television & Home Video* (April 1979), 9; and Istead, untitled consumer advertisement, *Television & Home Video* (Winter 1978), 42. On the operations of Michael Barratt, see Upton, 'Electric Blues', 25. See also Graham Wade, 'Michael Barratt – where is he now?' *Television & Home Video* (February 1981), 37–41; and also Anon., 'Michael Barratt – Home Video Producer', *Video World* 1.7 (November 1979), 33.
26. Salomé Aguilera Skvirsky, *The Process Genre: Cinema and the Aesthetic of Labor* (Durham, NC: Duke University Press, 2020), 2.
27. Michael Barratt, 'Comment', *Television & Home Video* (April 1979), 5.
28. See Barton, 'Who's doing what in audio visual', *Cinema TV Today* 10112 (7 December 1974), 9. See also Istead, untitled consumer advertisement, *Video & Audio Visual Review* (May 1978), 21.
29. UK Film Council, 'A short note on UK cinema admissions during recessions, 1970 to 2007', UK Film Council (16 September 2008), available at: http://www.bfi.org.uk/sites/bfi.org.uk/files/downloads/uk%E2%80%93cinema%E2%80%93admissions%E2%80%93during%E2%80%93recessions%E2%80%931970%E2%80%932007.pdf. See also Simon Blanchlard, 'Cinema-going, going, gone?', *Screen* 24.4/5 (July 1983), 108–13. Information at 109.
30. As Sheldon Hall explains: 'Throughout the decade [the 1970s], it was usually possible for viewers at least in some parts of the country to see a film every night of the week and in some cases to have a choice among several (video recorders not becoming widely available until the late 1970s)'. See Sheldon Hall, 'Feature Films on British Television in the 1970s', *Viewfinder Online* (13 November 2015), available at: http://bufvc.ac.uk/articles/feature-films-on-british-television-in-the-1970s/fullpage (accessed 4 April 2018).
31. Michael Barratt quoted in Anon., 'Michael Barratt – Home Video Producer', 33.

32. Heikki Hellman and Martti Soramäki, 'Economic concentration in the videocassette industry: a cultural comparison', *Journal of Communication* 35.3 (September 1985), 122–34. Quotation at 124.
33. Leonard Cassini, 'Pre-Recorded Video', *Video World* 1.5 (1979), 60–2. Quotation at 60.
34. The 'collage' approach was in fact borrowed from the distributors of Super 8 and 16mm film reels, which tended to foreground diverse imagery in their promotional material to reflect the broadness of their catalogues. Distributors such as Mountain, Derann and Walton typically adopted this approach. All would eventually move into home video.
35. Intervision Catalogue (1978/9), n.p.
36. Intervision Catalogue (1978/9), n.p.
37. Intervision Catalogue (1978/9), n.p.
38. Intervision Catalogue (1978/9), n.p. Added emphasis.
39. Intervision Catalogue (1978/9), n.p. Added emphasis.
40. Anon., '"Business is booming" says Intervision', *Video World* 1.3 (July 1979), 45, 65.
41. On the company's formation, see Anon., 'Anglo-American tie-up boosts video sales', *Screen International* 193 (9–16 June, 1979), 17; on its product range, see Anon., 'Pre-recorded news', *Video World* 1.4 (August, 1979), 61.
42. Nova Home Video Entertainment, untitled consumer advertisement, *Video World* 1.7 (July 1979), 29.
43. On Magnetic's history, including Fox's acquisition of the company, see Greenberg, *From Betamax to Blockbuster*, 52–6. For an example of contemporaneous industry reportage, in the British context, see Don Macpherson, 'Magnetic Video line up top features', *Screen International* 202 (11–18 August, 1979), 13.
44. Hokushin, untitled consumer advertisement, *Television & Home Video* (August 1979), 28. See also Barton, 'Who's doing what in audio visual (Part 2 of 4)', 9; Hokushin, untitled consumer advertisement, *Video World* 2.3 (March 1980), 41. Hokushin was originally slated to be the UK distributor of Fox's video titles. On the deal and its collapse see Ian White, 'Indie pioneers staying ahead', *Television & Video Retailer* (11 August, 1983), 9.
45. Rank Video Library, untitled consumer advertisement, *Television & Home Video* (January 1980), 72.
46. Videorama Ltd, untitled consumer advertisement, *Television & Home Video* (November 1979), 56.
47. Mountain ad, *Video World* 2.1 (January 1980: 51); Derann ad, *Video World* 2.4 (April 1980), 37.
48. Woodstock Video, untitled consumer advertisement, *Television & Home Video* (March 1980), 8.
49. Inter-Ocean Video, untitled consumer advertisement, *Television & Home Video* (April 1980); Video Instant Picture Company, untitled consumer

advertisement, *Television & Home Video* (April 1980), 62. Thank you to Mark McKenna for pointing me to the early VIPCO ad.
50. Art Features, untitled consumer advertisement, *Television & Home Video* (May 1980), 58; Carnaby Video, untitled consumer advertisement, *Television & Home Video* (May 1980), 51.
51. Vision on Video, untitled consumer advertisement, *Music & Video* (July 1980), 50. See also Home Video Supplies, untitled consumer advertisement, *Video World* 2.7 (July 1980), 12. On the history of the company, see Anon., 'HVS freshens up for summer', *Television & Video Retailer* (May 1982), 50. See also Taboo, untitled consumer advertisement, *Video World* 2.7 (July 1980), 46; and Dapon, untitled consumer advertisement, *Video World* 2.7 (July 1980), 65.
52. See, for example, Brent Walker Video Ltd, untitled consumer advertisement, *Television & Home Video* (September 1980), 29.
53. Anon., 'New UK company', *Video World* 2.10 (October 1980), 7; Anon., 'More Blood More Gore', *Music & Video Review* 6 (October 1980), 14.
54. 21st Century Video, untitled consumer advertisement, *Video World* 2.11 (November 1980), 22–3. See also Anon., 'Tapes cut by VCL', *Television & Home Video* (December 1980), 17.
55. WCI Home Video, untitled consumer advertisement, *Video World* 2.11 (November 1980), 45.
56. See, for example, TCX, untitled consumer advertisement, *Television & Home Video* (September 1980), 44; Intercity Video, untitled consumer advertisement, *Television & Home Video* (December 1980), 62.
57. TCR Video, untitled consumer advertisement, *Television & Home Video* (December 1980), 45.
58. Anon., 'Mean Streets on video', *Television & Home Video* (December 1980), 21.
59. Intercontinental Video, untitled consumer advertisement, *Television & Home Video* (December 1980), 40.
60. CIC, untitled consumer advertisement, *Television & Home Video* (December 1980), 10.
61. Mountain Video, untitled consumer advertisement, *Video World* 2.1 (1980), 51; Mountain Video, untitled consumer advertisement, *Television & Home Video* (June 1980), 72.
62. Derann Audio Visual Catalogue (4th edition, 1981), n.p.
63. 21st Century Video, untitled consumer advertisement, 22.
64. See Vision On Video, untitled consumer advertisement, 38; and Hokushin, untitled trade advertisement B, *Television & Home Video* (August 1981), 76.
65. By 1981, major companies involved in the UK business comprised Warner Bros, Magnetic, CIC, MGM/CBS, PolyGram Video, and EMI Videogram Productions (later Thorn-EMI).
66. On the US context see McDonald, *Video and DVD Industries*, 114; see also Wasser, *Veni, Vidi, Video*, 82–91.

67. Such cinemas were known colloquially as 'fleapits' in the UK and Australia and 'grind houses' in the US. For a useful overview of exploitation cinema see Ernest Mathijs and Jamie Sexton, *Cult Cinema: An Introduction* (Oxford: Wiley-Blackwell, 2007), 145–54. For discussion anchored specifically to the British context, see I. Q. Hunter, *British Trash Cinema* (London: British Film Institute, 2011), and on the etymology of 'flea pit' and 'grind house' respectively, see David Church, *Grindhouse Nostalgia: Memory, Home Video and Exploitation Film Fandom* (Edinburgh: Edinburgh University Press, 2015), 73–118; and Dean Brandum, 'Temporary Fleapits and Scabs' Alley: The Theatrical Dissemination of Italian Cannibal Films in Melbourne, Australia', in Austin Fisher and Johnny Walker (eds), *Grindhouse: Cultural Exchange on 42nd Street, and Beyond* (London: Bloomsbury, 2016), 53–72.
68. Anon., 'London's top ten', *Screen International* 277 (31 January–7 February 1981), 1. See also Colin Vaines, 'Hitting home with the punch-lines', *Screen International* 277 (January–February 1981), 7.
69. Tigon Film Distributors, untitled trade advertisement, *Screen International* 238 (26 April 1980), 24. See also Leon Hunt, *British Low Culture: From Safari Suits to Sexploitation* (London: Routledge, 1998), 32.
70. For example: VPD distributed numerous films handled theatrically by its parent Inter-Ocean Films, such as *Exit the Dragon . . . Enter the Tiger* (Tso Nam Lee, 1976) – which did 'excellent business' in British cinemas due to being similar to *Enter the Dragon* – in 1981. See Anon., 'Latest newcomer to cassette scene', *Television & Home Video* (February 1981), 9. VIPCO licensed a series of popular horror films from Miracle Films, including *Zombie Flesh-Eaters* (Lucio Fulci, 1980) in 1981, which had enjoyed some theatrical success when released as the A-feature on a double bill with *The Toolbox Murders* (Dennis Donnelly, 1978), having set 'a New Year's high' at the Odeon cinemas of Nottingham and Newcastle in March of the previous year. See Anon., 'Zombies on the march', *Screen International* 232 (15 March 1980), 16.
71. See, for example, Anon., 'Exploiting exploitation: Intervision's path to profits', *Broadcast* 1128 (5 October 1981), 32.
72. Peter Speiser, *Soho: The Heart of Bohemian London* (London: British Library, 2017), 7.
73. Hunt, *British Low Culture*, 24. For examples of contemporaneous news coverage see, for example, John Cunningham, 'Sleazy soho falls back on soft porn', *The Guardian* (8 October 1977), 15; and Nicholas de Jongh, '"100 raids" on Soho sex film clubs', *The Guardian* (28 September 1978), 2.
74. Thompson quoted in Hunt, *British Low Culture*, 24.
75. See, for example, Graham Wade, 'Soho goes video', *Television & Home Video* (May 1980), 31–5. This is not the most objective of articles, yet it does capture rather effectively the attitude held by several journalists and media pundits regarding the circulation of such material in Britain, and offers insight into the production and importation of adult films for the British

market. See also Wade, *Film, Video and Television*, 24; and Upton, 'Electric Blues', 33–4.
76. Nicola Lockey, 'Who's behind *Electric Blue*', *Video World* 3.12 (December 1981), 50–3. Quotation at 50. See also Upton, 'Electric Blues', 31.
77. Wade, 'Soho goes video', 33.
78. For a comprehensive examination of pornography and stigma see Georgina Voss, *Stigma and the Shaping of the Pornography Industry* (London: Routledge, 2015).
79. See for example Intervision's subsequent catalogue of 'adult' titles: 'The Video at Midnight Collection' (c.1980).
80. Intervision Catalogue (1978/9), n.p. Added emphasis.
81. As Intervision's Richard Cooper is keen to explain when asked by the adult magazine *Fiesta* why Intervision, while advertising sexploitation films in the pages of the magazine, refrains from trading in hardcore pornographic material: 'In the high street . . . the type of retail outlet we are going for is highly respectable and they would no way handle the stuff . . . [W]e have to be very careful of our own image.' Quoted in Tony Slinn, 'Video Porn' *Fiesta* 14.1 (January 1980), 14–9. Quotation at 17.
82. Wade, *Film, Video, and Television*, 24.
83. Macpherson, 'Magnetic Video line up top features', 13. See also Magnetic Video, untitled consumer advertisement, *Video World* 1.7 (November 1979), 18.
84. See WCI Video, untitled consumer advertisement, 45. The moniker 'WCI Home Video' did not actually make it onto the packaging of Warner Bros releases; by the time the videocassettes made it onto the market, its video division had been renamed 'Warner Home Video'.
85. Companies launching in 1981 include: Astra Video, Go Video, Iver Film Services (Videorama rebranded), Kingston Video, Precision Video, Video Unlimited and Starcurve, ABC Video, British Home Video, Capricorn, Ciroshire, Hello Video, Fletcher (distributing the slide and 8mm Techno Film label), Red Tape Productions, Video Network, Videoform, Videomedia (and the Zodiac label), the Jaguar Video label launched by World of Video 2000, the Picture Time, Sport on Video, Cinema Features, Family Video and 21st Century labels launched by VCL, Gulf Video Centre and the Ocean Shore Video and Omni Video labels, the Video Co, PMA Video, Euro Video Club (EVC), Vidpics, Red Tape Productions and Video Programme Distributors (VPD, now distributing Inter-Ocean and handling releases from the US company Media Home Entertainment). Nineteen eighty-one also sees the launch of the major company PolyGram's video label, Spectrum, and the move into video by one of Britain's long-standing distributors of 8mm reels, Walton (discussed in some detail below).
86. Derann Audio Visual, untitled consumer advertisement, *Video World* 2.4 (April 1980), 37.
87. Derann Audio Visual, Catalogue, 1st edition (1981), n.p.

88. Peter Dean, 'Derann, Derann', *Television & Video Retailer* (3 November 1983), 24–5. Citation at 25. See also Derann Audio Visual, 'Derann Backs Dealers with Quality Video & Promotion', Supplement issued in *Video Business* 1.12 (January 1982), 3.
89. Dean, 'Derann, Derann', 24.
90. Derann Catalogue (1981 revised edition), n.p.
91. Walton Video, 'Aiming to be Britain's most Professional Team. Walton Video – The Professionals [sic.] Choice', supplement issued in *Video Business* 2.8 (June 1982), 3.
92. Walton Video, 'Aiming to be', 3.
93. Anon., 'Movie Pacts with CBS-Fox', *Video Business* 3.31 (26 September 1983), 4.
94. Gibson quoted in Walton Video, 'Aiming to be', 3. On Gibson's career in movies see Walton Video, 'An Excellent Line-up of Vast Skill and Experience. Walton Video – The Professionals [*sic*] Choice', supplement issued in *Video Business* 2.8 (June 1982), 6.
95. Walton Video, 'An Excellent Line-up', 6.
96. Walton Video, 'Aiming to be', 3.
97. Peter Alilunas, *Smutty Little Movies: The Creation and Regulation of Adult Video* (Berkeley: University of California Press, 2017), 11.
98. Alilunas, *Smutty Little Movies*, 11–14.
99. Alilunas, *Smutty Little Movies*, 9. For a broader discussion about consumer anxieties associated with video's inferior quality to, for example, 35mm film, see Michael Z. Newman, *Video Revolutions: On the History of a Medium* (New York: Columbia University Press, 2014), 50–61.
100. Alilunas, *Smutty Little Movies*, 11.
101. See, for example, Cal Vista Video, untitled Promotional Booklet, *Popular Video* (April 1981).
102. Wade, 'Soho goes video', 31–5.
103. Alilunas, *Smutty Little Movies*, 9.
104. See Oliver Carter, 'Original Climax Films: historicizing the British hardcore pornography film business', *Porn Studies* 5.4 (2018), 411–25.
105. John Gill, 'The Sex on Your Telly', *Music & Video* (January 1981), 42–5. Quotation at 42.
106. Gill, 'The Sex on Your Telly', 43.
107. See, for example, VIPCO, untitled consumer advertisement, *Music & Video* (July 1980), 5.
108. Probe Products, untitled consumer advertisement, *Popular Video* (December 1981), 68.
109. Peters clearly takes his cue from Astronics Tele-Cinema, an American company from which he most likely licensed his first releases, and apes his company name. See, for example, Astronics Tele-Cine, untitled consumer advertisement, *Hustler* (July 1979), 8. Thanks to Peter Alilunas for alerting me to this source.

110. TCX, untitled consumer advertisement, *Music & Video* (March 1981), 14. Added emphasis.
111. French Label, untitled consumer advertisement, *Video Review* (August 1981), 34–5. Quotation at 34.
112. French Label was one of several labels handled by David Hamilton Grant, a well-known film distributor with historic connections to the sex film industry. See Mark McKenna, *Nasty Business: The Marketing and Distribution of the Video Nasties* (Edinburgh: Edinburgh University Press, 2020), 63–5.
113. An early advert for VIPCO's range of sexploitation titles adopts a similar strategy. The advert is careful to note that the company's releases have been 'given a *definite* X certificate'. While titles such as *Hot Sex in Bangkok* (Michael Thomas, 1974), *Bed Hostesses* (Michael Thomas, 1972) and *Caged Women* (Jess Franco, 1975) are promoted for their 'strong' sex scenes, they are said to be 'selected . . . from hundreds passed by the censor'. See VIPCO, untitled consumer advertisement, *Television & Home Video* (April 1980), 62. Added emphasis.
114. Video Top Twenty, *Screen International* 351 (10 July 1982), 15.
115. Anon., 'Intervision – on top of the world', *Screen International* 263 (18–25 October 1980); Anon., 'Intervision in UA scoop', *Screen International* 257 (6–13 September 1980), 1.
116. Upton, 'Electric Blues', 35.
117. Upton, 'Electric Blues', 35.
118. Mountain Video, untitled consumer advertisement, *Video World* 2.1 (January 1981), 51.
119. Hokushin, untitled consumer advertisement, *Television & Home Video* (February 1982), 71.
120. PMA Video, untitled consumer advertisement, *Video World* 2.2 (February 1982), 10.
121. Starcurve, untitled consumer advertisement, *Popular Video* (March 1982), 10.
122. Julian Stringer, 'Introduction', in Julian Stringer (ed.), *Movie Blockbusters* (London: Routledge, 2003), 1–14. Quotation at 1. Peter Hutchings argues that, in the British context, Hammer Films were particularly adept at making 'a film appear more expensive than it actually was.' Peter Hutchings, *Dracula* (London: I. B. Tauris, 2003), 35.
123. Barbara Klinger, 'Digressions at the Cinema: Reception and Mass Culture', *Cinema Journal* 28.4 (1989), 3–19. Quotation at 5.
124. Stringer, 'Introduction', 4.
125. Paul Grainge, 'Branding Hollywood: studio logos and the aesthetics of memory and hype', *Screen* 45.5 (Winter 2004), 344–62. Citation at 348.
126. Magnetic had traded in Fox titles as an independent in the US since 1976, before being bought out by the major in 1978. See Wasser, *Veni, Vidi, Video*, 98. WCI Home Video launched in the US in January 1980. See, for example,

WCI Home Video, untitled trade advertisement, *Billboard* 92.1 (5 January 1980), 36–7.
127. Hokushin, untitled consumer advertisement, *Video World* 2.3 (March 1980), 41.
128. McKenna, *Nasty Business*, 99. For an example of branding inconsistency see Inter-Ocean Video, untitled consumer advertisement, *Video World* 2.4 (April 1980), 47.
129. See Intervision, untitled consumer advertisement, *Video Business* 1.8 (December 1980), 13.
130. The image, one assumes, is intended to represent the titles *Men of Sherwood Forest*, *Aladdin's Lamp* and *Treasure Island*. See Intervision catalogue (1978/9).
131. Chris Lightfoot and Richard Gerstman, 'Brand Packaging', in Susannah Hart and John Murphy (eds), *Branding: The New Wealth Creators* (Basingstoke: Palgrave, 1998), 46–55. Quotation at 46.
132. Magnetic Video UK, untitled trade advertisement, *Variety* 297.10 (9 January 1980), 184.
133. Intervision, untitled consumer advertisement, *Video Review* (January 1981), 39.
134. For examples of branding uniformity, see Rank Video Library, untitled consumer advertisement, *Video Review* (January 1981), 25; Hokushin, untitled consumer advertisement, *Video Review* (January 1981), 2; Vampix (Videomedia), untitled consumer advertisement, *Video Review* (February 1981), 33; Inter-Ocean Video, untitled consumer advertisement, Video Review (May 1981), 2; Guild Home Video, untitled consumer advertisement, *Video Review* (September 1981), 49; 21st Century Video (VCL), untitled consumer advertisement, *Video Review* (October 1981), 105; Home Video Productions, *Video Review* (November 1981), 57.
135. For example, both Cinehollywood and Fletcher Video did this. See VPD (Cinehollywood), untitled trade advertisement, *Video News* 1.7 (November 1981), 14–15; Fletcher Video, untitled trade advertisement, *Video Business* 1.12 (January 1982), 14–15.
136. See Iver Film Services, catalogue (1981). See also Iver Film Services, untitled consumer advertisement, *Popular Video* (April 1981), 26.
137. Chris Moore, 'IFS showing How Determined Promotion Can Beat Pirates', *Video Business* 2.10 (July 1982), 36.
138. McKenna, *Nasty Business*, 101.
139. Moore, 'IFS', 36. See also Graham Wade, 'Banking on Blockbusters', *Television & Video Retailer* (February 1982), 54–6. Citation at 54.
140. Grainge, 'Branding Hollywood', 346.
141. Peter Dean, 'The Cover-up Job', *Video Retailer* (30 June 1983), 26.
142. Barry Lazell, '"JAWS" was the chart champion in 1981', *Video Business* 1.12 (January 1982), 6. On Intervision and *Alligator* see Anon., 'Intervision on biggies trail', *Screen International* 336 (27 March 1982), 40. On the

'*Jaws*ploitation' phenomenon, see I. Q. Hunter, *Cult Film as a Guide to Life: Fandom, Adaptation and Identity* (London: Bloomsbury Academic, 2016), 77–96.
143. See, for example, Anon., 'Warners arrive – and feature films take off', *Video Business* 1.1 (February 1981), 11, 14.
144. Anon., 'Survey predicts a £200 million retail business this year', *Video Business* 1.12 (February 1982), 5.
145. Anon., 'Global Video Supplies: service with a smile', *Video News* 1.7 (November 1981), 19, 24. Quotation at 19.
146. Journalist Gerry Gable speaking on *The London Programme*, 'Video Crime', London Weekend Television (13 December 1979), available at: https://lolaclips.com/footage-archive/itv_archive/ITV-01-0722/screener_the_london_programme_video_crime.
147. Newman, *Video Revolutions*, 52.
148. Market rationalisation is covered in detail in Chapter 3 of this book.
149. Wasser, *Veni, Vidi, Video*, 80.
150. Newman, *Video Revolutions*, 43.
151. Newman, *Video Revolutions*, 43–4.
152. Newman, *Video Revolutions*, 44.
153. For example, Mountain adopted this strategy when promoting *Smokey and the Hotwire Gang* (Anthony Cardoza, 1980) and *Nobody's Boy* (Yugo Serikawa, 1970). Mountain Video, untitled consumer advertisement, *Video World* 2.5 (May 1980), 31. The strategy was also adopted by Precision Video, for example, when advertising its release of *Borderline* (Jerrold Freedman, 1980). See Anon., 'Precision movie hits the market before release to cinemas', *Video Business* 2.4 (April 1982), 12.
154. Hokushin adopts this tactic in reference to films such as *No Place to Hide*, *Shalimar*, *Angels Die Hard*, and *Gregory's Girl*. See Hokushin, untitled consumer advertisement, *Video Today* (March 1982), 88.
155. Cinema Features (VCL), untitled consumer advertisement, *Video World* 4.1 (January 1982), 20.
156. See, for example, Adrian Hope, 'Is video killing the cinema?', *Television & Home Video* (July 1980), 22–8; and Anon., 'Video – a threat to the cinema?', *Video News* 1.5 (September 1981), 1.
157. Barbara Klinger, *Beyond the Multiplex: Cinema, New Technologies, and the Home* (Berkley: University of California Press, 2006), 3.
158. Thorn EMI, untitled trade advertisement, *Video News* 1.7 (November 1981), 38.
159. Newman, *Video Revolutions*, 28.
160. Carnaby Video Club, untitled consumer advertisement, *Video World* 2.1 (January 1980), 13.
161. See, for example, Anon., 'The day the telly went blank', *The Observer* (5 September 1999), available at: https://www.theguardian.com/business/1999/sep/05/columnists.observerbusiness2.

162. Anon., 'Will ITV's loss be video's gain?', *Broadcast* 1022 (27 August 1979), 16.
163. Anon., 'ITV strike boosts home video market', *Broadcast* 1029 (15 October 1979), 22–3.
164. Maggie Brown, *A Licence to be Different: The Story of Channel 4* (London: British Film Institute, 2007), 10.
165. Hobson, *Channel 4*, vii.
166. Hobson, *Channel 4*, 2.
167. Hobson, *Channel 4*, vii. See also Brown, *A Licence to be Different*, 53–71.
168. Brown, *A Licence to be Different*, 10.
169. Electric Blue, untitled consumer advertisement, *Television & Home Video* (March 1980), 16.
170. An IPC ad from December 1979 reads 'The exciting alternative to the same old predictable television programmes this Christmas.' IPC Video, untitled consumer advertisement, *Television & Home Video* (December 1979), 48. Similar, a Mountain Video advert reads: 'SEE IT ON YOUR TV WHILST YOUR NEIGHOBUR WATCHES RUN OF THE MILL PROGRAMMES.' Mountain Video, untitled consumer advertisement, *Television & Home Video* (July 1980), 45. Such strategies were also adopted by hardware companies and video clubs. For example, Granada, asks consumers 'What's on the fourth channel tonight?', Video City encourages people to buy into video and thus 'Get Your 4th Channel Now', and Leisuremail offers 'quality pre-recorded cassettes of programmes that you can't see on ordinary TV'. See Granada, untitled consumer advertisement, *Television & Home Video* (October 1979), 19; Leisuremail, untitled consumer advertisement, *Television & Home Video* (March 1980), 46; and Video City, untitled consumer advertisement, *Television & Home Video* (February 1980), 71.
171. See 'Test Cards and Ceefax', BBC [online], available at: http://www.bbc.co.uk/archive/testcards_ceefax.shtml?chapter=1 (accessed 6 April 2018).
172. *Television & Home Video*, untitled consumer advertisement, *Television & Home Video Annual 1981* (December 1980), 42.
173. Intervision, untitled consumer advertisement, *Video & Audio Visual Review* (May 1978), 21.
174. Anon., 'Video goes to market', *Broadcast* 1201 (28 March 1983), 35.

CHAPTER 2

# Shrugging Off the Recession

> If, like me, you're not quite in the upper echelons of the expandable-income bracket, there *is* an alternative to busting your bank balance every time you want to acquire a movie on video. Simply rent one for a few days.
> Martin Hodder, 'Tape rental – here's why it makes sense', *Video Review*

In 1978, when Intervision established its mail order video club and what, ostensibly, was the first British video shop, Britain was on the verge of recession. Between mid-1979 and the beginning of 1981, 'manufacturing output fell by 19.6 per cent' and '23 per cent of all manufacturing jobs were lost'.[1] At this time, 'one worker in 10' was 'jobless', while sales of consumer goods such as alcohol, cigarettes and cars were in decline.[2] This period of recession also, conversely, marked the dawning of a new age of leisure industries (culminating in the opening of Europe's biggest shopping complex, the Metro Centre in Gateshead, Tyne and Wear, in 1987), during which video grew exponentially, with the market doubling in value between 1980 and 1981, and new video libraries – whether mail order companies or physical shops – began springing up to meet demand.[3]

The growth of video clubs and shops and, by extension, the popularity of video as an entertainment medium, needs to be set alongside broader shifts in economic change fostered by the New Right in Britain during the 1980s. Writing in the US context, Frederick Wasser employs the term 'harried leisure' to explain the boom in popularity of video in the 1970s and 1980s, which, he suggests, was a consequence of 'rising affluence' amongst North Americans.[4] Watching video, in other words, could fit around busy work schedules as more people, including a greater number of women, entered employment. 'The VCR', Wasser argues, 'fit in with the new fragmented patterns of family life'.[5]

In Britain the context was different. Home penetration of the VCR grew immeasurably despite the *falling* levels of employment among less well-off social groups.[6] One reason cited for this is that, as more people were laid

Figure 2.1 The managing directors of Intervision, Richard Cooper (L) and Mike Tenner (R), standing outside their headquarters/video rental outlet in Holland Park, London, 1979. Photographer unknown. Credit: Popular Film and Television Collection.

off work, severance money was used to acquire consumer electronics: an area of expenditure that, contra the cost of food and homebuying, had not risen in any drastic sense for a decade or so.[7] As Julian Upton writes, Britons were well accustomed to renting consumer electronics or buying through hire-purchase agreements. '[B]y making machines available for rental at £16–17 a month', he writes, high-street retailers such as Radio Rentals 'brought them into homes that would not previously have been able to afford them.'[8] This also explains why renting video software (the pre-recorded cassettes themselves) appealed over outright purchasing. While prices to rent cassettes were far from consistent (as I discuss in some detail below), when priced to buy – around £40–£50 (c.£150–£200 today) – they were prohibitively expensive for most.[9]

The many programme distributors discussed in the previous chapter ensured that a wealth of material was available to feed the appetite of video-hungry Britons. However, a question remains. How did those with an interest in pre-recorded software go about accessing such material? The present chapter seeks to address this. It is primarily concerned with setting the scene of video renting in its infancy, tracing the development of the business and the culture it fostered between 1978 and mid-1982, from the first mail order clubs to shops where individuals could browse and rent tapes over the counter (and, it must be said, from under it). It begins by examining the social, cultural and economic context that led to the establishment of these operations, and how, collectively, they helped make video a recessing-beating industry. The chapter then pivots to discuss some of the swelling controversy around the independent video trade in the wake of reports of video piracy and how this, among other factors, sealed the image of the independent video trader as unseemly, downmarket and unprofessional: a stereotype the business would struggle to shake as the years progressed.

## Milk and honey

The explosion in video clubs and shops was symptomatic of the dire straits of the British economy in the late 1970s. Margaret Thatcher's project of denationalisation and privatisation fostered an individual-driven, 'pro-capitalist enterprise culture' of self-betterment, one that was enabled by various enterprise initiatives – including the Enterprise Allowance and Loan Guarantee schemes – designed (purportedly) to benefit those workers searching for new career opportunities.[10] The free-market philosophy of Thatcher's Conservative government looked towards what the Prime Minister herself termed future 'princes of industry' or 'self-starters': 'people who have fantastic ability to build things and create jobs'.[11] This rhetoric appealed to the everyday aspirations of Britons – 'who come, as it were, "from nowhere"' – to better their own situation (a situation which, for many, had been worsened by the same neoliberal agenda).[12] By 'taking the initiative', the story went, one could gain financial security and better one's life, the lives of those one employed and the economy.[13]

In *Trash or Treasure?: Censorship and the Changing Meanings of the Video Nasties*, Kate Egan argues that the philosophy of the self-starter underwrites the operations and promotional strategies of the first video distributors.[14] It is a term equally applicable to the thousands of video retailers established in Britain between 1980 and 1982 – those 'small firms' that the Thatcherite agenda, as one that pushed back against the large-firm unionised sector 'which many policy-makers ... believed contributed to ... poor competitiveness and hence the growth in employment', hoped to nurture.[15] However, unlike many of the first distributors – who, as Chapter 1 indicates, already had firm footing either within the AV sector or in film distribution – numerous clubs and shops were managed by people new to the sector and, certainly, new to self-employment, with 'little experience of business'.[16] Many were 'forced [into] entrepreneurship' as a consequence of, for example, redundancy or asylum seeking.[17] Others came to video as a means of expanding their business interests. Regardless, in the late 1970s and early 1980s, video stood as an open door to an unconquered land of milk and honey.

It was in part the reticence of the major high-street retailers to fully embrace video, or for those that did to fail to make a big success of it, which drew aspiring dealers to the business. Major electronics chains such as Granada, Rumbelows, Telefusion and Rediffusion held back from stocking video software at the outset of the boom, while chain stores W. H. Smith and Woolworths, having experimented with video for a couple of years, then withdrew from rental for a period, such was the popularity of independent dealerships.[18] A scheme launched in 1980 by Thorn (a major electronics company), Video at Home, saw greater success throughout Thorn-owned electronics hardware chains Domestic Electric Rentals (DER), Multibroadcast and Radio Rentals. However, while by 1982 the scheme was one of several operating through multiples (including, for example, Rediffusion's Video View operation), together they accounted for a mere 5–10 per cent of the entire rental business.[19]

Numerous factors explain the failure of the high-street multiples to dominate the video market at this early stage of the business's history. The range of stock available in these stores was limited in comparison to that being offered by independent video libraries, and evinced a gross underestimation of the appetite for video that was to grow throughout 1981 and 1982.[20] Video at Home, for example, offered consumers approximately 100 titles in 1980. This was a figure that paled in comparison to the 200-plus that Intervision was offering, the 160 available through The Video Club and the 1,500 offered by Video Unlimited.[21] Moreover, while Video at Home was present 'in all High Streets', its reach did not extend to suburban or rural areas where Intervision and Video Unlimited were supplying racks of cassettes to smaller electronics shops, bookshops, music shops, newsagents and green grocers (where videos were 'nestling among the Bisto and the Brobat').[22] In short, the major high-street retailers did not yet adequately meet the demand for a business that was exploding across various demographics, social strata and regions. Industry watchers were therefore quick to advocate video as a market where the independent trader could – indeed *would* – flourish.[23] Without the fear of serious competition from the multiples (a situation that would, within a year or two, change), the nascent video business was presented as a viable option for those out of work, or, indeed, to those presently self-employed in adjacent retail sectors who were 'feeling the pinch' of the recession and seeking supplementary income.[24] The numbers spoke for themselves: video was one of a handful of growth industries running 'counter to the . . . climate of recession' in 1980 and 1981.[25]

There were two options available to the budding video dealer. Establishing one's own mail order video club proved an attractive proposition at first due to the minimal financial outlay it required. The primary cost was the cassettes themselves – costing around £1,000 (c. £4,000 today) per twenty-five cassettes, including library cases, catalogues, order forms and membership cards – in addition to relatively inexpensive adverts placed in the rear sections of newspapers and new consumer magazines such as *Video World* and *Video Review*.[26] Staffing or rental charges did not always apply, nor was expensive signage or branding required, for many such business were operating out of domestic households. This was true, for example, of the Video Exchange Club: a library boasting 'thousands' of titles, all the while operating from a semi-detached house in Essex.[27] Such mail order clubs showed that, in theory, anyone could enter the video business, and there is anecdotal evidence to suggest that there was much success to be had by adopting this approach. For example, another operation, The Video Club, having started life in 1979, was boasting about attracting 500 new members per week in 1981,[28] while other firms had boomed beyond all recognition, including Video Unlimited, which started life at a residential address in 1980 stocking titles from Intervision and other companies, but, by late 1981, was a thriving independent distributor in its own right.[29]

It soon became apparent that, while mail order firms proffered a no-frills means of entering the video trade for aspiring business folk, a good consumer experience was not always guaranteed, and such operations became stigmatised. It was common across the piece for clubs to request advance cash payments of considerable sums. Club members would pay a membership fee, typically in the region of £85 (c. £350 today), that would entitle individuals to either a set or an unlimited number of video rentals for a twelve-month period, with the only additional cost being the price of postage (around 80p or £3.50 today).[30] Joining clubs in the early months of the video boom, when few mail order clubs had amassed credible reputations, was therefore considered a risky business. Consumer magazines warned consumers about falling foul of 'unscrupulous advertiser[s who] can take your cash and just disappear'. Other stories, of exchange clubs supplying its members with titles alternative to those requested, were also pervasive. For some, mail order clubs merely amounted to 'a small ad that promises much' but ultimately fails to deliver.[31] The spectre of mail order pornography and piracy was also mobilised to steer consumers away from postal clubs.[32]

Mail order clubs would soon give way to a consumer preference for retail outlets that one could visit in person.[33] Video shops, whether trading solely in video cassettes/hardware, or outlets where video served as an add-on to another lines of product (such as those Intervision and Video

Figure 2.2 Catalogues of two of the earliest mail order video clubs, The Video Club and Video Unlimited, 1980. Credit: Ian Richardson.

Unlimited supplied in the early days), enabled consumers to experience video as a tangible medium, to browse, choose and acquire their cassette of choice immediately. There were, of course, *some* similarities between the shops and the mail order clubs. Most required a membership fee and charged an additional fee per cassette for between one to three nights' rental. But even then, there were huge discrepancies between shop policies. Memberships fees were wildly inconsistent. Some clubs offered an annual membership from £25–£50 (c.£100–£200 today), depending on the outlet. Others offered a lifetime membership, with some charging as little as £5 (c.£20) and others as much as £100 (c.£400). Rental prices were more consistent – varying between £2 (c.£8) and £5 (c.£20) for an evening's rental, or around £6 (c.£23) for three days (prices were, at times, set by the distributors) – but as a rule one could expect to pay a little more if the membership fee was low, or less in the opposite scenario.[34] It was also the case that renting from shops bore some risks: there were some stories of shops springing up, taking people's money and disappearing without a trace, for example.[35] But, for most, the pros of in-person rental outweighed the cons. Being able to visit premises to select a title proved favourable because it was more convenient than having to wait days or weeks for a cassette to arrive at one's door, and was certainly perceived as being less hazardous than sending money and valuable videocassettes through the post.

While in the beginning no one video outlet was the same as another, there were nevertheless elements of consistency that quickly became staples of the video shop's 'material character'.[36] Titles tended to be categorised in some semblance of order – what Herbert, writing in the US context, describes as a video store's 'architecture of classification' – such as by genre, distributor or alphabetically.[37] Customers would typically be able to browse empty video boxes in the front of the shop, or, if the premises were very small, peruse flattened box-covers in folders or similar. In most scenarios, the valuable cassettes remained behind the counter, out of the public's reach.[38] One might also find in smaller outlets – where stock was at times surplus to space – a list of titles at the front of the shop, to be browsed as one would a food menu in a takeaway. Regardless of the specific approach of each outlet, however, video shops normalised video rental as a consumer activity that was presented to the public in a manner more in keeping with their day-to-day experiences as consumers of cultural goods.[39]

## 'Experience the high profitability for yourself!'

Establishing a video shop, or embracing video as part of an established business, appealed greatly to existing and aspiring business folk, not least because those who were already experimenting with stocking video software were enjoying unprecedented levels of success.[40] In this context, video was viewed as an easy win for aspiring business owners, or those with established businesses who were struggling. Thatcher's 'rags to riches' narrative was pushed in the trade and consumer press, and those working in the business looked to appeal to the public to help video grow.

The story of Carnaby Video, a wholesaler and chain of video shops established in 1979, is a good example of the narrative that Britons might better their luck by venturing into video during the recession. Founded by managing director Joseph Pina in August 1979, Carnaby joined Intervision as another of the earliest pre-recorded videocassette retailers in Britain, operating out of one shop, 26 Carnaby Street in central London, and offering cassettes for both rental and sale.[41] Within a year, Pina moved the company into wholesaling (while retaining his initial retail outlet, and opening a further two), and, shortly after, became Europe's biggest video wholesaler.[42] This success was, however, short-lived. By the end of 1981, the company was in the hands of the receiver, before being bought out

Figure 2.3 One of Joe Pina's stores: The Video Cassette Shop, Charing Cross Road, London, 1981. Photographer unknown. Credit: Popular Film and Television Collection.

by one its newest rival wholesalers, Wynd-Up.[43] The failure of Carnaby to survive after amassing such huge profits was indicative of the rate at which video was booming, the number of tapes released on a weekly basis, and also the number of new distributors and wholesalers emerging as the market entered its rationalisation period in 1982. Pina's company was among many firms not to exercise caution during this period, carried away by self-made success and the notion that the nascent video market was 'recession-proof'.[44] (The next chapter will show how this assumption, while pervasive, was far from true.)

Regardless of the fate it would eventually meet, the significance of Carnaby to the present discussion, and specifically Pina as the face of the company, is that, from the outside looking in, the company embodied the key components of the New Right's 'pro-capitalist enterprise culture',[45] pushed 'the gospel of enterprise' to the trade and consumer press with vigour,[46] and in so doing created a sense that video provided a road out of the recession for everyday Britons.[47] Pina was presented – and, indeed, self-identified – as someone who, with very little in the way of resources but with an abundance of ambition, found huge success quickly during the fraught economic period. At a time when retail was otherwise slumping, video was booming, and Pina was keen to present himself as one of the industry's first real success stories: a *prince of industry* to be in awe of and to inspire.

The Carnaby success story first appears in the inaugural issue of the trade periodical *Video Business* in February 1981.[48] The headline, 'From a tiny retailer to a wholesale success', indicates the social and economic climate of contemporary Britain and the narrative Thatcher would proceed to push, summarising growth ('from . . . to . . . ') and an individual's drive for self-betterment ('a tiny retailer'). The article progresses to discuss the partnership at the heart of the company, between Pina and John Whelan, who is said to bring 'experience of retailing' to the table.[49] Yet it is Pina, as managing director, who is emphasised as the company driver. Any retail experience Pina may or may not have is not acknowledged; rather, Pina is the *brains* of the operation – the one with 'the big ideas' – having established the company on his own and successfully predicting the extent to which video 'would snowball in the High Street'.[50] The key to Carnaby's success (it would appear from this description at least) is having the confidence and ambition to think big and – crucially for those being hit hardest by the recession – beyond one's current situation. Indeed, in terms of the New Right, such confidence – the ability to stand 'on your own feet' – was crucial to realising the 'princes of industry' narrative.[51] As Corner and Harvey have it, self-starters 'thrive on the excitement of competition and the stimulus of commerce'.[52] Pina's 'big ideas' were therefore presented as being enough for him to lead in the infant video software industry, outweighing the necessity for a history in business. The resultant image is that of a passionate everyman 'taking the initiative' and, through resourcefulness and hard work, 'getting things done'.[53]

The consequence of Pina's vision is evidenced by the success the reader is told he has amassed in a matter of months: three retail outlets, a '2,500 square foot warehouse', twenty-six staff, and the status of being 'probably the UK's largest wholesaler of pre-recorded videocassettes'. By framing Pina as an everyman with ideas and ambition, listing his achievements and the speed at which they were attained as evidence of them, he is hereby presented as an archetypal self-starter, who 'comes from nowhere', creates jobs, and in the process 'make[s] it to the top'.[54]

Pina was keen to capitalise on this image, to reach out across the faltering retail sector and beyond, to make winners of others and further his own business interests in the process. Consequently, Carnaby's 'rags to riches' narrative would remain central to Pina's self-image as his company expanded into 1981. From late 1980 Carnaby had experimented trading in 'special dealer packs': two different combinations of twenty video titles designed to entice people into the video business by, in essence, providing them with twenty desirable cassettes, catalogues and point-of-sale material. The service was aimed at those already working within retail wanting 'to move into video software but [who] lack[ed] the knowledge of the market'.[55] This was a service originally provided on a word-of-mouth basis. Yet as the recession took a tighter grip of the retail sector in early 1981, Pina seized an opportunity to reach out to a greater number of dealers, taking it upon himself to write to them personally expressing the benefits of video, and the money to be generated by accepting Carnaby's help in establishing a video sideline of their own. His strategy comprised a typed letter and a full-colour leaflet. Key to the message was the ease with which one could reimage one's faltering business through video rental and sales. In so doing, Pina reinforced the opportunities of free enterprise deemed so intrinsic to the Thatcherite project. The strategy adopted two strands: at once stressing the growth of video a major market, and also that small-time independent dealers are the ones best suited to propel its growth and reap rewards from it.

The letter is a culmination of statistics and statements about the growth of home video's popularity and claims to the role everyday tradespersons can play in contributing to that growth and, in the process, their own wealth. Video's 'profit growth', the first sentence informs the reader, 'is the highest of any product within the UK', before going on to explain that 'Local availability is proving to be the key to success for all types of outlets'. Here, video is framed as a sector of 'mass popularity', yet one that is driven not by major retailers, but, conversely, everyday tradespersons reliant on 'local' footfall. The future of this growth industry, thus, is at the grassroots level, and therefore an opportunity for individuals – with Carnaby's help – to seize.

The rhetoric continues across the accompanying leaflet. Adorning the cover is a photograph of Pina, wearing a suit, smiling and looking outwards. The leaflet embodies the individualism of the Thatcher years. The story is not one of teamwork, but of personal ambition and leadership; the legend beneath the image blaring '*I* had just one shop, a couple of staff and a little spare capital'.[56] With very 'little', one could have success with video, staff of one's own and, perhaps more than '*just* one' outlet: again feeding into the narrative that risk and ambition lead to prosperity.[57] Anyone, allegedly, can do this. Pina's is the face of a relatable person who, against the odds, turned his life around through video.

The boom in independent shops, and the narrative of success that was being propelled not by the high-street multiples but by everyday individuals, continued throughout 1981 – culminating in the formation of a representative body for the independent dealer, the Video Trade Association

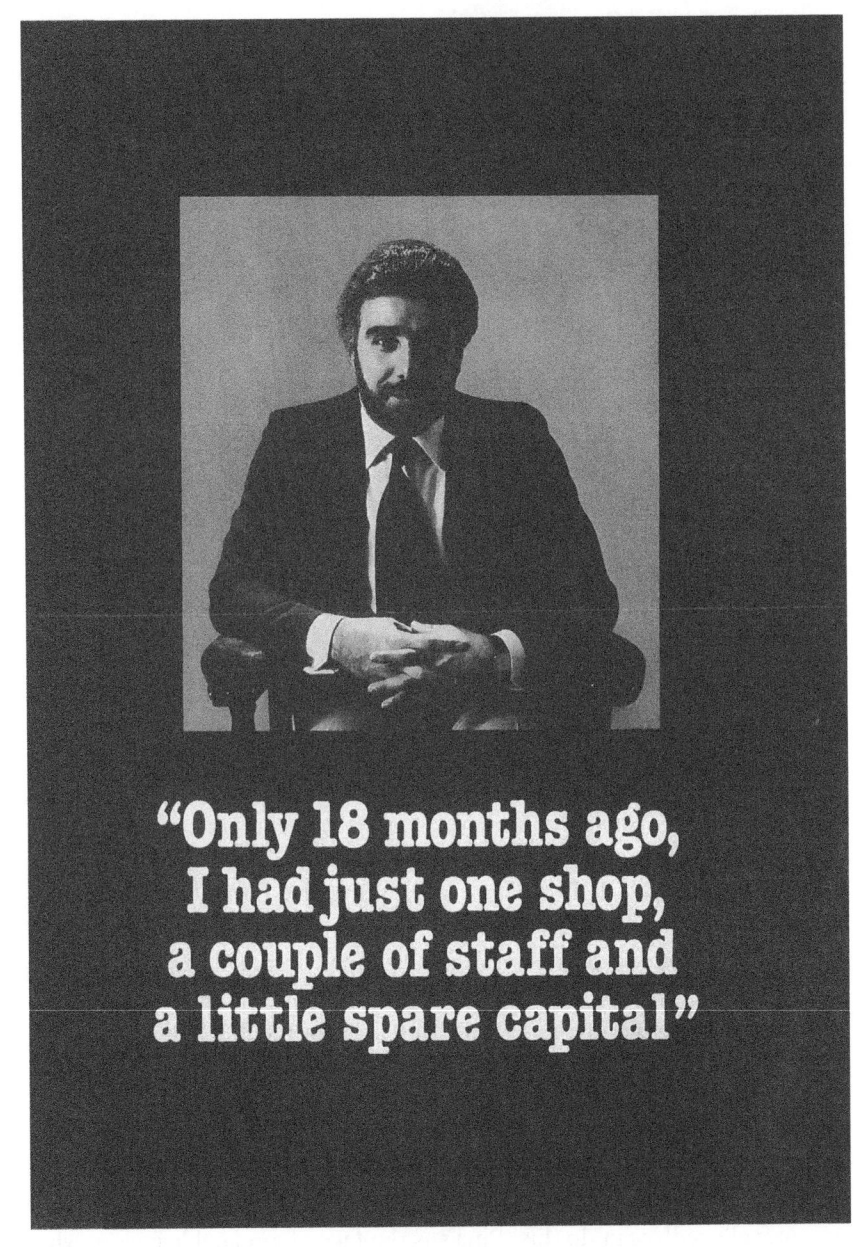

**Figure 2.4** A prince of industry: Joe Pina of Carnaby Video. Credit: Popular Film and Video Collection.

(VTA).[58] The first Home Video Show, a trade show at which distributors advertised their wares in the hope of striking deals with retailers and vice versa, had evidenced video's gravitational pull as a recession-beating industry, attracting people from as diverse a range of backgrounds as greetings card retail, carpet and upholstery sales, off licences, used car sales, the building trade, bakery, hairdressing and tour operation.[59] Meanwhile, new wholesalers were promoting a similar narrative to Carnaby, such as Video Unlimited, said to have grown '[f]rom a bedroom to a warehouse in two short years'.[60] Similarly, other companies were following in the footsteps of Carnaby, by advertising 'VIDEO FILMS AS A BUSINESS', promoting video as a '"fun" field of enterprise' that was both 'highly profitable' and 'easy to run'.[61] Such adverts once again spoke to the layperson, as means of enticing those out of work or looking to bolster their current business – to 'make your fortune', as an early advert for the wholesaler PMA had it – while squarely aligning with Thatcher's enterprise initiative, and the New Right's notion that work is something that should be enjoyed.[62]

## 'Ethnic minorities go for video'

The preceding analysis has offered an assessment of how video became a viable business opportunity for individuals from a range of employment backgrounds. What it has not done, however, is accounted for *cultural* nuances that, in various ways, affected the video business for many tradespersons and consumers. As the previous chapter suggests, the video boom was fuelled, chiefly, by a demand for western films – by which I mean films produced in the western region of the globe and not films in the 'western' genre (per se).[63] Yet there was also a large, and forever growing, market for non-English movies among the UK's diverse migrant population, specifically those of the South Asian diaspora.

The migration of South Asians to British shores dates back to the early twentieth century, but has notable significance in the partitioning of India and the dissolution of the British Raj in 1947 (resulting in the statelessness of many across the Bengal–Punjab divide), various bouts of political turmoil in East Africa (including the end of British Colonial rule in Kenya and the proceeding African nationalist agenda pushed by Prime Minister Jomo Kenyatta), and the expulsion of 50,000 Asians from Uganda by prime minster Idi Amin in 1972.[64] These significant political events occurred amid an economic boom period for Britain following the end of World War II, of which 'the large-scaled immigration of migrant workers' from the Indian subcontinent played a key role.[65]

Many South Asian immigrants residing in Britain gravitated towards video retail in the late 1970s and early 1980s because, as ethnic minorities, they 'suffered disproportionately' when unemployment spiked, as they were 'often concentrated in the most vulnerable jobs', which tended to demand long hours and offered low pay.[66] Self-employment was an 'outcome of a struggle against economic disadvantage and discrimination', with video in particular appealing for several reasons.[67] Film culture was, and still remains, a hugely significant pastime for Britain's Asian communities, specifically involving films produced out of Bollywood.[68] The growth in popularity of Bollywood movies among South Asians in Britain since the 1950s led to the development of many 'specialist Indian cinemas' by the end of the 1970s, 120 of which screened Hindi films on either a full- or part-time basis.[69] The first Indian cinemas catered for a community whose experiences and interests were not adequately represented on domestic television, or catered for by other 'leisure/culture facilities'.[70] In some areas, such venues are said to have 'attracted' Asian businesses to their vicinity, which 'in turn attracted Asians who moved into the respected areas'.[71] Seen in this way, Hindi cinemas became hubs around which communities grew. The nascent video market can attribute its buoyancy to the culture that such venues fostered; as with elsewhere in the country, supplanting the high cost of a 'family outing to the cinema' with a cheaper alternative.[72] Bringing about the 'collapse of Hindi cinema exhibition' in Britain, video was now a 'regular family leisure activity',[73] offering first-generation migrants an opportunity to reflect nostalgically on their old home life while exposing their British-born children to elements of their native culture.[74] As with specialist cinemas before them, video offered migrants one means of reconnecting – or rather, maintaining a connection – with their heritage: as Rajinder Dudrah has it, to 'engage further with their diasporic sense of selfhood'.[75]

British Asian video shops in areas of cities such as Leicester and Birmingham in the Midlands, while similar in some respects to those operated by their white British counterparts, foregrounded an Asian cultural experience – one governed by the heritage of their owners and the communities they were serving – not found in other, predominantly white, areas of the cities. Characteristics of all video shops such as membership/rental fees and stock categorisation were features of Asian outlets too, but the range of Indian Hindi-language films far exceeded those available at non-Asian dealerships, most of which did not stock any.[76]

This had not always been the case. In 1979 and 1980 Intervision and Carnaby advertised Asian films – usually bundled under the loose (and most of the time frankly inaccurate) 'Arabic' or 'Arab' labels – in their shops alongside other genres.[77] Yet this soon changed when the companies set up their distribution and wholesale divisions in earnest. Following the rapid uptake of video by South Asian shopkeepers and entrepreneurs in 1979/80, non-English films were abandoned by the companies whose success in the English-language market was skyrocketing. It was of course commonplace for Asian shops to stock English-language videos, which were as popular as ever, and indeed many of the major wholesalers (all of which dealt primarily in English-language fare) had contracts with these outlets. But the wide range of Indian stock made Asian dealerships stand out among communities in areas of cities where many South Asians lived and worked.[78]

Writing in the US context, Joshua M. Greenberg argues that early video stores sought to instil in their clientele a sense of familiarity anchored to the individuals' formative experiences of film viewing. A key means of doing so, he reveals, was for stores to sell snacks that one had come to expect at movie theatres; to, as he has it, 'duplicate' the 'theatre experience'.[79] Popcorn was one such product, with video retailers sometimes going so far as to install popcorn machines on the shopfloor, akin to those found in cinema lobbies.[80] The sweet snack, one retailer is quoted as having argued, 'is part of' the 'aura' of movie-going: it 'makes people feel good'.[81] While the meshing of sweet snacks and video retail was not as common in the western British video shop as it became in the late 1980s when the market became more corporatised and US-influenced, from the outset of the video boom Asian video retailers were situating video alongside food and other products designed to command an 'aura' of familiarity that would make their South Asian customers 'feel good'.[82] The 'aura' of Asian shops, however, was not of cinema-going (per se), but rather of a non-western cultural experience in a broader sense. This was an inevitable consequence of Asian shopkeepers incorporating video into their established businesses, selling, for example, 'types of food and clothing unknown' to their native British counterparts.[83] One would therefore find sections of 'the ubiquitous corner shop' established by first-generation migrants given over to a rack of videocassettes, complementing other culturally specific commodities.[84]

Pioneer Video Emporium in Leicester is one such example. Its history is typical of its cultural moment. Established in the late 1970s by the Rathods, a family of Ugandan Indians expelled by Idi Amin, Pioneer began its life on Narborough Road (one of several areas in the city where migrant families live and set up businesses to this day) as 'Dave Pan & Sweets Centre', a confectioner and tobacconist trading in specialist Indian sweets and 'pan' (or 'paan' – a combination of betel leaf and areca nut, for chewing).[85]

**Figure 2.5** Archive news footage of Dave Pan & Sweets Centre
(later Pioneer Video Emporium), Leicester, c.1982. Source: BBC News.

Following the rapid uptake of video by ethnic minorities, the shop began stocking Asian and English-language video titles as a sideline, eventually changing its name, yet retaining its confectionary and paan, when video became its primary customer draw.[86] The shop, like other Asian businesses throughout the city, was emblematic of factors anchored to the experience of South Asian diasporic communities, in that, by foregrounding culturally specific video films and consumables, it contributed to a shared 'ethnic consciousness', articulating 'distinctiveness' through the products it sold to the community of which its owners were also a part.[87] If, as Gurharpal Singh has it, 'the core feature that defines the Indian diaspora is its collective imagining of India', 'of emotions, links, traditions, feelings and attachments', then Pioneer Video and its contemporaries went some way in bringing together cultural elements that fed into this imaginary.[88] The shop symbolises the 'common history' of many Asian entrepreneurs whose businesses were brought about as a consequence of their lives having been uprooted. Such establishments thus bore the fruits of shared experiences.

The shop name is significant to the owners' articulation of their heritage to their customers. As with many East African Asians who were expelled from Uganda, the Rathods were 'forced to leave their [business]', the

Pioneer Customs Agency, 'behind'.[89] The reappropriation of 'Pioneer' into their new business venture into video retail, and as a name specific to the family of migrants, serves as a bridge between the family and their past lives in Uganda, as a reminder of their heritage and how they managed, like so many of their contemporaries, to flourish in local business as 'an unexpected minority in the UK'.[90] Succeeding in business in a culturally alien environment allowed South Asians 'to recapture some of the self-esteem lost' as a consequence of Amin's Asian expulsion.[91] The reuse of 'Pioneer' in this new environment thus embodies the defiance and pride temporarily perturbed by the family's forceful uprooting as a reassertion of their past business success. The addendum 'Video' speaks comparatively to both the present moment and the future, to the role that the Rathods would continue to play in helping maintain native cultural experiences through communal relations fostered by the retail of South Asian video films, sweets and paans, and the role this combination played for so many businesses in 'maintaining culture and traditions reminiscent of back home'.[92]

## 'Rip Off Video Club'

The romantic image of video being propelled by normal, everyday people servicing their communities was not one held by all. For example, the assumed pervasiveness of pornographic videocassettes discussed in the previous chapter reflected badly on independent dealers. Another looming factor affecting the image of video shops was video theft, or 'piracy'. Since the earliest stirrings of the video boom, a key concern of the major film studios was that video allowed individuals to make duplicate copies of copyrighted materials – a concern usually directed at the VCR's ability to record television programmes owned by the major American networks. These concerns were present in Britain too, albeit more so the alleged ubiquity of illegally duplicated pre-recorded material. Indeed, it was estimated in 1982 that 70–80 per cent of all commercially available videos in Britain were illicit copies.[93]

Independent video shops, so ubiquitous they now were, were typically held accountable. There is no doubt some truth in this. However, it is important to understand the many factors that led video dealers to trade in pirated goods. It is conceivable, in the early days at least, that some of those working as video dealers did not fully comprehend the law – never mind its application to video technology. Video was, after all, a new medium that both the industry and consumers were just starting to understand, and there was much discussion in the trade press about the industry lacking formal regulation: this latter scenario is what encouraged some distributors to, for example, release uncut prints of films censored for cinema release onto video, or trade in hardcore pornographic material. But it was also inevitable, given that many dealers often had no experience in running any business, that naive mistakes were going to be made. Percy Brown, head of the Motion Picture Export Association of America (MPEAA), was in 1981 prepared to give some video pirates the benefit of the doubt. Speaking with the consumer magazine *Popular Video*, he explained that piracy was common among 'workers who have been made redundant, who have been persuaded to put all their money into running a video club', because said individuals lacked business acumen or knowledge of the laws protecting intellectual property and copyright.[94] Notwithstanding the air of classism in Brown's assessment, in this context the entrepreneurial spirit of the self-starter is seen to trump the demands of the law because mistakes, Brown seems to suggest, are inevitable in such a formative stage of the business.

Such accounts, however, were in the minority. The dominant image of video piracy in 1980–1 was a shadow economy propelled by US crime syndicates rapidly infiltrating Britain's retail sector. Indeed, in 1980, London Weekly Television's (LWT) current affairs show, *The London Programme*, ran a report on so-called 'video crime', which claimed that the 'criminal potential of video was first realised' in the US by the Mafia.[95] It proceeds to argue, via the support of talking heads from law enforcement and major software distributors, that pirate video was but one component in a vast network of criminal activity including drug trafficking, gunrunning, smuggling and hardcore pornography. 'It's a very very big business', Tony Seaman of 20th Century Fox tells the reporter, 'and videocassettes are a part of that business'.

The bridge between the Mafia and the public, such reports intimated, was the 'small scale dealer'.[96] Indeed, the press – including the video consumer press – tended to depict or write about video pirates in a manner that compounded the industry's associations with Thatcherite enterprise initiatives. After all, if the video business was awash with individuals who had 'come from nowhere', then this could also, by such logic, include criminals. However, far from princes of industry, pirates were sketched as 'cowboys', 'wideboys' and 'spivs': longstanding stereotypes of affluent, ostensibly working-class men involved in petty criminality. This allowed reportage to emphasise the covertness of piracy – it was happening at the margins, i.e. not on the high street – while at the same drawing attention to the culpability of otherwise legitimate dealers in furthering the agenda of gangland criminality. Such stereotypes were familiar to the public given their presence in sitcoms of the period, such as *Minder* (1979–94), where the character of Arthur Daly (George Cole) strives to make a 'fast buck' through various covert get-rich-quick schemes,⁹⁷ and *Only Fools and Horses* (1981–96), where market trader Del Boy (David Jason) is characterised as 'part of a coterie of duckers and divers and bit-of-this, bit-of-that merchants'.⁹⁸ Yet while framing pirates in this manner drew from a culture whereby such character types were, for the most part, endearing and central to their shows' appeal, in the real world such types were considered by case-makers to be at odds with the enterprise culture that Thatcher endorsed. As Stephen Baker and Paddy Hoey argue of Arthur Daly, '[in *Minder*] there is no porousness in the dividing line between the opportunistic urban working class and the sophistication of the middle class'. Thus, while Arthur and by extension the pirate video dealer 'resonate', on the one hand, 'with the privatising, deregulating, free-market zeal of the Conservative government', they both ultimately embody 'unrespectable, working-class entrepreneurship', from which 'upward mobility' is inhibited by a 'glass ceiling'.⁹⁹

The downmarket image of the opportunistic, 'small scale' pirate video dealer pervades across the consumer press of the period. For example, in a 1981 issue of *Popular Video*, a satirical cartoon accompanies an article about the 'risks' of video rental. The image, set in the Wild West, shows a cowboy – the proprietor of the 'Rip Off Video Club' – hiding from the local Sherriff whose badge bears the Warner Communications logo and whose gun has 'COPYRIGHT' engraved into the barrel.¹⁰⁰ The message is clear: the law is on the side of the big corporations, who can use it at any time to take out the low-level, opportunistic, chancers who seek to obstruct their expansion by trading in illicit wares. Another article, this time for the consumer magazine *Video World*, attempts something similar, characterising video piracy as peddled by small-time gangsters in the image of Arthur Daly. 'If Arthur Daly was up with the times', the opening paragraph reads, 'he'd be into dodgy video.' The article is accompanied by a Daly-style caricature, a gangster in a pin stripe suit and trilby, holding up a copy of the then legally unavailable *Rocky III* (Sylvester Stallone, 1982), adjacent to the headline 'All Right My Son' – a known Daly catchphrase.¹⁰¹

Piracy being a cog in the underworld machine, potent though the idea was, was only part of the story. Oftentimes, such transgressions, while pervasive, were not anchored to a network of organised criminality. In fact, there is anecdotal evidence to suggest that, as video boomed throughout 1981 and into 1982, 'back-to-back' piracy – whereby individuals make their own copies of tapes using domestic VCRs – was increasingly practised by dealers who, for the most part, were otherwise legitimate. Ramon Lobato notes in his pivotal study *Shadow Economies of Cinema: Mapping Informal Film Distribution* that industry claims as to piracy's interconnectedness with underworld activity, from drug trafficking to gun smuggling to terrorism and so on, were and remain routinely unsubstantiated.[102] Moreover, claims regarding the detrimental impact of piracy on the formal media economy – on sales, for instance – are widely controversial given that, among other reasons, 'piracy's subterranean and disreputable nature means attempts to quantify', for example, industry losses, 'are inevitably speculative'.[103] Such spin is nevertheless widespread, and works to reinforce the logic that propels the industry's 'war' on illegal copying which, as Lobato argues, 'needs to be understood as a public relations exercise aimed at reinforcing a deferential relationship to copyright and showing the vulnerable side of a powerful industry'.[104] This enables the anti-piracy lobby to propagate claims as to the harm that piracy does to the legitimate film industry (i.e. corporate Hollywood),[105] all the while negating the harm caused by the legitimate film industry to those who, for instance, comprise the distribution supply chain: in the present context, video dealers.

Indeed, by 1982 video tradesfolk were becoming increasingly vocal about the unfair terms that the major distributors were trading on. Competition was especially fierce during this period as the market, now crowded with both product and video outlets, approached rationalisation (see Chapter 3). Copies of the majors' desirable films were very expensive, and, in many cases, were not eligible to be bought outright due to distributor-imposed restrictions. In fact, most of the majors had begun *leasing* titles to dealers, routinely making it so that the most desirable of releases could only be acquired if a dealer agreed to lease several less popular titles; usually up to twelve at a time and typically for a minimum period of six months. For many of the less-resourced video dealerships the policy was unreasonable, because:

> [it] serves to increase the lack of flexibility to the dealer by forcing him [*sic*] to stock a range of titles (not all of which can be said to be blockbusters) for a longer of period of time than he [*sic*] would choose. These titles must be pushed upon library members for rental at the expense of titles paid for in full simply to ensure that they pay for themselves.[106]

Faced with these terms, some turned to piracy to outstep them.

It was a choice that had political implications. As Lobato argues, 'while film industry lobbyists decry piracy', it is possible to interpret it 'as a form of subversion' or *resistance* to the onslaught of market dominance by corporate forces.[107] It was, after all, the majors who had 'forced' independent retailers to take such drastic action by imposing such a stringent policy. As one dealer has it, writing in the letters pages of *Video Business*, the majors 'need look no further than the end of their avaricious noses' for an explanation as to why illegal copying was on the rise. The prices were too high and the terms of acquirement for the dealer were unfair.[108] Another argues despairingly, that, under present leasing terms, '4500 rentals are need to break even' if he is to keep his reasonable £2 per night rental charge.[109] Piracy – which might amount to maintaining contracts with major distributors, ordering the minimum number of cassettes, and then making 'back-to-back copies as custom demands'[110] – was a strategy that could ease the pressure. It would certainly negate having to lease twenty-four titles to get two copies of a sought-after film. Trading in illegal wares thus enabled the small dealer to recalibrate the market, to re-level the playing field, and to reduce prices to more easily compete with their main rivals who were already seeing the financial rewards of stocking pirated copies of films.[111] Piracy in this way was a means by which small dealers could obstruct market domination from corporations whose trading terms were deemed exploitative.[112] It provided a way for the independent dealer to 'survive'.[113]

Given the growing market for non-English-language films, chiefly among South Asians, piracy also provided a means of *access* to material that was otherwise unavailable or very expensive to acquire through formal means.[114] The leading Hindi films rights owner, Esquire Video, did not establish UK offices until 1982.[115] Till then, legal copies of Hindi films had to be imported from Esquire's Bombay (now Mumbai) headquarters. In practice, this was a complicated and costly affair. Issues of technological incompatibility also came into play. Orson Video, a formal Hindi film distributor operating in 1981, initiated its UK presence via a distribution deal with Sony, meaning that its first video releases were available only on the Betamax format, as Sony had yet to adopt the VHS system.[116] While legitimate Orson and Esquire cassettes were available from many video outlets, piracy ultimately proved a more convenient option for many South Asian dealerships, because it meant quicker title acquisition, lower outlay and the ability to trade in the two most popular software formats.

The ubiquity of piracy within ethnic areas led to South Asian video dealers being written about in the trade and consumer press with suspicion or contempt, at times framed as illegitimate tradespeople whose greed outweighed their desire to provide a quality service. 'Quality' in such discourse, however, is a moveable feast, and provides another reason as to why pirated cassettes were so appealing to South Asian retailers. Key to most anti-piracy narratives of the time is that illicit copies of works were of inferior quality to legitimately released cassettes, in terms of the clarity of the image, sound and so on.[117] Yet it was reported at the time that pirated copies of Indian films tended to be of 'superior quality' compared with those released formally by above-the-board distributors such as Esquire and Orson.[118] Indeed, while some illegal duplication happened in houses using domestic VCR machines and from $n$th-generation copies, a bulk of such material was also being covertly duplicated using industry-standard machines, from dozens of the 'video facility' companies operable in London and elsewhere.[119] Given this, the 'quality' of videos offered to Asian consumers by Asian video dealers in all likelihood far exceeded that being alleged in the trade and consumer press. To this end, while allegations of opportunism and 'rip off' culture can be levelled at any pirate, they hold weight when levelled against ethnic minorities of South Asian descent in the British context, who have historically and in many contexts been discursively positioned an '"alien" threat to the "British way of life"'.[120]

In Richard Dyer's study, *White*, the author remarks that whites are typically perceived as a non-race, at least by whites themselves: 'Other people are raced, we [whites] are just people.'[121] He continues, 'We (whites) will speak of, say, the blackness or Chineseness of friends, neighbours, colleagues, customers or clients . . . but we don't mention the whiteness of the white people we know.'[122] British consumer and trade periodicals reflect the notion that whiteness is invisible. White video retailers, thus, are never racialised – they are, in Dyer's words, 'the white people we know'. Even when the press discussed cowboys in the mould of Arthur Daly or Del Boy (white men), such caricatures give petty criminals an air of familiarity – *relatability*, even. This is to say that the race of white petty criminals is never given as a reason for their behaviour. The opposite is true of South Asian video dealers, who are racialised and invariably 'Othered', singled out as either being different from or offering a lesser service than the white mainstream of British video retail.[123]

In Britain, racist attitudes towards South Asian migrants are entrenched in the country's colonial history. As Roger Ballard argues in the context of Indian migration specifically, while the British Raj ceased to exist in the mid-1940s, the 'British indigenous majority' assume that 'British ways of thinking and acting' are 'innately superior to all things Indian'.[124] Inherent suspicion or wariness of South Asians might provide an additional reason why Hindi video films took such a hold within minority communities but not anywhere else, because, as Barrett and McEvoy explain, in the late 1970s, whites ceased buying into 'ethnically changing areas'.[125] Though whites did indeed live among South Asians, a dominance of video films unknown and in a language alien to them commanded them to seek their video entertainment elsewhere. The actions of South Asian pirates within 'significant ethnic enclaves'[126] thus posed, for some, a threat to an image of upstanding 'British' dealerships striving for legitimacy.

The perceived relationship between South Asian video dealers and video piracy began following reports in UK periodicals of widespread piracy overseas, namely in the Gulf region, 'the prime destination for immigrant manpower from across the world, of which South Asians have undoubtedly become the predominant group'.[127] The Middle East, an article for *Television & Home Video* claims in early 1981, is 'the largest market per capita for pre-recorded cassettes'.[128] This context was different to the narrative of Mafia-led piracy. Why? Because, as *Video World* explains, in the Middle East 'there are no copyright laws'.[129] In other words, piracy in the Middle East was practised not by the criminal underworld, but rather by *everyone* – it was (much to dismay of British journalists) a cultural norm. The tone of articles differs from fascination to ambivalence to contempt, yet there is unanimity across the piece: the video operations in the Middle East are less 'professional' than in the West and it is right to condemn such practices, if present in the UK.[130]

Printed adverts in British newspapers and magazines advertising pirated wares from Asia and the Middle East fuelled this discourse. One such company, Gulf Video Centre (GVC), took out a full-page advertisement in the pages of *Television & Home Video*, boasting that it has 'The Biggest [video] Library in the Gulf', and that, of 'The top 100 all-time film rental champs', GVC is offering '81 of them' on videocassette. The ad is ambiguous and deliberately so: it does not specify the eighty-one titles that GVC stocks. Rather, interested parties must send away for a 'complete' list of 'over 1600 American, English, Indian and Arabic Films'.[131]

A means by which South Asian piracy is presented as a threat, is that it is described (in a manner comparable to the Mafia) as operating on the fringes of legitimate video culture. For example, trade periodicals feature barely any content about legitimately released Hindi films on video, despite the presence of genuine Esquire and Orson imports throughout the country. The absence of such releases from the trade and consumer magazines in terms of features, reviews or advertising reinforces the contemporaneous 'institutionalized disdain and ignorance' that Hindi films face from western 'critics, academics and film enthusiasts', which, as Marie Gillespie argues, 'is not only a symptom of racism but feeds directly into it'.[132] Given the extent to which the market for legitimately released Hindi films is placed on the periphery of discussion or, more often than not, ignored entirely, creates a schism in the consumer and trade press between, on the one hand, the legitimate video business constituting English-language films traded by reputable storeowners and, on the other hand, an illegitimate video business awash with piracy, facilitated by South Asian dealers.

Such distinctions are manifested geographically in trade and consumer press coverage. South Asian piracy, thus, is framed as happening on the periphery of city centres, e.g. in areas where South Asian migrants live and run their businesses. Leicester, for example, is singled out in an article published in *Video Business* as a city of 'appalling piracy', with the South Asian community facing the brunt of the blame, standing in contrast to the 'legitimate' operations in more respectable areas such as 'the centre of town'.[133] While the article is complimentary about the city in other ways, from its 'famous covered market' to its 'handsome' Haymarket Centre, and credits a number of professionally run video retailers (including Orbit in the city centre, which 'gleams with well-laid-out videos'), areas of the city populated by South Asians and ethnic video stockists are discussed less favourably. A symbolic rift is hereby created between the city's British heritage and unseemly goings-on in the present by its migrant population. One dealer interviewed, John Langham of Leicester Video, speaks of the 'Asian market' as a 'separate thing' to the 'English' market. This is despite Asian dealers quoted in the same article – such as the owner of B. B. Star Video, Bhupendra Jalhan – trading in both Asian and English titles, and other dealerships in the city advertising 'LATEST ENGLISH & INDIAN FILMS'.[134] By failing to acknowledge the fluidity of both markets amid Leicester's migrant communities, Langham reinforces the notion that 'separate' is also to be read as 'alien'; and, by implication, a threat to the legitimate – and implicitly 'white' – way of business.

Another article, this time in the consumer magazine *Video World*, singles out Leicester as emblematic of the country's piracy 'horror story'.[135] The authors begin by identifying Leicester's '16 per cent Indian population', describing 'whole areas ... given over to curry restaurants, sari shops and so on'. They then proceed to educate the reader about 'the notorious' Melton Road, a long street at the edge of the city populated largely by South Asian families and representing a core area of Asian business, where 'Rental outlets include such unlikely sources as tailors and green grocers'. 'It seems', the authors deduce, 'that just about everybody is into the act.'[136] By introducing Leicester to the reader in this way, the authors succeed in Othering South Asians on account of their culture and business practices, of which piracy serves as an additional factor in the community's stigmatisation. Through prefixing the denigration of Melton Road with a general description of the ethnic population of the city and the commonplace cultural signifiers to be found there, the authors reinforce the pervasiveness of racial stigmatisation that is typically associated with working-class areas that are home to migrants and asylum seekers.[137] While the authors acknowledge other cities where piracy is said to be rife, Leicester is the only example to be discussed in any detail, and one of two whose ethnic make-up is acknowledged (the other being Birmingham – another city with a comparatively high percentage of South Asians). Consequently, the lasting impression from the article is that Leicester serves as good an example as any of a city where piracy – an operation being peddled by a community at odds with mainstream standards – is rife.

Framing piracy squarely as a malicious criminal enterprise ignores the divergent factors that drew the first video dealers to it. Piracy, despite its unseemly associations, should still be anchored to the philosophy underwriting the economic context of the video boom. Reports that almost 80 per cent of the market was given over to pirates was shocking to some, but it was a figure that nevertheless spoke to the popularity of a booming new market where demand for product was very high. In this context piracy might best be thought of as 'free enterprise': 'a flourishing of commercial activity catering directly to market needs'.[138] Whether opted for by shopkeepers due to ignorance, ill intent, protest or because the UK market was ill equipped to cater for a culturally diverse consumer society, video piracy nevertheless evinced entrepreneurialism (of an 'evasive' sort) that was self-starter in spirit, and responded to the market demands that everybody working in it – from the Hollywood majors to the trade associations and beyond – was striving to comprehend.[139]

This chapter has shown how the first video dealers made video rental a recession-beating industry, from mail order clubs to the boom in video shops, and the formal and informal processes that collectively made video such a success between 1979 and 1982.

In the years that followed, independent dealers found the stigma of piracy – and pornography, and a post-1982 boom in horror films – difficult to overcome. Subsequent chapters of this book explore these issues in detail, but, in short, industry bodies and affiliates looked upon some independent dealers as a thorn in the side of an otherwise legitimate video business. In response to growing concern that the piracy situation was getting worse, a new organisation was formed to 'take over' from trade organisations such as the British Video Association (BVA), the MPEAA and the Society for Film Distributors to oversee 'all law enforcement activities against copyright infringement': the Federation Against Copyright Theft (FACT).[140] Within a year of its founding, FACT successfully lobbied the government to toughen punishments both for pirates and dealers found trading in illicit copies.[141] Prior to FACT's intervention, under the Copyright Act 1956, pirates could face a maximum penalty of £200, a figure which, in the words of the BVA's Norma Abbott, was 'as absurd as Al Capone being charged with parking on a double yellow line'.[142] Given that the punishment, in the eyes of the industry at least, was negligible, distributors initially policed the matter themselves by, for example, sending representatives to shops throughout the country, seizing illegal stock and then closing their accounts.[143] Other attempts saw both journalists and people from the industry confronting individuals trading in pirate wares, at times recording illegal transactions. One such example, an edition of the BBC's *Newsnight* programme broadcast in 1981, sees actor Andrew Sachs, one of the co-stars of the popular BBC comedy series *Fawlty Towers* (1975–9), confront a pirate and demand royalties from him.[144] However, due to pressure from FACT lobbyists, an amended version of the Copyright Act was passed in 1983. Pirates could now face unlimited fines and up to two years' imprisonment for trading and/or manufacturing illegal copies.[145]

The piracy issue was significant, but it was one of several that would negatively impact the reputation of independent video dealers in the coming years. By mid-1982, some sources were reporting that outlets were suffering countrywide, and that the business was no longer as brisk as it had been merely months prior. *Video World*, for example, reported that, in the first half of 1982, 400 video shops had gone out of business, with a further 400 projected to go the same way 'in the next six months'.[146] As the remaining chapters of this book detail, this period saw the market for pre-recorded video entertainment reach saturation point, and a resulting plethora of industry-wide shakeouts. Around the same time, press reports began coming in about an upsurge in the popularity for violent horror films – what journalists described as 'video nasties' – which, moral case-makers argued, looked to 'deprave and corrupt' the people who, they alleged, comprised the genre's core audience: children. As with piracy, blame was laid at the feet of small-time video dealers for allowing such material into the hands of the innocent. Despite it being the case that, much of the time, the reportage was a toxic concoction of exaggeration and untruths, a moral panic was soon in full swing, and the princes of industry who had propelled the nascent video rental business were now, according to some case-makers, enemies of the people.[147]

## Notes

1. John Hill, *British Cinema in the 1980s: Issues and Themes* (Oxford: Oxford University Press, 1999), 6.
2. Lindsay Vincent, 'Britain turns on to a £1 billion plaything', *The Observer* (12 April 1981), 17.

3. Vincent, 'Britain turns on', 17. On the 1980s as the 'age of leisure', as well as a discussion about the development of the Metro Centre, see Ken Warpole, 'The age of leisure', in John Corner and Sylvia Harvey, *Enterprise and Heritage: Crosscurrents of National Culture* (London: Routledge, 1991), 133–45.
4. Frederick Wasser, *Veni, Vidi, Video: The Hollywood Empire and the VCR* (Austin: University of Texas Press, 2011), 77.
5. Wasser, *Veni, Vidi, Video*, 80.
6. Nigel Willmott, 'Mom & Pop Shops, Largely Non-Video, Mob Brit. HV Show', *Variety* 302.8 (25 March 1981), 2/172. Citation at 172.
7. Anon., 'You can afford it', *Video World* 1.2 (June 1979), 16.
8. Julian Upton, 'Electric Blues: The Rise and Fall of Britain's First Pre-recorded Videocassette Distributors', *Journal of British Cinema and Television* 13.1 (2016), 19–41. Quotation at 37.
9. Price adjustments made here and elsewhere in the chapter are calculated using the Bank of England's Inflation Calculator, accessible here: https://www.bankofengland.co.uk/monetary-policy/inflation/inflation-calculator.
10. John Corner and Sylvia Harvey, 'Introduction: Great Britain Limited', in John Corner and Sylvia Harvey (eds), *Enterprise and Heritage: Crosscurrents of National Culture* (London: Routledge, 1991), 1–20. Quotation at 7. It is argued that 'Between 1983 and 1988 . . . The Enterprise Allowance Scheme helped 325,000 individuals become self-employed. The Loan Guarantee Scheme aided more than 19,000 businesses from 1981 to 1987, providing £635 million in loans.' See Charles Dellheim, *Inc.* (undated), available at: https://www.inc.com/magazine/19960701/1725.html (accessed 2 February 2021).
11. Thatcher quoted in Corner and Harvey, 'Introduction', 7.
12. Corner and Harvey, 'Introduction', 8.
13. Corner and Harvey, 'Introduction', 7.
14. Kate Egan, *Trash or Treasure? Censorship and the Changing Meanings of the Video Nasties* (Manchester: Manchester University Press, 2007), 50.
15. Marc Cowling and Peter Mitchell, 'The evolution of UK self-employment: a study of government policy and the role of the macroeconomy', *The Manchester School LVX.4* (September 1997), 427–42. Quotation at 428.
16. Robert MacDonald, 'Welfare dependency, the enterprise culture and self-employed survival', *Work, Employment & Society* 10.3 (September 1996), 431–47. Quotation at 433.
17. MacDonald, 'Welfare dependency', 433.
18. Anon., 'Two big multiples pull out of rental business', *Video Business* 2.14 (mid-September 1982), 1.
19. Anon., 'Two big multiples', 1.
20. Joseph Pina, *Running a Successful Video Club – Confidential Video Report* (London: Visionwell, 1983), 3–4.
21. See Intervision, untitled consumer advertisement, *Video World* 2.2 (February 1980), 5; The Video Club (Catalogue, April 1980); Video Unlimited, untitled consumer advertisement, *Television & Home Video* (February 1981), 36.

22. On Intervision's business contracts see, for example, 'A True Story', *Music & Video* (August 1980), 17. On Video Unlimited's business contracts see Video Unlimited (Exchange Club Catalogue, December 1980). On the Video at Home range, see Mark Hodder, 'Tape rental – here's why it makes sense', *Video Review* (February 1981), 55–7. Citation at 55–6.
23. An editorial for *Television & Home Video* captured the optimism of the consumer electronics trade from the outset: 'It is not as if you can leap into your local WH Smith and hoist one [a videocassette] off a rack, or pop round to Boots or the Wonder of Woolies or M&S'. See Richard Whittington, 'Pre-recorded software', *Television & Home Video* (Winter 1978/1979), 43–6. Quotation at 43.
24. Pina, *Running a Successful Video Club*, 4.
25. Bert Baker, '50% growth for cassette biz', *Variety* (14 January 1981), 206.
26. Pricing information taken from Carnaby Video/Wholesale leaflet (c.1981).
27. See Video Exchange Club, untitled consumer advertisement, *Video Review* (December 1980), 78.
28. Anon., 'Laskys and Rumbelows to sell Video Club kits', *Video News* 1.4 (August 1981), 8.
29. On the expansion of Video Unlimited see Brian Mulligan, 'From a bedroom to a warehouse in two short years', *Video Business* (October 1981), 23. See also Video Unlimited (Exchange Club Catalogue, December 1980) and Video Unlimited (Distributor Catalogue, 1981).
30. See, for example, Hodder, 'Tape rental – here's why', 57.
31. Stuart Dollin, 'Tape rental jungle', *Video Review* (October 1981), 76–80. Citation at 79–80.
32. Dollin, 'Tape rental jungle', 76.
33. Pina, *Running a Successful Video Club*, 7.
34. Information taken from a variety of sources, including Dollin, 'Tape rental jungle', 79, and Hodder, 'Tape rental – here's why', 55–7. Speaking as part of the documentary *Bad the Sadist Videos* (2005), Bill Best of London's Star Video states that 'we were doing so well in the beginning, we were charging £50 per head membership . . .'
35. See, for example, Nigel Cawthorne, 'How not to get video clubbed', *Video World* (November 1982), 45.
36. I'm lifting the term 'material character' from Daniel Herbert, *Videoland: Movie Culture at the American Video Store* (Berkeley: University of California Press, 2014), 123. Many of us of a certain age will have memories of video shops. The following descriptions are based on mine, supplemented by conversations I have had with many others over the years, as well as descriptions given in Pina, *Running a Successful Video Club*, 9–13.
37. Herbert, *Videoland*, 58–67.
38. Pina, *Running a Successful Video Club*, 10.
39. For a discussion of the American context, Herbert, *Videoland*, 27.
40. See Willmott, 'Mom & Pop Shops', 8–9.

41. Anon., 'From a tiny retailer to a wholesale success', *Video Business* 1.1 (February 1981), 8.
42. Carnaby Video, Promotional Leaflet (1981).
43. Anon., 'Wynd Up in Vid Bid', *Variety* 13.304 (4 November 1981), 40.
44. Willmott, 'Mom & Pop Shops', 9.
45. Corner and Harvey, 'Introduction', 7.
46. MacDonald, 'Welfare dependency', 434.
47. Corner and Harvey, 'Introduction', 7.
48. Anon., 'From a tiny retailer to a wholesale success', 8.
49. Whelan quoted in Anon., 'From tiny retailer to a wholesale success', 8.
50. Anon., 'From tiny retailer to a wholesale success', 8. It would later materialise that Pina had run a printing business and that, by chance, Intervision was a client. This, he later told a consumer magazine, was what first alerted him to video as an industry likely to boom. See Anon., 'Rags to riches on Carnaby Street', *Popular Video* (July 1981), 18.
51. Corner and Harvey, 'Introduction', 7.
52. Corner and Harvey, 'Introduction', 7.
53. Corner and Harvey, 'Introduction', 7.
54. Corner and Harvey, 'Introduction', 8.
55. Anon., 'From a tiny retailer to a wholesale success', 8.
56. Carnaby leaflet (c.1980/1).
57. Carnaby leaflet (c.1980/1). Added emphasis.
58. Julian Petley, *Film and Video Censorship in Modern Britain* (Edinburgh: Edinburgh University Press, 2011), 17.
59. Willmott, 'Mom & Pop Shops', 2.
60. Mulligan, 'From a bedroom to a warehouse, 23.
61. Centre Video, untitled consumer advertisement, *Television & Home Video* (September 1981), 44.
62. PMA Video, untitled trade advertisement, *Video News* 1.4 (August 1981), 12.
63. However, for what it's worth, film westerns were very popular on video. In *Running a Successful Video Club*, Pina argues that, along with horror, actions and blockbusters, westerns 'are the best renters' (14).
64. Ram Gidoomal, *The UK Maharajahs: Inside the South Asian Success Stories* (London: Nicholas Brealey Publishing, 1997), 6–9.
65. Roger Ballard, 'The South Asian presence in Britain and its transnational connections', in Bhikhu Parekh, Gurharpal Singh and Steven Vertovec (eds), *Culture and Economy in the Indian Diaspora* (London: Routledge, 2002), 197–222. Quotation at 197.
66. Giles A. Barrett and David McEvoy, 'Temporal and geographical variations in ethnic minority business', in Leo-Paul Dana (ed.), *Handbook of Research on Ethnic Minority Entrepreneurship: A Co-evolutionary View on Resource Management* (Cheltenham: Edward Elgar, 2007), 337–59. Quotation at 338. See also Ballard, 'The South Asian presence', 200.

67. Barrett and McEvoy, Temporal and geographical variations', 337. See also Trevor Jones, 'Small business development at the Asian community in Britain', *Journal of Ethnic and Migration Studies* 9.3 (1981), 467–77.
68. Tejaswini Ganti, *Bollywood: A Guidebook to Popular Hindi Cinema* (London: Routledge, 2013).
69. Lucia Krämer, *Bollywood in Britain: Cinema, Brand, Discursive Complex* (New York: Bloomsbury, 2016), unpaginated ebook.
70. Marie Gillespie, 'Technology and tradition: audio-visual culture among South Asian families in West London', *Cultural Studies* 3.2 (1989), 226–39. Quotation at 228.
71. Krämer, *Bollywood in Britain*, unpaginated ebook.
72. Krämer, *Bollywood in Britain*, unpaginated ebook.
73. Gillespie, 'Technology and tradition', 228.
74. Gillespie, 'Technology and tradition', 236.
75. Rajinder Kumar Dudrah, 'Vilayati Bollywood: popular Hindi cinema-going and diasporic South Asian identity in Birmingham (UK)', *The Public* 9.1 (2002), 19–36. Quotation at 20. See also BBC Report on Asian Video in Leicester, c.1982, available at: http://drjohnnywalker.co.uk/rewind-replay-resources.
76. For example, despite one Midlands shop boasting of stocking 'over 5,000 VHS and Betmax films', all were English-language titles from well-known independent and major distributors. Quotation taken from *Fox's Video News*, debut newsletter of Nottinghamshire-based video club (December, 1982). The newsletter features photographs and the names of managers and employees, all of whom are white Britons.
77. See, for example, Whittington, 'Pre-recorded software', 43.
78. Charles Robinson, 'Energetic scene of over 60 shops and "appalling piracy"', *Video Business* 2.8 (June 1982), 24.
79. Joshua M. Greenberg, *From Betamax to Blockbuster: Video Stores and the Invention of Movies on Video* (Cambridge, MA: MIT Press, 2008), 84.
80. Greenberg, *From Betamax to Blockbuster*, 82–4.
81. Nestlé spokesperson cited in Greenberg, *From Betamax to Blockbuster*, 84.
82. The influence of North American retail on the British video market is discussed in detail in Chapter 6, in relation to the Ritz, Hollywood Nites and Blockbuster chains of shops.
83. Jones, 'Small business development at the Asian community in Britain', 473.
84. Ballard, 'The South Asian presence', 202.
85. The following information regarding Pioneer Video is taken from personal correspondence between the author and the shop's owner, 'Pops' (7 April 2014). On Amin's 'Asian expulsion' see, for example, Chibuike Uche, 'The British Government, Idi Amin and the Expulsion of British Asians from Uganda', *Interventions* 19.6 (2017), 818–36.
86. For an example of early reportage on the popularity of video among ethnic minorities in Britain, see Graham Wade, 'Ethnic minorities go for video', *Television & Home Video* (July 1980), 14–15.

87. Gurharpal Singh, 'Introduction', in Bhikhu Parekh, Gurharpal Singh and Steven Vertovec (eds), *Culture and Economy in the Indian Diaspora* (London: Routledge, 2003), 1–12. Quotation at 3.
88. Singh, 'Introduction', 4.
89. Spinder Dhaliwal and Peter Kangis, 'Asians in the UK: gender, generations and enterprise', *Equal Opportunities International* 25.2 (2006), 92–108. Quotation at 93.
90. Dhaliwal and Kangis, 'Asians in the UK', 93.
91. Dhaliwal and Kangis, 'Asians in the UK', 93.
92. Dhaliwal and Kangis, 'Asians in the UK', 93.
93. Graham Wade, *Film, Video and Television: Market Forces, Fragmentation and Technological Advance* (London: Comedia, 1985), 24. For the purposes of the present discussion, 'piracy' is used here to refer to all forms of illegal video copying. However, there was a period when industry bodies such as the BVA sought to distinguish between different sorts of criminal duplication. The various types comprised 'advance piracy', where a 'video is made of a film that does not exist in video form'; 'counterfeiting', 'when an illegal copy is made to simulate a legitimate video'; and 'crude back-to-back copy[ing]' where 'no attempt is made to simulate packaging and is usually a small amateurish operation'. Norman Abbott quoted in Basil Comely, 'Video achieves spotty adolescence', *Broadcast* 1189 (20 December 1982), 22–3. Quotation at 22.
94. Percy Brown quoted in Brian Oliver, 'Housewives and jobless are prey to video thieves', *Popular Video* (December, 1981), 16.
95. The full programme is available to stream on YouTube and can also be accessed at: http://drjohnnywalker.co.uk/rewind-replay-resources.
96. Tony Seaman quoted in *The London Programme*.
97. Stephen Baker and Paddy Hoey, 'The Picaro and the Prole, the Spiv and the Honest Tommy in Leon Griffiths's *Minder*', *Journal of British Cinema and Television* 15.4 (October 2018), available at: https://www.euppublishing.com/doi/abs/10.3366/jbctv.2018.0440.
98. Stephen Wagg, '"At ease, corporal": social class and the situation comedy in British television, from the 1950s to the 1990s', in Stephen Wagg (ed.), *Because I Tell a Joke or Two: Comedy, Politics, and Social Difference* (London: Routledge, 1998), 1–31. Quotation at 28.
99. Baker and Hoey, 'The Picaro and the Prole'.
100. Paul Haigh, 'How to find your way around video clubs', *Popular Video* (April, 1981), 58–9.
101. Nick Lloyd and Charles Robinson, 'All right my son?', *Video World* (October 1982), 42–7. Quotation at 43.
102. Ramon Lobato, *Shadow Economies of Cinema: Mapping Informal Film Distribution* (London: British Film Institute, 2012), 72.
103. Lobato, *Shadow Economies*, 73.
104. Lobato, *Shadow Economies*, 73–4.

105. Independent dealers were routinely written about as the enemy. For example, Intervision withheld the distribution of *Alligator* (Lewis Teague, 1980) from independents dealers until the film had completed its theatrical run because 'we are unable to control geographical distribution once it is available to the independent trade'. See Anon., 'Intervision gives the multiples first bite at Alligator movie', *Video Business* 2.4 (April 1982), 5.
106. Grant Endersby, 'At £2 a night 4500 rentals are needed to break even', *Video Business*, 1.12 (March 1982), 34.
107. Ramon Labato, *Shadow Economies of Cinema: Mapping Informal Film Distribution* (London: British Film Institute, 2012), 80.
108. Colin Louch, 'How "greedy" film companies can help make video healthy and respectable', *Video Business* (letters pages) 2.8 (June 1982), 50.
109. Endersby, 'At £2 a night', 34.
110. Abbott (of the BVA) quoted in Comely, 'Video achieves spotty adolescence', 22.
111. H. Parker, '"I tried to report a case of piracy – but nobody wanted to hear my story', *Video Business* (letters pages) 2.8 (June 1982), 50.
112. Labato, *Shadow Economies*, 81.
113. Comely, 'Video achieves spotty adolescence', 22.
114. Labato considers the 'piracy as access' question in relation to territories 'where accessing media legally is not an option' (82). He includes 'South East Asian mediascapes' as one example. In the present context, I am choosing not to restrict 'piracy as access' to such scenarios, as the forthcoming analysis attests.
115. Anon., 'Indian film catalogue gives Esquire a solid foothold in UK', *Video Business* 2.17 (November 1982), 48.
116. Anon., 'Bombay Video', *Video Review* (November 1981), 27.
117. Haigh, 'How to find your way around video clubs', 58–9. Citation at 59; Oliver, 'Housewives and jobless are prey to video thieves', 16.
118. Anon., '"Roti, Kapda Aur Films" – the new order of basic human needs', *Organiser* (14 December 1980), 11–12.
119. See *The London Programme*.
120. Gillespie, 'Technology and tradition', 226.
121. Richard Dyer, *White* (London: Routledge, 2002 [1997]), 1.
122. Dyer, *White*, 2.
123. Such attitudes are of course indebted to the 'ethnocentric bias' upon which 'Othering', as a discursive, stigmatising process, depends. See Jean-Francois Staszak, 'Other/otherness', in Rob Kitchin and Nigel Thrift (eds), *International Encyclopaedia of Human Geography* 8 (Oxford: Elsevier, 2009), 43–7. Quotations at 43 and 44.
124. Ballard, 'The South Asian presence', 198.
125. Barrett and McEvoy, 'Temporal and geographic variations', 342.
126. Barrett and McEvoy, 'Temporal and geographic variations', 342.

127. Prakash C. Jain and Ginu Zacharia Oommen, 'Introduction', in Prakash C. Jain and Ginu Zacharia Oommen (eds), *South Asian Migration to Gulf Countries: History, Policies, Development* (London: Routledge, 2016), 1–14. Quotation at 4.
128. Graham Wade, 'Move to the Rights', *Television & Home Video* (February 1981), 17–18. Quotation at 18.
129. Alan Puzey, 'Video Middle East', *Video World* 2.1 (January 1980), 30–2. Quotation at 30.
130. Puzey, 'Video Middle East', 30–2.
131. Gulf Video Centre, untitled consumer advertisement, *Television & Home Video* (August 1980), 54.
132. Gillespie, 'Technology and tradition', 232.
133. Robinson, 'Energetic scene of over 60 shops', 24.
134. Quotation taken from generic video sleeve issued by Pioneer Video Emporium, Leicester, c.1980s.
135. Lloyd and Robinson, 'All right my son?', 43.
136. Lloyd and Robinson, 'All right my son?', 43.
137. See, for example, Ade Kearns, Oliver Kearns and Louise Lawson, 'Notorious places: image, reputation, stigma. The role of newspapers in area reputations for social housing estates', *Housing Studies* 28.4 (2013), available at: https://www.tandfonline.com/doi/full/10.1080/02673037.2013.759546.
138. Labato, *Shadow Economies*, 74.
139. On 'evasive entrepreneurship', see, for example, P. J. Boettke and C. J. Coyne 'Entrepreneurship and development: cause or consequence?', *Austrian Economics and Entrepreneurial Studies* (2003), 67–87; and Niklas Elert and Magnus Henrekson, 'Evasive entrepreneurship', *Small Business Economics* 47.1 (June 2016), 95–113.
140. R. E. T. Birch, 'Piracy's Growth In UK Spawns Org To Wage War', *Variety* 309.11 (12 January 1983), 191, 198. Quotation at 191, 198.
141. FACT was not the only organisation of its type, but was (and remains) without question the most influential. In 1980, the BBC, the Society for Film Distributors and the Independent Television Companies Association (ITCA; a trade body representing the interests of the ITV channels) set up the Video Copyright Protection Society. By 1986, however, the Society was no longer operable for reasons that, while not clear, likely pertain to the success of FACT, and there being no need for two organisations fighting the same cause. On the formation of the VCPS see Anon., 'BBC/ITCA video copyright group', *Stage and Television Today* 5177 (3 July 1980), 18.
142. Abbott quoted in Comely, 'Video achieves spotty adolescence', 22.
143. Oliver, 'Housewives and jobless are prey to video thieves', 16.
144. See an edition of the BBC's Newsnight c.1981, available on YouTube or at http://www.drjohnnywalker.co.uk/rewind-replay-resources.html.
145. Colin Vaines, 'Piracy action is welcomed by CEA', *Screen International* 400 (25 June 1983), 12.

146. Cawthorne, 'How not to get video clubbed', 45.
147. For concise overview of the video nasties moral panic, see Julian Petley, '"Are We Insane ?": The "Video Nasty" Moral Panic', *Recherches sociologiques et anthropologiques*, 43.1 (2012), 35–57, available at: https://doi.org/10.4000/rsa.839.

CHAPTER 3

# Threats and Benefits

> The Video Explosion has created a confusing number of companies who are jostling for your business. Some offer excellent services or products, while others seem to spring up overnight only to disappear just as quickly.
> Walton Video, 'Aiming to be Britain's most Professional Team',
> *Video Business* supplement (June 1982)

By the beginning of 1982, the future of the video market was in the balance. Major distributors were making strong advances in software penetration: the top five rented titles of 1981, for example, were all major studio productions.[1] Independent distributors, consequently, were feeling the pressure. However, for all that bigger organisations such as CIC – whose video release of *Jaws* (Steven Spielberg, 1975) was the most rented title of 1981 – and the likes of Thorn/EMI and Warner – companies that, along with CIC, dominated that year's sales charts – media reportage around home video tended to focus squarely on the output of independents, specifically videos released within the horror, exploitation and sexploitation modes: what journalists and moral campaigners described as 'video nasties'.[2] Indeed, media reportage of grisly marketing campaigns conducted by comparatively small outfits such as Astra, VIPCO and Go to promote exploitation titles such as *Snuff* (Michael Findlay, 1976), *The Driller Killer* (Abel Ferrera, 1979) and *SS Experiment Camp* (Sergio Garrone, 1976), which included the foregrounding of violent imagery, suggestive taglines and claims as to the 'strong uncut' nature of the films, compounded the idea that video distributors were hellbent on operating beyond the realms of public decency.[3]

The video nasties panic, leading to the eventual banning of thirty-nine videocassettes under the Obscene Publications Act 1959 (OPA), would spark significant changes within the video industry; namely the passing of the Video Recordings Act 1984 (VRA), which stipulated all videos must be certified by the BBFC prior to being released to the general public.[4]

Yet the video nasties panic was by no means the only problem, nor for that matter the most imminent, for the video business in 1982. When the panic was first initiated by the media in May, the most immediate threat to both distributors and dealers was the impending rationalisation of what, by this point, was a very crowded marketplace.[5]

Whereas in 1978 there was a mere handful of distributors offering a small amount of product to a small number of customers, by 1982 there were over eighty distributors collectively supplying approximately 7,000 titles to 'almost 10,000' video dealerships throughout the country.[6] By the end of the year, some sources reported that videos were available from some 25,000 outlets across the country.[7] A market recently celebrated by the consumer press for its 'diversity' was now, according to some journalists, 'chaotic',[8] as distributors and video shop owners scrambled to find new means of making their product distinctive to credibly rival their many competitors. Distributors that would have released between twelve and twenty titles in one go in 1981[9] were now having to 'cut back' and release only two to five at a time,[10] while the video dealers that found themselves buying 'virtually every film that was released' in the late 1970s – because (like the rest of the business) they were 'not sure what they were doing'[11] – were now having to 'cherry-pick' specific titles that (they hoped) would guarantee a profit.[12] Clearly something needed to change if the business were to last. A potential solution was for distributors to shirk their broad, randomised approach to targeting customers, and instead target newly emerging (or hitherto unexploited) demographics.

This chapter is concerned with how this strategy was optimised. First, focus is given to independent companies and the economic strategies employed to market videocassettes specifically to children. The majority of distributors were by 1982 carrying a range of videos intended for children (so-called 'kidvids') ranging from age-appropriate feature films to cartoons to non-fiction education videos. Others dealt exclusively in children's programming.[13] Many independents went to great lengths to exploit this market and, amid video nasty hysteria, appeal directly to youngsters. Discussion then moves to major companies. They too had to find means of riding out rationalisation, given that it was largely agreed in that trade, due to video's popularity since the late 1970s and the wide range of titles now available on the UK market, that studios had used up the majority of the quality titles on their roster and, as a result, had to exercise creativity in handling material not typically associated with such large companies. To this end, several majors looked to exploit negative media coverage of the video nasties for their own ends, capitalising on the widespread media reportage by buying directly into these areas, so as to profiteer from an area traditionally associated with their 'opportunistic' independent counterparts.[14]

## Video nicies

It was said at the time that video nasties threatened 'the welfare of children', that they could 'damage their minds, soil their souls' and turn them into 'society's future murderers and rapists'.[15] This was certainly the impetus that drove moral campaigners such as Mary Whitehouse, the National Viewers and Listeners Association (NVLA) pressure group, and British journalists, in their condemnation of violent videos. However, though it was common for campaigners to denigrate video companies for handling such titles, it would be unreasonable – and, frankly, at odds with business logic – to suggest that video distributors completely disregarded children's welfare. It would also be erroneous to assume that most independents felt pressure to move into children's programming as a means of offsetting negative media attention by overtly distancing themselves from the video nasties. While there were a small number adopting this strategy, many had a buoyant children's range long before the 'nasty' furore had begun. Indeed, the consumer press had been running extended features on children's tapes for years.[16]

What is undoubtedly true is that kidvids were yet to receive the levels of exposure so far granted to feature-length movies. Rationalisation changed this for the independents, providing the impetus for the trade's first industry-wide push on kidvids – which also happened to be the first industry-wide push on any single genre – in early summer of 1982. With some in the trade believing that feature films were likely to go out of fashion very quickly as the video-renting public quickly moved from one 'overnight hit' to the next, children's entertainment, as a genre yet to be fully exploited, was anticipated to have more staying power.[17] By targeting a child audience directly, distributors and dealers wished to stabilise their businesses because, unlike '"[f]lavour of the month" blockbuster titles',[18] children's videos were hoped to generate repeat viewings and have a longer shelf life as a consequence.[19]

These predictions were given credence by a number of contemporaneous empirical studies. One revealed that 'children watch almost as much video material as adults'.[20] Another claimed that the core VCR market was made up of people aged between twenty-three and thirty-five: 'precisely those people who have the most young children'.[21] With one distributor, Richard Price Television Associates (RPTA), claiming to have sold 2,000 copies of its cartoon anthology, *Video Play-box 1* (Leslie Pitt, 1980), in 1981 alone,[22] kidvids were expected to have the commercial staying power to help companies survive rationalisation. Children's tapes were deemed to be so popular that a number of children-only membership clubs were established (such as KIDEO[23] and Junior Video at Home[24]) to accommodate the slew of products being offered by almost every distributor, including subsidiaries of majors such as WHV, MGM/UA, Rank Home Video and CIC; independents such as Intervision, Guild, Astra, Go, Fletcher, Home Video Productions, VCL, Videomedia and Derann; British subsidiaries of foreign independents such as Video Tape Centre (VTC), ACE Europe and Media; and local 'special interest' labels including ArTel (which had the aptly named 'KidVid' series), and Longman Video (an offshoot of an historic educational publisher). The kinds of kidvid being released at this time were just as varied as their distributors, yet two primary strategies were typically adopted in marketing them.

The first was to promote kidvids as having a function beyond that of mere entertainment: assertions that were especially welcome in response to pro-censorship case-makers who claimed that videos were at best mindless, and at worst dangerous. Conversely to such claims, children's video entertainment was promoted by independents as *beneficial*, as being able to supplement parenting, by keeping children occupied when schools were closed during half-term and summer holidays. In select cases, a video's alleged educational value was promoted, as a further marker of value. The second strategy was to place kidvids in a cheaper price bracket than feature films and product offered by major companies such as MGM – which stocked a number of widely popular *Tom and Jerry* cartoons – and Rank – which was handling Disney's UK distribution at the time. It is worth considering both of these strategies in detail.

## The purported benefits of kidvids

In 1982, Intervision, ran an ad promoting its first ever full-colour children's entertainment catalogue. 'When the weather is unreliable, so are the kids', it professed. The ad was published in *Video Business* in the lead up to the national school summer holiday period (hence the knowing hat-tip to Britain's notoriously bad weather), which would see state schools close for six weeks and thus leave parents with the task of having to find childcare arrangements or other means of keeping their children occupied. Television's offerings for kids across the summer were, according to one consumer magazine, sparse: 'TV programmes offer a choice of sport, cookery or maths with the Open University.' Video might therefore 'relieve boredom for children on rainy days'.[25] Intervision's ad, published

Figure 3.1 Intervision's first ever children's catalogue. Credit: Ian Richardson.

in conjunction with a special report on the rise in popularity of children's videos, appeared to be communicating to storeowners – and, by extension, their customers – that videos provided an easy solution to the stresses that the school holidays can cause parents, and keep demanding children engaged when the schools could not. Indeed, 'Finding family entertainment is child's play', allegedly, thanks to the company's diverse range of children's programming, none of which (it was claimed) had ever been shown on TV or in British cinemas (such as the animated features *Rip Van Winkle* [Will Vinton, 1978], *Treasure Island* [Will Vinton, 1976] and *Jack and the Beanstalk* [Gisaburo Sugii, 1979]).[26]

Intervision's approach to marketing children's fare was indicative of practices across the board, with the majority of distributors using empathetic rhetoric in their marketing to appear in line with parental needs. For example, ADB Video appeared to be offering its customers virtual childcare, when it promoted the animated characters of *Fables of the Green Forest* (Director unknown, 1978) and *Tales of La Manca* (Kunihiko Yuyama, 1980) as 'ENGLAND'S NO.1 BABYSITTERS'.[27] Other distributors presented themselves as a remedy for inevitable school holiday tedium by homing in on the assumed completest impulses of demanding children by releasing multi-volume series. This was true, for instance, of Mountain, which promoted the launch of its nine-title Cartoon Collection

– including *Nobody's Boy* (1970), *Party Laughs* and *Fun Time* (both 1982) and others – as a solution to 'school holiday boredom',[28] while ACE Europe spread the five-part 1930s serial 'The Phantom Creeps' (1939) across two volumes of *Childrens [sic] Fun Show* (c.1982). Others simply foregrounded programme duration: the front cover of *Tiny Tots Fun Time* (c.1982), for example, promises to 'keep your kids amused for hours!', while the cover for the 120-minute *Cartoon Spectacular* (1982) offers 'a gigantic helping of youthful entertainment to interest, amuse and captivate'.

Some companies adopted more ambitious means to stimulate the minds of young people, by promoting their kidvids as novel and, in some cases, interactive. For instance, in late 1982 Go Video – under its 'Kidivid' label – released *The Bumper Fun Video Annual Volume 1* (various, 1982), which was modelled on the widely popular comic book 'annuals' that were marketed at Christmastime and typically featured a range of stories featuring popular characters from notable child weeklies, such as the *Beano* and the *Dandy*. *The Bumper Fun Video Annual Volume 1*, similar to Go's more rudimentary *Video Comic* from 1980, was comparable to a comic annual on the grounds that it contained a compendium of cartoon stories featuring popular characters such as Superman, Laurel and Hardy and Felix the Cat. Similarly, Channel Video's release of *My Video Party* (Director unknown, 1983) – yet another compendium of cartoons and other vignettes, first promoted in early 1983 – was sold with a 'colouring and activity pad' that children were supposed to use when instructed during the programme, to complete 'puzzles' and 'dot-to-dot' activities.[29]

These examples demonstrate how distributors used their knowledge of surplus time and a prospected lack of stimulus for British children to present their kidvid ranges as being able to provide a service that extended beyond the usual parameters of entertainment. However, another – arguably more daring – tactic exploited by companies during weeks of school closure was to foreground the alleged educational benefits of children's videos in advertising. One such distributor was VCL who, under its Family Video label, re-released its *Animal Kingdom* video from 1981 (directors and dates unknown) during the Christmas period of 1982: a cassette that was promoted as 'educational' on the grounds that it was allegedly 'filmed on location in Africa',[30] and that it would, one is to assume, have exposed some British children to cultures that they would have been unfamiliar with. (These claims of verisimilitude were made in spite of the fact, that, as the video cover rightly stated, *Animal Kingdom* was comprised of 'entertaining, yet educational, *cartoons*' and not live action sequences.)[31] Similarly, during the two-week Easter break in March 1983, VCL lined up a number of cartoons for release, again

**Figure 3.2** Go Video brings a children's comic to life in *Video Comic*. Credit: Popular Film and Television Collection.

**Figure 3.3** Copies of Channel Video's My Video Party came with supplementary activities for children to complete. Credit: Popular Film and Television Collection.

under the pretence of 'education', including *Ivanhoe* (Leif Gram, 1975) and *The Black Arrow* (Leif Gram, 1973). Neither of these cartoons was originally produced with the British education system in mind. They are, in fact, Australian TV movies. Yet VCL keenly publicised their pedagogical benefits regardless. For example, promotional copy provided to the trade press singled out the historical elements of *The Black Arrow* ('set in the turbulent 15th century with the War of the Roses in full flow'), using its grounding in British history to validate the company's claim that its cartoons were produced 'not only with an eye to entertainment but with an eye to education too'.³² Likewise, Home Video Productions (HVP) marketed its August 1982 releases of *The Adventures of Reddy the Fox* (Director unknown, 1978), *The Adventures of Buster the Bear* (Director unknown, 1978) and *The Adventures of Ultraman* (various, 1979), with the kind of rhetorical questions used to assess schoolchildren's literacy comprehension in contemporaneous storybooks: '*Why* is Reddy Fox in trouble with Farmer Brown's Sheep?'; '*Who* won't let Buster Bear share his fish?'; '*Will* Ultraman save the universe?'³³ As with the aforementioned VCL releases, these programmes were not originally created for young British audiences: *Reddy the Fox* and *Buster the Bear* are Japanese adaptations of two classic stories by the American author Thomas W. Burgess, while *Ultraman* was a Japanese TV show from the 1960s–1970s. Yet HVP heavily pushed their potential to educate, perhaps in light of growing concerns surrounding the availability of foreign horror films in British video shops,³⁴ telling the trade press that, in spite of the videos' non-British origins, '"Americanisms" [*sic*] have been Anglicised so as to not confuse our minors [*sic*] spelling efforts'.³⁵ In so doing, the company presented itself as an organisation that had the welfare of the nation's children at the forefront of its business practices and thus, unlike those more disreputable companies being reported on by the media, could be trusted to deliver age-appropriate material of benefit to child audiences.

Perhaps the most notable of all efforts to promote the pedagogical potential of video during this period came from Longman Video, a company established in late 1982 as a subsidiary of the educational book publisher Pearson Longman. Founded to target children and other special interest markets,³⁶ it had education at the vanguard of its marketing agenda. Longman's promotional material repeatedly drew on the company's scholarly history, using its reputation to connote moralistic qualities such as care, reliability, and trustworthiness: qualities associated with people of high social standing, not least school teachers. For example, in Longman's first trade campaign, an ad in *Television & Video Retailer* explained to readers how the company was 'backed by 250 years' experience of providing entertainment and information for all ages'.[37] Identifying binaries between the old (Longman's legacy in educational publishing) and the new (its associations with the booming video market), as well as between entertainment (stimulus) and information (education) worked to present the company as one that not only had longevity and historic success, but was also in tune with the way that technology was headed and the benefits it could provide for children and their families. Not wishing to appear a distributor out for profit at all costs, Longman positioned itself as a video brand that could communicate successfully with children, and as a company that, by offering *'specially crafted* programmes of *quality* for children from pre-school to teenage level',[38] took a much more measured approach to video than (it is implied) other distributors of the period. Being the first company to secure a distribution deal with a high-street book wholesaler, Bookwise, further worked to underscore Longman's commitment to doing for home video what it had been doing for educational books for the last two and a half centuries.[39]

With promises of video programmes for a wide age range and a drive to exploit video's potential as a new means to occupy the nation's young, companies such as ADB, Go, VCL, HVP and Longman went to great lengths to convince people of the benefits of video with titles that would keep children not only entertained (and thus, as in the case of some of the companies mentioned above, out of their parents' hair), but schooled as well. However, for all that education and stimulus were thought to be of key interest to consumers, there was another – and arguably more crucial – actor that had to be heeded if kidvids were to be as popular as distributors hoped: namely, how much said products were going to cost consumers.

## Quality and affordability

Videos, generally speaking, were not cheap commodities. In 1982, feature films that were released onto video could retail to the general public for as high as £60 per cassette (approximately £190 today), and were typically rented out from shops for anywhere between £1.50 and £4.00 per night (around £5.00 to £13.00 today).[40] As a result, it remained uncommon for people to *buy* videos. However, in light of the kidvid's assumed 'repeatability' factor, and as a means of incentivising parents to purchase videos outright, distributors would, in most cases, price their children's videos lower than their other releases. For example, in December 1981 and January 1982, the consumer magazine *Popular Video*, in association with Polygram's Spectrum distribution label, ran a Christmas-themed campaign, offering the likes of *Noddy Goes to Toyland*, *Animals at Work and Play* and *Daily Fabel* for £19.95 '[e]xclusively for *Popular Video*'s Readers'.[41] Similarly, VCL – whose 'Cartoon Carousel' range included animated versions of *Robin Hood* (Zoran Janjic, 1971), *A Christmas Carol* (Leif Gram, 1970) and *Moby Dick* (Richard Slapczynski, 1977) – and ArTel Video – whose 'KidVid' range included various *Tin Tin* and *Fred Bassett* cartoons – trade-priced their kidvids at £16.00 and £16.20 respectively.[42] CIC 'lined up *Woody Woodpecker and his Friends*, at £18.50',[43] Mountain and Longman marketed their kidvids at the competitive price of £19.95,[44] while Fletcher Video, in the run-up to Christmas 1982, 'pegged' the prices of its *Popeye the Sailor Man* cartoons 'back to £29.95',[45] as Derann had done with its release of *Tales of Magic* (date and director unknown) earlier in the year.[46] Cheaper pricing was achievable because most of the content featured on kidvids was relatively old, dating mostly from the 1930s to the 1970s,[47] meaning that it was either very cheap to license, or, in the case of public domain material, free.[48] As a result, budget pricing could be justified, as it was assumed a healthy profit could still easily be made.[49]

Low pricing had two desired consequences. In one respect, it was designed to increase appeal with VCR owners in a flooded market. As mentioned in the previous section, children's videos were a relatively new commodity, so cheapness was hoped to translate into broader product exposure, especially during summer and at Christmas and Easter, when time is pressed and gifts are bought. Also, the fact that such films were purchasable at a lower cost contributed to the projected flexibility of the kidvid: if a tape was bought by a member of the public, it could be watched again and again, without it ever having to be returned to a rental outlet, avoiding costly late fines in the process.

It is important to note that, while the affordability of the children's videos was central to their appeal, it was also crucial for the distributors to ensure that people's perception of the quality of the material was not affected by the cheap price tag. One means of doing this was for companies to release children's programming that was likely to be relatable to those parents who would be purchasing or renting the videos on their child's behalf. Thus, Mountain's release of Max Fleischer Studio's *Superman* cartoons from the 1940s 'performed . . . well' in the summer of 1982,[50] no doubt due to the superhero's longstanding legacy in children's popular culture, as well as the recent success of the live action family blockbuster, *Superman II* (Richard Lester and Richard Donner, 1980). Similarly, ACE Europe released a series of compendium videos including *Childrens* [sic] *Fun Show* parts 1 and 2, *Kids Cartoon Hour*, *Kids Cartoon Capers*, *Fun Parade* and *The Bugs Bunny Show*, featuring a mix of live action serials and cartoons dating as far back as the 1930s, ranging from Dick Tracey, Superman, Popeye, Felix the Cat, as well as Bugs Bunny and Daffy Duck; Video brokers released a series of Laurel and Hardy cartoons; RPTA's 'Playbox Fairy Tales' series traded on the 'classic' status of stories by the likes of Hans Christian Anderson and the Brothers Grimm, including: *Beauty and the Beast* (Fielder Cook, 1976), *The Magic Well* (director and date unknown), *The Little Match Girl* (director and date unknown), *The Mermaid Princess* (director and date unknown) and *Thumbelina* (director and date unknown) – some of which were voiced by Peter Hawkins, who was best known for providing the voice of Captain Pugwash in the popular children's cartoon from the 1960s;[51] and, in the summer of 1983, Select Video released a series of notable classics likely to resonate with parents, including *Popeye and Friends in Outer Space* (various, 1961), *Lassie* (various), *Zorro* (various), *The Lone Ranger* (various) and *Flash Gordon* (various).[52]

Some companies went to great lengths to stress that their products' quality was akin to their corporate counterparts, in spite of their videos being a fraction of the cost of those offered by major distributors. A case in point is Fletcher Video. All of its children's features released in 1982 were acquired from Rankin/Bass Productions, a company that had some success with its critically acclaimed adaptation of *The Hobbit* in 1977. However, rather than capitalising on this relatively recent success, Fletcher instead employed a tactic that had been utilised by Mountain and Intervision as early as 1980, and drew on factors more likely to encourage sales among parents and kids, stressing to the trade press how its forthcoming kidvids 'compare[d] very favourably with Walt Disney products'.[53] There are number of reasons why the Disney comparison was useful. Perhaps most obvious is Disney's status as a pivotal family brand, whose identity 'rested on the legacy and value of the classic animated feature films produced by the company over several decades'.[54] It therefore made business sense for Fletcher, which was a relatively small outfit, to draw direct comparisons between itself and the American monolith. Also, and to Fletcher's advantage, Disney's video output by 1982 was very limited. Indeed, amid the debacle with Sony over the Betamax system's capacity to duplicate copyrighted material,[55] Disney remained fearful of piracy and prioritised the release of compilation videos of old cartoons and serials over the release of its more cherished features, which it could repeatedly re-release in cinemas to large box office returns.[56] As a result, none of the available Disney videos, in spite of their being official branded products, carried the weight of the company's most iconic, bankable fare, comprising mostly of anonymous compendiums such as *Cartoon Festival* parts I,

II and III (all 1981). Fletcher, thus, was able to fill a void in the market by releasing videos that were not simply 'comparable' in style to well-known Disney animation, but, in some instances, were in fact alternative versions of fables that had been made popular in cinemas by Disney itself, including *Pinocchio* (Giuliano Cenci, 1971), *Cinderella* (Bass and Rankin, 1970), *Sleeping Beauty* (Bass and Rankin, 1972), *Snow White* (Bass and Rankin, 1972), *Robin Hood* (Bass and Rankin, 1972) and *Alice In Wonderland* (Bass and Rankin, 1972). Such releases, it was hoped, would resonate with parents: they may not have carried the cachet of the classic Disney versions, but they were the closest things available to British consumers at that time.

Another string to Fletcher's bow was that the Disney Corporation had, at this point – unlike Fletcher (and most other independents) – refused to make its videos available for sale to the general public: they could only, as per a rigid leasing agreement with wholesalers, be rented out.[57] As discussed in the previous chapter, the leasing system remained risky for owners of smaller shops who had to stock fewer titles than their bigger rivals, and who relied on a greater turnover of titles to keep their catalogues fresh and appealing to their clientele.[58] Something else for shop-owners to bear in mind was the ongoing discussion in the trade press that the video market had become over-saturated. Therefore, Fletcher, by releasing videos that were not only destined to be familiar to parents and children alike because of their Disney associations, would have no doubt appealed to the storeowners at this time, who, due to market pressures, did not want to restrict themselves to stringent contracts that may not result in the profits they yearned for. Stocking Fletcher products was a much safer bet because, as with other titles released by the majority of UK independents, if one title was not performing as well as it hoped, it could be sold on to a member of the public with no fear of legal repercussions.[59]

Fletcher, by releasing the aforementioned kidvids, tapped in to the wants of video dealers and the general public, not only by recognising the appeal of children's content, but also by offering a product akin to those of the major studios. Indeed, its summer 1982 range of children's cartoons allegedly 'sold out in 36 hours', with the company having sold a reported 5,000 units to 'nearly every wholesaler' in the country.[60] At a time of market uncertainty, this would appear to indicate the value being placed on children not as morally corrupt or deviant, but, rather, as *children*. Tapping into childish wants and characteristics – the sort that the press feared were being lost through exposure to home video from small unregulated firms – was, conversely, a central component to the kidvids' success.[61]

**Figure 3.4** Fletcher Video plugged a gap in the market by offering consumers adaptations of fables made popular by Walt Disney Studios. Credit: Kevin Hall.

## Carving a slice of the action: power selling 'blood and guts'

By the summer of 1983, the children and family video market was booming at an unprecedented level. Kidvids reportedly accounted for 6–7 per cent of the 'overall video market'.[62] Many companies were now foregrounding children's titles in their promotional materials. This was true of Mountain and Atlantis, the former of which had reportedly 'doubled its turnover' since deciding to specialise in children's programming at the beginning of the year, with one notable title, the animated SF fantasy *Techno Police* (Masashi Matsumoto, 1982), said to have sold 7,500 copies; while the latter (a much newer company) claimed that it had sold 2,500 copies of the live action feature, *Treasures of the Snow* (Mike Pritchard, 1980).[63] In response to these levels of popularity, 'more concentrated promotional campaigns' were initiated 'by majors and independents alike',[64] including, for example, Intervision, whose new 'Halo Collection' of re-releases consisted of family-centred films 'guarantee[d] to please even Aunt Edna'.[65]

However, while the children's market hinted towards a degree of stability for independent distributors, press reportage continued to swell around the alleged ubiquity of video nasties. As press reportage increased, the sector was aided by the free exposure, and the demand for the kinds of film being described in lurid detail shot up.[66] As with the recent boom in kidvids, horror films that could be sold as 'nasty' became of real business interest.[67]

The positive correlation between media reportage and horror/exploitation's popularity explains why numerous independent companies looked directly to the furore as a business opportunity. Just as exploitation film distributors of yesteryear would appeal to cinemagoers with advertisements foregrounding present-day social ills and stories 'ripped from the headlines', the video nasties provided distributors with a contemporary panic from which to profiteer.[68] Indeed, the 'strong market trends' that independent horror and exploitation represented in Britain at this time encouraged distributors to supplant 'innocuous cover illustrations on sleeves' with 'hardened-up' imagery in a manner that directly aligned them with films making headlines and the companies distributing them.[69] Such strategies of so-called 'power selling' – of using bold, graphic artwork – were in fact encouraged in the trade press at this time as yet another means of quelling the advancement of the majors and riding out rationalisation, irrespective of the media kickback.

Go Video's promotional campaign for the 'Nazisploitation' film *SS Experiment Camp*, depicting a topless woman crucified in front of a Nazi general, is a case in point.[70] While the campaign prompted several

**Figure 3.5** *Cannibal Holocaust* and *SS Experiment Camp*: promotional images that secured the reputation of Go Video as a leading 'power-seller'. Credit: Ian Richardson.

complaints from the general public, and helped spawn 'mirror images' of itself and its fellow distributors 'in the censorious press', it also – along with the marketing for the violent Italian jungle caper *Cannibal Holocaust* – cemented Go as an effective and resourceful distributor that understood the wants of the market and, above all else, one that knew how to shift product in it.[71] In spite (or perhaps because) of the negative media publicity, Go's strategy was unequivocally successful: its bold packaging was reproduced to accompany articles about the nasties more so than that of any other distributor.[72] For industry commentators, as far as marketing campaigns were concerned, the company was a standout operation given its knack for generating 'much media and public attention'.[73] *Video Retailer*, following trade reports of the company spending £60,000 on promoting a package of eight films,[74] commended Go's managing director Des Dolan for 'recognizing that the majors hold many trump cards with their relationships with the big film studios', noting that by 'cleverly exploiting' newly emergent markets 'from nasties through to weepies', Dolan's smaller firm presented an admirable challenge to them.[75] On account of its 'straight-forward marketing philosophy', the company's turnover had increased by 200 per cent since its founding in 1981.[76] By tapping into exploitable markets, Go was able to mobilise recognition from the industry as a 'major independent'. And, thanks to the reputation it had amassed following its handling of *SS Experiment Camp* and *Cannibal Holocaust*, it was able to outwardly project an image of a company enjoying success when the majors statistically had much wider appeal. For Go's many competitors it was clear: power selling videocassettes, especially those with a 'nasty' bent, was central to Go's accomplishments, and therefore something that should be mimicked.[77]

Numerous companies looked to replicate the success of Go and the other main rival power-sellers making the headlines, Astra and VIPCO.[78] Given that horror was so widely featured within the media, distributors expected their edgier titles to sell better. As such, in their marketing, some would equate a film's 'nasty' elements with its bankability, and anticipate the returns dealers would likely amass if they chose to stock it. Thus, Merlin Video, in an ad published in the summer of 1982 promotes *Massacre at Central High* (Rene Daalder, 1976) and *Death Threat* (Jack Starrett, 1976) as 'Death-ridden' and 'Violence-drenched', denoting their anticipated popularity with the bellowing headline 'CARVE YOURSELF A SLICE OF THE ACTION', and an image of a bloodied knife stabbing into a wad of cash.[79] Another example sees Media promote four cassettes, including the film *Demented* (Arthur Jeffrey, 1980) – said to feature 'blood chilling' scenes of castration and murder – as 'HORROR . . . that will make you cringe, and', to the foreseen glee of retailers and its distributor, 'come back for more'.[80]

By late 1982, the popularity of such titles was taken as a given by some companies, with 'nasty' being adopted by the consumer press as shorthand for gory independent horror films. For example, *Video Viewer* magazine launched a 'New Nasties' review section in late 1982 featuring reviews of numerous recent horror films, drawing attention to their grisliest 'stomach churning' scenes,[81] and assessing their effectiveness and appeal to 'splatter fans'.[82] Arcade Video's decision to promote *Don't Go in the House* (Joseph Ellison, 1979) simply as 'another nasty', and World of Video 2000's choosing to release the 1967 American horror film *Night Fright* (James A. Sullivan) as *The Extra-Terrestrial Nastie*, further attests to the perceived popularity of 'nasty' horror films during this period, and the extent to which the term itself was seen as a means to generate profit.[83]

However, as the popularity of horror video grew, so did the caution of some distributors. As Julian Petley and others have noted, the outwardly provocative nature of such marketing – in what was a sensitive political climate – likely contributed to a rising number of raids on video shops by police officers and subsequent prosecutions, beginning with the banning of *Death Trap* (Tobe Hooper, 1976) and *The Driller Killer* in August 1982,

# THREATS AND BENEFITS

## CARVE YOURSELF A SLICE OF THE ACTION

You shouldn't need reminding just how popular hard action movies can be.

Films like "Halloween" and "Assault on Precinct 13" have been steady sellers – and renters – ever since they were first launched.

Now Merlin introduces another two: "Death Threat" and "Massacre at Central High".

Variously described by the film trade press as *"Death-ridden"*, *"Violence-drenched"* and *"Good value for addicts of action"*, they have proved successful in the States where they attracted a strong cult following.

These films have just been launched in the UK. A colour campaign is already running in the consumer press.

"Death Threat" and "Massacre at Central High" can be ordered direct from VCL, or through your local wholesaler.

Either way, act now and make sure you carve yourself a large slice of the action.

Distributed for Merlin by VCL Video, VCL House, Dallington Street, London EC1 Tel: 01-251 6131

**Figure 3.6** Merlin Video encourages dealers to stock two 'hard action' videos. Credit: Martin Myers/Popular Film and Television Collection.

and the continuous seizing of various titles from shops and warehouses.[84] This climate led some distributors to think strategically, albeit not to cease releasing horror videos. After all, the genre was very popular; so much so that industry watchers claimed horror movies were 'outpacing everything except blockbuster films'.[85] Instead, it meant companies augmenting their practices to reflect more accurately a willingness to acknowledge the heightened legal climate, and the pressure being placed on the trade by the BVA to toe the line of the law by ceasing to trade in potentially obscene material.

Within trade and consumer discourse a distinction therefore had to be made between videos that were simply 'horror' and those that were 'nasty': the former constituting films that were frightening, perhaps violent or featuring sexual content, but which were acceptable in the eyes of the law; the latter signifying films of an extreme, and thus legally precarious, nature. Given the lack of clear legal guidance, confusion abounded about what actually constituted an illegal video during this time; a list of offending titles was not made available to dealers until July 1983,[86] and even then, titles were frequently added and dropped by the Director of Public Prosecutions.[87] Nevertheless, distributors went to great lengths to do the 'right' thing, and promote their law-abiding statuses.

Video Programme Distributors (VPD) was one such company.[88] Following the seizure and successful prosecution of its release of Wes Craven's violent exploitation film *The Last House on the Left* (1972) in March 1983, company MD Brian Payne took it upon himself to take a 'hard look' at his catalogue, and identify any 'borderline' cases. Thus, he submitted another of the company's 'strong' releases, *Cannibal Ferox* (Umberto Lenzi, 1981, on the Replay label), to the BBFC for certification as part of a new voluntary censorship scheme, established by the BVA to try and regulate the industry prior to the passing of the VRA the following year (this scheme is discussed at length in the following chapter). For VPD, it was hoped that *Cannibal Ferox*, now heavily cut and with an official '18' certificate, would prevent further misgivings with the law.[89] Similarly, Video Film Organisation (VFO), upon its release of *Madman* (Joe Giannone, 1981) and *The Horror Star* (Norman Thaddeus Vane, 1981), is reported by *Video Retailer* as being 'determined to do anything to avoid police activity',[90] and is thus 'submitting all new titles for video release to the British Board of Film Censors'.[91] Here the weight that distributors believed a legitimate certificate from the BBFC to carry in the prevention of prosecution is apparent; this was a belief shared by many of their contemporaries.[92] Given that video shop owners often spoke to the popularity of 'blood and sex' and, in one specific instance, videos described (like VPD's Payne) as 'borderline' video nasties,[93] the legitimacy of the BBFC certificate was, it was hoped, a seal of approval that would dissuade trading standards officers from seizing their videocassettes. In actuality, a BBFC cinema certificate did not offer much in the way of protection at all. As Peter Kruger, head of the Obscene Publications Squad, pondered to *Video Business* in 1983, 'a judge might decide that a film with a certificate was alright for cinemas but not for home video'.[94] In spite of this, and in a manner similar to sex video distributors a few years earlier (see Chapter 1), there remained something to be gained from courting legitimacy in this way. Given that horror and exploitation films were making money, companies had to find a balance between trading in genres that were popular and avoiding trouble with the law.

A means of protection, it appeared, was to have the status of a major, well-respected company: one that could set itself apart, reputation-wise, from lesser-known independents. It is therefore significant that the recently merged CBS/Fox – CBS Records and Twentieth Century Fox – would begin adopting the tactics of independent distributors as the nasties panic unfolded, by buying up horror and exploitation films and then marketing them in a sensational fashion. The looseness with which the term 'video nasty' was applied was incentive enough for the major to trade in titles of the 'borderline' variety: films that were either similar to those identified in the press as 'official' video nasties, or films that were offered by companies seen to be doing good business in this area. This strategy was part of a much broader operation to help the company cope in an uncertain market. Key to this plan was softening the ruthless image of major companies in the eyes of video dealers by aligning with the operational practices of independent distributors.

## CBS/Fox and 'borderline nasties'

When CBS/Fox launched its video operation in March 1982, it appeared on the face of it to be another instance of two big companies combining forces to aid in steady monopolisation; creating, as *Video Business* had it, 'overnight, a major new force in the industry'.[95] And, in keeping with the character of a ruthless major, the new company began its operation by implementing a number of policies thought unfair by video dealers. Price hikes, tiered-pricing schemes and leasing agreements aligned CBS/Fox squarely with practices that made the likes of WHV, RCA/Columbia, and Disney so unpopular in the trade.[96] However, as rationalisation set in, CBS/Fox made some radical steps to break away from the norm as defined by its major counterparts, and align itself to the operations of most independent companies. The strategy, it was hoped, would strengthen CBS/Fox's relationship with dealers, and consequently its market position.

The company's first step was to listen to its customers and drop the widely unpopular leasing policy, 'derestricting' its titles and making them available for dealers to buy outright. This policy meant that, as rationalisation kicked in, shopkeepers could now pick and choose which CBS/Fox titles they wanted and, as with those of their independent counterparts (such as Fletcher, discussed above), could sell them on if their rental popularity slumped.[97] This was a move believed to be widely unpopular with other major companies – but this was, of course, CBS/Fox's aim. Derestricting titles indicated that CBS/Fox recognised the plight of the struggling dealer, showing that a major could appear friendly and empathetic for a change. CBS/Fox was at once distinguishing itself from the majors, while simultaneously broadening its market share.[98]

Second, the company moved to increase its share further by taking control of the fledgling wholesale sector and raising trade margins for 'the big six': Centre Video, S. Gold and Son, Lightning, Terry Blood, Relay and Wynd-Up.[99] Collectively, these companies supplied most of Britain's video shops with stock. By going into exclusive partnership with them, CBS/Fox's managing director, Steve Mandy, claimed to be 'giving them the terms they need to survive properly', as numerous other wholesalers had recently gone out of business. The deal also served to benefit his own company of course, 'streamlining distribution' of CBS/Fox titles to 'ensure [it is] able to exercise a degree of control over [its] own product'. The arrangement also looked to incentivise dealers to stock CBS/Fox cassettes ahead of other companies, given that, under the new agreement, 'every dealer in the UK stocking CBS/Fox or distributed titles' would be the beneficiary of a 'full merchandising service' that would 'ensure that every CBS-Fox title . . . receives . . . promotional support', thus 'maximising the product's rental or sales potential'.[100] Given that dealers and distributors alike were struggling to make their titles stand out in a saturated market, CBS/Fox's promises to support shopkeepers in such a manner, and take an active role in helping them push their product during this uncertain time, was welcomed by the trade.

Third, CBS/Fox looked to expand further by, as mentioned above, growing its catalogue and tapping into markets that major companies tended to avoid: namely, low-budget, independently produced horror and exploitation films. To achieve this the company came to 'manufacturing, sales and distribution agreements' (hereafter MSDAs) with numerous independent distributors. Mandy was explicit with the trade about his intentions, citing the 'new policy' as a 'means of filling the product gap in the CBS/Fox range presently being avidly pursued by so-called independents'.[101] Though he did not say it in as many words, this was a move no doubt inspired by the spike in popularity in horror and exploitation films in the wake of the video nasties panic.[102] With more money behind him than the independents, Mandy could, by recruiting a number of small rivals, encompass a greater market share, by using the lower-end independents to saturate an area of the market untouched by its major counterparts.

MSDAs were reached with companies that had wide product ranges with films in a variety of genres, but inevitably included a number of more sensational, attention-grabbing titles promoted in a bold, exploitative fashion. Its deal with Pyramid Productions, for example, was made with the intention of packaging hitherto unknown independent genre films in attractive sleeves: 'in effect . . . selling covers'.[103] Heading up Pyramid was Maurice 'Mo' Claridge, the former managing director of power-selling indie Atlantis Video.[104] At Atlantis, Claridge oversaw several of the company's aggressive marketing campaigns, including those used to promote the science fiction films *Clonus* (Robert S. Fivesome, 1978) and *Plague* (Ed Hunt, 1978). According to Claridge, such releases 'turned Atlantis into a high-profile' independent in early 1983.[105] Key to Pyramid's success, *Video Business* maintained, is '[s]ensational' imagery and 'target[ting] . . . releases to public demand', with the latter appearing to necessitate the former.[106] Pyramid's covers, which display bold fonts and colourful graphics, were typical of the period, as were the low-budget films that the company handled. Thus, an illustration of a severed hand floating through a graveyard is used to promote the horror film *The Demons of Ludlow* (Bill Rebane, 1983); a menacing, wide-eyed woman brandishing a knife is used to sell another horror film *The Forest* (Don Jones, 1981); and an image of a man firing a machine gun promotes the blaxploitation film *Street War* (John Evans, 1974). Such releases speak to CBS/Fox's desires to ride out rationalisation, achieving 'maximum mileage' out of independent films that were unlikely to be familiar to video consumers.[107] Sensational campaigns could compensate for their anonymity as they always had done, and prove attractive to shopkeepers in the process.

One finds further evidence of this tactic across several of the other videos released via CBS/Fox's MSDAs, which, more boldly than Pyramid, show the company handling more violent titles (or films where violence was a central element of their promotional materials). Its deal with Premier Video is a case in point.[108] The box art of Premier's release of, for instance, the spaghetti western *A Town Called Bastard* (Robert Parish,

1971) depicts, in the background, three corpses hanging from gallows and, in the foreground, a man firing a gun above a blood-splattered sign baring the film's title.[109] Of similar intent is the promotional ad used to promote Premier's release of the high-octane, made-for-TV sports drama, *The Deadliest Season* (Robert Markowitz, 1977), depicting a angry-looking hockey-player brandishing his stick as one might a weapon above a short synopsis outlining the film's 'bloody' content. The goal in both of these instances, as with Pyramid's broader strategy, is clear: to lure in dealers and consumers using sensationalism – in these instances promises of violence and controversy – with CBS/Fox aiming to achieve, as the strapline for *The Deadliest Season* has it, 'BIG BUSINESS' in the process.[110]

The foregoing examples evidence CBS/Fox's willingness to adopt the strategies of power-selling independents: casting its net wide, and broadly focusing on sensationalism and violence to sell its material. Yet there are other instances where the company adopted more specific, localised approaches to align itself with borderline nasties. First, it looked to ape a specific company, VIPCO, whose marketing of controversial films was a regular feature of the tabloid press. Second, it moved to acquire several films that were particularly resonant with an issue that was a named concern of Whitehouse, the BVA and government officials: depictions of sexual violence.

Writing in 2007, Kate Egan appraises the operations of VIPCO, and the success it went onto accrue in the 1990s as a company dealing in (often heavily censored) sell-through re-releases of video nasties. As Egan argues, VIPCO's second incarnation 'appears . . . reliant on the legacy of nasty titles, in order to articulate and promote its historical legitimacy',[111] presenting the company, as its official website declared, as 'Pioneers of the Video Nasty!!' and the 'Oldest and Greatest Horror Video Label in the world!!'[112] However, as early as 1982 VIPCO had an established brand, and was well known in the trade largely for having initiated the video nasties furore with its gruesome covers for *The Driller Killer* and *Death Trap*, and it was common to see VIPCO advertisements for these titles reproduced in media reportage.[113] Beyond press coverage of the company, VIPCO was also known within the trade for the popularity of its other horror releases and its approach to marketing them, including the soon-to-be outlawed *Zombie Flesh-Eaters* (Lucio Fulci, 1979) and *The Bogey Man* (Uli Lommel, 1980).[114] An examination of CBS/Fox's agreements with the independent companies Psycho Video and Adam Corporation are indicative of VIPCO's influence on the major's promotional strategies, and speaks further to the lengths that CBS/Fox was willing to go to co-opt the horror/exploitation market.

Consider, for example, the promotional material for Psycho's first release, the Australian exploitation film *Magee* (Gene Levitt, 1978), which echoes that of the widely reported-on VIPCO title *The Driller Killer*. Like the title of *The Driller Killer*, as Egan notes, which appears in 'large red-lettering' on its respective advert 'with an illustrated drill bit slicing through the middle of the title', 'Magee' is also rendered red, with a hunting knife striking through the first 'E'.[115] Featuring a knife in this way draws parallels with VIPCO, in a manner likely intended to register with consumers: here is another film in which an everyday functional item is used to perform grisly acts. It is telling, however, that the photograph used on the box art of *Magee* forgoes anything comparable to the image of a victim being drilled in the head. The image adorning *Magee*'s cover is, simply, a headshot of the titular character. To this end, while the film's logo suggests violence, the anodyne photograph works to temper the box art's potential to fully transgress standards of moral decency and thus, using the industry logic of the time, present it as a film that will attract consumers (but hopefully not law enforcement).

The consumer ads for Psycho's second release, *The Turn of the Screw* (Dan Curtis, 1974), and those used to promote the Adam Corporation's release of *Beyond the Living Dead* (John Davidson, 1973), have the same aim. Materials used to promote *The Turn of the Screw* directly echo the widely seen promotional materials for VIPCO's release of *The Bogey Man*, while those promoting *Beyond the Living Dead* ape VIPCO's box art for *Zombie Flesh-Eaters*. The main promotional images for *The Turn of the Screw* and *Beyond the Living Dead* are near-identical in their composition to their precedents albeit, as with *Magee*, lacking in blood or anything likely to trigger police interest. Thus, while the video cover for *The Bogey Man* features a priest holding a crucifix with blood streaming down his face, ads for *The Turn of the Screw* feature a bloodless image of the lead character holding a candle. As with *Magee* vis-à-vis *The Driller Killer*, *The Turn of the Screw* presents its title in a jagged, free-hand font comparable to that of *The Bogey Man*. Meanwhile, Adam Corporation's box art for *Beyond the Living Dead* replicates much of the main image used to promote *Zombie Flesh Eaters*, from the original's composition of rotting hands breaking through earth, foregrounding scattered headstones and a glaring sun, to the green/brown/blue/orange colour scheme. Absent is an image declaring 'STRONG UNCUT VERSION' as there is on the cover for *Zombie Flesh Eaters*. Rather, a red '18' certificate sits below the title, indicating that the film has a certificate from the BBFC, and thus is unlikely to lead to legal repercussions.[116] The adoption of this tactic helps anonymous exploitation films align with those generating headlines and/

**Figure 3.7** Aping VIPCO's branding: Psycho Video's *The Turn of the Screw* and Adam Corporation's *Beyond the Living Dead* echo the artwork of controversial horror videos, *Zombie Flesh-Eaters* and *The Bogey Man*. Credit: Popular Film and Television Collection/Daz Gordon.

or proving popular with audiences, and the reputation of a distributor known to deliver shocking fare, while at the same time employing strategies to maintain a safe enough distance from the video nasties controversy proper.

The alleged centrality to video nasties of what the *Daily Mail* described in May 1982 as 'sadistic attacks on women' grew gradual traction among campaign groups and media spokespersons throughout the first half of 1983.[117] By this point, Astra Video's releases of *I Spit on Your Grave* (Meir Zarchi, 1978) – a film in which a woman, having endured multiple gang rapes, rises to seek vengeance on her attackers – and *Snuff* (Michael Findlay, 1976) – which falsely claimed to depict the 'real' killing of a woman – had become two of the most visible of all nasties in press reportage. The press response to these films and others said to be like them denoted widespread reactions by organised feminists to the alleged negative representation of women in horror video. Thus, the British feminist periodical *Spare Rib* writes in July 1982 that, because of video, 'anybody can buy or hire films which show either simulated or real rape, mutilation and murder of women' and called for this alleged 'trade in women's bodies [to be] stopped'.[118] In January 1983 a group operating under the moniker 'Angry Women' launched an attack on a video shop in Yorkshire. In March, attendees at a conference organised by the Association of Cinematograph, Television and allied Technicians 'vote[d] unanimously to campaign against "video nasties" depicting violence against women'. In May, Channel 4 broadcast *A Gentleman's Agreement?*: a 'feminist look' at video regulation.[119] Given the increasing vocalisation of feminist campaigners at this time, and the media attention they were getting, CBS/Fox responded to the climate by releasing more films in the vein of *I Spit On Your Grave* and its contemporaries.

Its deal with London-based Films International is indicative of this. Along with several dramas, westerns and kidvids, Films International handled the little-seen British horror film *Dark Places* (Don Sharp, 1973), and went on to promote it in a style evocative of named-and-shamed video nasty distributors.[120] *Dark Places* had appeared on video in Britain once before, first released by the independent HNP in late 1982, with a video cover comprising four full-colour stills from the film.[121] As a collage of images that, on the face of it at least, appear arbitrarily selected, HNP's artwork is very different to the 'excessive ... marketing campaigns' that would then lead to the '*image* and *idea* of the [video] nasties' in British popular culture.[122] The one bloody image, of a woman lying dead, tied to a bed with a knife protruding from her abdomen, is set against three others that are decidedly more innocuous: a medium close-up of a man and woman staring into each other's eyes; two individuals standing in a garden; a man staring at an axe. Promotional materials for the video nasties were, as per Justin Wyatt's theorisation of Hollywood marketing in the 1980s and 1990s, typically 'high concept', comprising 'strong, singular images' designed to 'make an immediate impression on the potential viewer'.[123] HNP's artwork for *Dark Places*, however, veers more towards 'low concept' marketing: it 'conveys little about the film's plot',[124] and is not easily 'reducible' to a consumer in a manner comparable to the single-image advertisements used to promote, for example, *The Driller Killer*, *SS Experiment Camp* or *Cannibal Holocaust*.[125] It is therefore significant that the artwork used to promote the later Films International release of *Dark Places* adopts a high concept approach. Comprised solely of the aforementioned image of the dead woman on the bed – the contrast heightened to emphasise the redness of the blood upon her yellow sweater – the cover, typical of other video nasties, draws consumers to its 'frozen moment of violent spectacle'.[126] At a time when horror videos were said to 'exploit extreme violence, particularly towards

**Figure 3.8** Remarketed as a 'nasty': the first and second video releases of *Dark Places*, a British horror film. Credit: Tony Earnshaw/Popular Film and Television Collection.

women, and show', among other things, 'murder [and] rape', CBS/Fox's choice to promote *Dark Places* in a manner redolent of these precise elements appears deliberately contrived.[127] So too does the inclusion of the tagline, 'There's more than death waiting for you in dark places', which sits boldly above the main image. In the context of the film's original video release the tagline is vague and problematic, especially given that two of the stills are photographs shot in broad daylight. In the context of the Films International release, however, when anchored solely to the image of a defenceless stabbing victim strapped to a bed, the tagline suggests the threat, or inevitability, of sexual assault. Given the alleged ubiquity of 'rape' and 'mutilation' in popular contentious videos of the period, Films International's promotion of *Dark Places* appears retroactively engineered to hit video nasty criteria and, thus, directly profiteer from the controversy.[128]

Materials used to promote Odyssey's release of *Born Innocent* (Donald Wrye, 1974), a made-for-TV film set in women's detention centre, further illustrate this strategy. The box art homes in on the film's several scenes of sexual violence, while using the star image of lead actress Linda Blair as a means of bolstering its contrived edginess. On *Born Innocent*'s cover, the legend 'SHE WAS BORN TO BE BRUTALISED' sits above an image of youthful-looking Blair (here playing, as the plot synopsis informs us, a fourteen-year-old) and carries an evident double meaning. In a direct sense it serves to anticipate the one-sentence summary that sits at the bottom of the image pointing to Blair's adolescence and the physical and mental trauma she endures throughout the film: 'The abuse and savage humiliation of a young girl in detention.' In another broader respect the tagline also draws on Blair's stardom, specifically her status as the child actress who famously portrayed Regan, a young girl possessed by a demonic spirit in the widely controversial horror film *The Exorcist* (William Friedkin, 1974). Blair had, since the release of *The Exorcist* in 1973, become synonymous with the film as someone whose childhood was now corrupted on account of her playing such a role.[129] This was central to press discourse upon *The Exorcist*'s theatrical and later video release. In the context of *Born Innocent*, Blair's star image lends credence to the film's alleged brutality and power to shock, drawing once again upon Blair's youthful innocence and vulnerability and juxtaposing this notion with mature themes designed to shock an adult audience, while the cover's focus on scenes of violent sexual abuse – the summary suggests that there's nothing more to the film than this – directly situates the film alongside contemporary video nasty marketing and reports expressing concerns about 'films which specialise in extreme violence'.[130]

CBS/Fox's numerous MSDAs with independent companies granted the major a foothold in an industry undergoing drastic change. It enabled a major company, ostensibly distanced from the independent sector, to profiteer and increase its market share by diversifying, while its counterparts remained preoccupied with blockbuster titles. Consequently, such agreements enabled the company to do good business in a market sector that no other major was tapping into, all the while maintaining its glossy corporate image by keeping a degree of distance from the alleged filth merchants whose company logos adorned the video sleeves. The extent to which this distance was imperative to CBS/Fox is evidenced by how the company took action following the trade response to adverts promoting two films it was handling on behalf of a new independent, Avatar Communications, in the summer of 1983: *The Violators* (Jeff Hathcock, 1983) and *Pieces* (Juan Piquer Simón, 1981). The advertising materials for both films represent the boldest ever commissioned by the major and, consequently, dealers worried that if they were to stock such titles, they would risk prosecution for handling obscene publications. The poster for *The Violators*, for example, depicts a man attacking a bare-breasted woman below the tagline 'THEY GAVE RAPE A BAD NAME', while the poster for *Pieces* depicts a woman being attacked by a chain saw in the shower above the strapline 'EVERY WOMAN PLAYED HER PART'. A letter penned by the recently formed Association of Video Film Dealers, encapsulates the feeling among retailers:

> At a time when the government is determining the form of legislation to impose of the video industry, we of the Association of Video Film Dealers consider most unfortunate the advertising copy produced by Avatar Communications for publicising the two films *Pieces* and *The Violators*.
>
> The task of the AVFD, among other national bodies trying to introduce a little calm rationality into the near hysteria being generated in Parliament over 'video nasties', is made all the more difficult by Avatar's insensitivity.
>
> In the current climate, any dealer displaying Avatar's material should not doubt the risk of prosecution.[131]

In response, CBS/Fox immediately withdrew *The Violators* and redesigned the artwork for *Pieces* (supplanting the nude woman with an image of a bloodied chainsaw). Steve Mandy then stressed to the trade press that, should any tapes be seized, the company would replace them at no cost to dealers. This guarantee, Mandy argued to *Video Retailer*, was 'designed to support the dealer, and give him [sic] the confidence he needs to carry on his business without worry about video nasties'.[132] Such a response is telling and is perhaps the best example of the major's willingness to court a 'borderline' nasty market. It recognises that CBS/Fox was aware that such material was on the radar of the police (and thus might be seized), while also evidencing a desire to maintain corporate responsibility as a major company with the best interests of its dealer base at heart. Trading in this way, by having its cake and eating it, allowed CBS/Fox to build a foundation upon, and withstand the pressure of, a turbulent market.

This chapter has shown how video distributors sought to augment their release strategies to survive market rationalisation, by concentrating on emerging genres, and by targeting their releases to new market sectors. However, these efforts, for some at least, would ultimately prove futile.

While the popularity of the kidvid and family genres remained for many independent companies a cause for optimism, and horror in particular was moving to become 'the most popular [video] subgenre' of 1983,[133] this was not enough to withstand the pressures being mounted on them by the ever-strengthening majors. Indeed, while an independent company, Palace, managed to top the video sales charts in 1983 with a horror film, *The Evil Dead* (Sam Raimi, 1981), it was the majors that dominated the charts overall, including numerous horror titles such as CIC's releases of *The Thing* (John Carpenter, 1982) and *The Sentinel* (Michael Winner, 1976), WHV's release of *Poltergeist* (Tobe Hooper, 1982), Thorn EMI's release of *Amityville II: The Possession* (Damiano Damiani, 1982) and CBS/Fox's release of *The Entity* (Sidney J. Furie, 1982).[134] The reality was, in a super-saturated market, videos released by independents were just not as appealing to consumers or to dealers, who pinned hopes on the familiarity and quality of major releases attracting people to their shops.

Conversely, deals with independents gave CBS/Fox a strong enough foothold to flourish. At the Video Software Show in September 1983, the company reported having sold 25,000 units of titles making up its MSDAs: 'almost certainly . . . a larger gross than any other major company taken during the three-day event'.[135] Such success, amounting to £750,000, enabled it to become the first British major to launch a film-buying programme (others tended to distribute their own in-house productions, or license films from other companies).[136] As Hellman and Soramäki note, by 1983, major companies were now in control of two-thirds of the British video market.[137] By comparison, the remaining third (around seventy-five companies trading in thousands of titles between them) were fighting a losing battle; consumers did not gravitate towards their titles and shops were reluctant to stock them. As a result, many independents went out of business.

Astra Video was among the first go. Despite the visibility of its widely advertised kidvid series *Choppy and the Princess*, the company folded in August 1983 with debts of £200,000.[138] Egan has argued that a key factor in Astra's demise was its reputation – in the video trade and news media – as a distributor of video nasties.[139] While it is true that Astra received considerable criticism in the press as a video nasty distributor and that, when its managing director announced that proceeds from the sales of Astra's release of *Choppy and the Princess* were to go to a children's charity the industry responded with cynicism, beyond these factors Astra's operation remained typical of most other struggling independents.[140] Its catalogue was very small (around forty titles) and Astra lacked the resources to renew it with the degree of regularity required to maintain fresh appeal. It simply could not compete with the films (in terms of quantity and quality) on the rosters of many of its competitors. It was evident from mid-1983 that, in the fierce market place, the company and numerous others were unlikely to withstand the rapid expansion of the majors.

Bev Ripley of Intervision captured the feeling in the trade in October 1983, explaining to *Screen International* that, since the industry's inception, consumers had been offered too much choice. He explains that, in just over three years, 'the video industry has used up 30 years of pictures':

> people want a film a week, not 350 films a month. We've used up so many good titles that now we're down to the real dross – and they're still pouring them out.[141]

Too much stock. Not much of it very good. Add to this the rising costs of video rights which, according to Ripley and others, were as expensive for the 'dross' as they were for blockbusters. In this climate independents were effectively priced out of the game, being unable to build up attractive, contemporary catalogues, while at the same time failing to make returns on their older material (which, in some instances, was repackaged and re-released to create an aura of 'the new').[142] Thus, June 1983 saw the demise of Fletcher, Walton and World of Video 2000, highlighting for one industry commentator 'the severe problems rapidly manifesting themselves before the smaller distributors'. 'The supply of existing video product for video use', he conceded, 'is rapidly drying up and prices are rocketing.'[143]

The demise of independents continued throughout 1984 and 1985 as the marketplace levelled out. Further challenges lay ahead, however. The next chapter explores these challenges. It considers the implementation of new legislation designed to combat video nasties, the Video Recordings Act 1984. It also examines how companies adapted as consumers drifted away from video renting due, among other factors, to increasing press coverage of the nasties and the stigma this created for British video dealers. New opportunities opened for independent distributors to diversify, including the development of the new video sales market.

## Notes

1. Barry Lazell, '"Jaws" was the chart champion in 1981', *Video Business* 1.12 (January 1982), 6.
2. On the rental and sales charts of 1981, see Lazell, '"Jaws", 6. On 'video nasties' see Julian Petley, *Film and Video Censorship in Modern Britain* (Edinburgh: Edinburgh University Press), 23–32; and John Martin's accessible breakdown of 'video nasty' reporting in the 'Nasty Times' section of *Seduction of the Gullible: The Truth behind the Video Nasty Scandal* (Liskeard: Stray Cat Publishing, 2007), 14–95.
3. Kate Egan, *Trash or Treasure? Censorship and the Changing Meanings of the Video Nasties* (Manchester: Manchester University Press, 2007), 47–77.
4. On the OPA in this context see Petley, *Film and Video Censorship*, 23–32.
5. David Graham, 'Video Film Kids Beat the X-Cert', *Daily Star* (7 May, 1982), 13. It is worth noting that the aforementioned news story precedes a report by the *Daily Mail* ('The Secret Video Show', 12 May 1982) that is often credited with instigating the panic. See Petley, *Film and Video Censorship*, 23.
6. Tim Smith, 'A temporary lull – or has software bonanza come to an end at last?' *Video Business* 2.10 (July 1982), 20. See also Brian Oliver, 'Has time come to reduce flood of new releases?' *Video Business* 2.10 (July 1982), 26.
7. Norman Abbott quoted in Basil Comely, 'Video achieves spotty adolescence', *Broadcast* 1189 (20 December 1982), 22–3. Quotation at 22.
8. Graham Wade, *Film, Video and Television: Market Forces, Fragmentation and Technological Advance* (London: Comedia, 1985), 24.
9. Distributors would typically release new titles in a quarterly cycle.
10. Oliver, 'Has time come . . .?', 26. The distributors covered in the article include 'major' companies such as CIC, EMI and Warner, as well as successful independents such as VCL, Go and Intervision.
11. These quotes are quite evidently hyperbolic, but they are also very much in keeping with the trade reportage cited elsewhere in this book. They are taken from a first-hand account of video shop ownership in Britain: Harry Pearce's self-published book, *Video Nasties: The True Story of Court Cases, Cock Ups & Collateral Damage* (2013), n.p.
12. Smith, 'A temporary lull . . .?', 20. See also Anon., 'Software overkill?', *Television & Video Retailer* (June 1982), 24.
13. 'Kidvid' was a term coined by US adult film producer/distributor Nigel Bloom, who pioneered children's video entertainment in the US with his Family Home Entertainment (FHE) label. See Frederick Wasser, *Veni, Vidi, Video: The Hollywood Empire and the VCR* (Austin: University of Texas Press, 2001), 107.

14. Julian Upton, 'Electric Blues: The Rise and Fall of Britain's First Prerecorded Videocassette Distributors', *Journal of British Cinema and Television* 13.1 (2016), 24–6.
15. Martin Barker, 'Nasty politics or video nasties?' in Martin Barker (ed.), *The Video Nasties: Freedom, Censorship and the Media* (London: Pluto, 1984), 7–38. Quotation at 7.
16. See, for example, Anon., 'The Christmas Video Show', *Music & Video* (December 1980), 54–79.
17. As Maureen Bartlett (managing director of Videomedia) explained to *Video Business* in July 1982: 'Many dealers have been neglecting the children's market . . . They have been a bit short-sighted. Children's tapes are not "here today, gone tomorrow" like feature films.' See Bartlett cited in Anon., 'Today's children are a visual, video generation', *Video Business* 2.11 (mid-July 1982), 12–13. Quotation at 12.
18. Anon., 'Software overkill?', 24.
19. Anon., 'Today's children . . .', 12.
20. Anon., 'Today's children . . .', 12.
21. Jan Maulden (head of Longman Video) quoted in Graham Wade 'Longman – a new chapter', *Television & Video Retailer* (November 1982), 52.
22. Anon., 'Today's children . . .', 12.
23. Anon., 'Kideo club in time for Christmas', *Television & Video Retailer* (November 1982), 9.
24. Anon., 'Another children's video club', *Television & Video Retailer* (January 1983), 8.
25. Anon., 'Keeping the children happy', *Practical Video* (undated 1982), 36.
26. Anon., 'Today's children . . .', 12.
27. ADB Video, untitled trade advertisement, *Video Retailer* (26 June 1983), 27.
28. Mountain Video, untitled trade advertisement, *Video Business* 2.11 (July 1982), 12.
29. Channel Video, untitled trade advertisement, *Television & Video Retailer* (March 1983), 23.
30. Anon., 'Children's market will make real impact – but caution is needed', *Video Business* 2.18 (mid-November 1982), 28.
31. *Animal Kingdom* video sleeve (VCL), Added emphasis.
32. Anon., 'Easter cartoons from VCL', *Television & Video Retailer* (April 1983), 15.
33. Home Video Productions, untitled trade advertisement, *Television and Video Retailer* (August 1982), 45. Added emphases.
34. Egan, *Trash or Treasure?* 86–7.
35. Anon., 'Distributors aware of children's holidays', *Television & Video Retailer* (August 1982), 21.
36. Wade, 'Longman – a new chapter in video?', 52.

37. Longman Video, untitled consumer advertisement, *Television & Video Retailer* (November 1982), 53.
38. Longman Video, untitled consumer advertisement, *Television & Video Retailer* (November 1982), 53. Added emphasis.
39. Anon., 'Longman opt for video retail – through bookshops', *Television & Video Retailer* (February 1983), 11. See also Paul Campbell, 'The Longman "way of thinking" will point the way to success', *Video Business* 2.17 (November 1982), 18.
40. 'The – Er – Beginners' Guide to Video', *Video World* (November, 1982), 43.
41. Spectrum, untitled trade advertisement, *Popular Video* (January 1982), 54.
42. On VCL's pricing see Anon., 'VCL feature cartoons', *Television & Video Retailer* (November 1982), 14; on ArTel's pricing see Anon., 'Anything to keep the kids quiet at the sign of the horse', *Television & Video Retailer* (March 1983), 25.
43. Anon., 'Children's market will make real impact', 28.
44. Anon., 'More quality tapes available – but careful ordering is essential', *Video Business* 2.18 (mid-November 1982), 34; Wade, 'Longman – a new chapter in video?', 54.
45. Anon., 'More quality tapes available . . .', 34.
46. Derann supplement, 15.
47. Anon., 'Children's market will make real impact', 32.
48. This accounts for why it was relatively common for several companies to release the same cartoons in different contexts. For instance, Fletcher, Mountain and Go all handled the Max Fleischer *Superman* cartoons from the 1940s, which, by the 1980s, were in the public domain.
49. Brian Oliver, 'Children's videos are growing up', *Kideo Business* (supplement issued with *Video Business* 3.22 (25 July 1983), 1.
50. Anon., 'More quality tapes available . . .', 54.
51. Anon., 'Fairy Tales', *Television & Video Retailer* (November 1982), 16.
52. Select Video Ad, *Kideo Business*, 3.
53. Anon., 'Silly season?', *Television & Video Retailer* (August 1982), 16. In May 1980, Mountain published an advert in *Video World* for the video release of a Japanese cartoon, *Nobody's Boy* (director unknown, 1970), in which it was compared to the Disney adaptations of *Snow White* and *Pinocchio* (see *Video World* 2.5 (May 1980), 31). A couple of months later, Intervision, in an advert for the film *The Great Balloon Adventure* (Richard A. Colla, 1978), went even further than Mountain, claiming that the film in question 'beats the best of Disney'. See *Video World* 2.8 (August, 1980), 67.
54. Paul McDonald, *Video and DVD Industries* (London: BFI, 2007), 117.
55. MacDonald, *Video and DVD Industries*, 116–18.
56. MacDonald, *Video and DVD Industries*, 117.
57. See, for example, Anon., 'Six more rental-only Disney movies', *Video Business* 2.10 (July 1982), 8.

58. See, for example, Paula Salvadori, 'Disney, Twentieth, RCA/Columbia – are they "on a different planet"?', *Video Business* (letters pages), 2.10 (July 1982), 38.
59. Joseph Pina, *Running a Successful Video Club* (3rd edition, London: Visionwell, 1983), 30.
60. Anon., 'Silly season?' 16.
61. Egan, *Trash or Treasure?* 90–5.
62. Oliver, 'Children's videos are growing up', 1.
63. Anon., 'Your company guide', *Kideo Business*, 4–8. Quotation at 4.
64. Oliver, 'Children's videos are growing up', 1.
65. Anon., 'No nasties', *Video Business* 3.22 (25 July 1983), 6.
66. See Martin, *Seduction of the Gullible*.
67. On the contemporaneous popularity of horror video see, for example, Anon., 'UK Buyers Like "Nasty" Cassettes', *Variety* 308.11 (13 October 1982), 42, 110; and also Malcolm Keen, 'Dracula bites again', *Video Review* (October 1982), 52–6.
68. See, for example, Eric Schaefer, *Bold! Daring! Shocking! True! A History of Exploitation Films, 1919–1959* (Durham, NC: Duke University Press, 1999), 108–9; and Peter Stanfield, *The Cool and the Crazy: Pop Fifties Cinema* (New Brunswick, NJ: Rutgers University Press, 2015). Kate Egan explores in great detail how video distributors adopted the promotional strategies of exploitation distributors of years gone by. See Egan, *Trash or Treasure?*, 47–77. See also Mark McKenna, *Nasty Business: The Marketing and Distribution of the Video Nasties* (Edinburgh: Edinburgh University Press, 2020), 72–96.
69. Anon., 'VTC fly with VIP jackets', *Television & Video Retailer* (April 1982), 36.
70. 'Nazisploitation' is a term typically given to a cycle of Nazi-themed European exploitation films from the 1960s and 1970s, though it is also on occasion used to describe more recent films. On the original cycle, see Julian Petley, 'Nazi Horrors: History, Myth, Sexploitation', in Ian Conrich (ed.), *Horror Zone* (London: I. B. Tauris, 2009), 205–26. For a further discussion of the term's pervasiveness across media and history, see Daniel H. Magilow, Kristin T. Vander Lugt and Elizabeth Bridges (eds), *Nazisploitation! The Nazi Image in Low-brow Cinema and Culture* (New York: Continuum, 2011).
71. Petley, *Film and Video Censorship*, 328. On Go Video's relationship to the video nasties panic see Petley, *Film and Video Censorship*, 24. On the company 'enjoying success' with *SS Experiment Camp* and *Cannibal Holocaust* see Anon., 'March video releases . . .', *Screen International* 335 (20–7 March, 1982), 17. On Go's knowledge of the market and the success of its marketing see Anon., 'New labels bow in – but accent is on quality before quantity', *Video Business* 3.21 (14 February 1983), 58–74. Citation at 64.
72. The media commonly reproduced the sleeves of *SS Experiment Camp* and *Cannibal Holocaust*, though some articles featured promotional material for

Go titles such as *Savage Terror* (Sisworo Gautama Putraand, 1978) and *Macabre* (Lamberto Bava 1980). See, for example, Peter Chippendale, 'How High Street Horror is invading the home', *The Sunday Times* (23 May 1982); Peter Chippendale, 'Video nasties to be prosecuted', *The Sunday Times* (8 August 1982), 3; Clare Dover, 'Children in video peril', *Daily Express* (12 October 1982), 5; and Brian James, 'We must protect our children NOW', *Daily Mail* (25 February 1983), 6.

73. Anon., 'Going . . . Going . . . GO!', *Television & Video Retailer* (December 1982), 36–8. Quotation at 37.
74. Anon., 'It's All Go – £60,000 spend to promote eight films', *Video Business* 2.13 (September 1982), 16.
75. Anon., 'Going', 37.
76. Anon., 'Going', 37.
77. Anon., 'Going', 37.
78. See, Chippendale, 'How High Street horror is invading the home'; Tony Dawe, 'This poison being peddled as home "entertainment"', *Daily Express* (28 May 1982), 7; Peter Chippendale, 'Watchdog is unleashed on video horror', *The Sunday Times* (30 May 1982).
79. Merlin Video, untitled trade advertisement, *Video Business* 2.10 (July 1982), 55
80. Media, untitled trade advertisement, *Video Business* 2.10 (July 1982), 60.
81. Anon., *Cataclysm* (1980) [Review], *Video Viewer* (September 1982), 60.
82. Liam T. Sanford, *Terror* (Norman J. Warren, 1978) [Review], *Video Viewer* (February 1983), 97.
83. Egan, *Trash or Treasure?*, 71. On *The Extra-Terrestrial Nastie* [sic] see McKenna, *Nasty Business*, 86–7.
84. As Petley, speaking in the documentary *Ban the Sadist Videos* (David Gregory, 2005), argues: 'The video industry does have some blame to take here for mounting advertising campaigns that were absolutely inviting the moral busybodies to get busy.' On *Death Trap* and *The Driller Killer*'s banning, see Alun Rees, 'Violent videos are outlawed', *Daily Express* (1 September 1982), 9.
85. Anon., 'UK Buyers Like "Nasty" Cassettes', 42, 110.
86. Anon., 'Nasties named by DPP in wake of rape case', *Video Business* 3.19 (4 July 1983), 1.
87. Egan, *Trash or Treasure?* 135.
88. Video Programme Distributors is not to be confused with the unaffiliated Sacramento-based firm, Video Products Distributors. For a short history of the latter see Daniel Herbert, *Videoland: Movie Culture at the American Video Store* (Berkeley: University of California Press, 2014), 160–1.
89. Anon., 'VPD offers cold comfort on "nasty" tapes', *Video Business* 3.2 (14 March 1983), 4.
90. Anon., 'VFO's Horror Story', *Video Retailer* 10 (14 July 1983), 1.
91. David Coe (Director of VFO) quoted in Anon., 'VFO's Horror Story', 1.

92. For example, the films on Videomedia's horror label, Vampix – such as *Eaten Alive* and *The Beyond* – all carried X certificates attained prior to their original theatrical distribution in the early 1980s, and displayed them on their covers.
93. Eddie White (manager of CS Unlimited Video, Cardiff) quoted in Charles Robinson, 'Making money out of blood, sex and budget Beta VCRs', *Video Business* 3.1 (14 February 1983), 42.
94. Kruger quoted in Paul Campbell, 'Police view of nasties', *Video Business* 3.12 (18 July 1983), 12.
95. Anon., 'New industry force as CBS and Fox link', *Video Business* 2.2 (March 1982), 1. A similar merger occurred between Thorn and EMI in 1979.
96. See, for example, Salvadori, 'Disney, Twentieth, RCA/Columbia'.
97. Anon., 'CBS/Fox drops lease scheme', *Video Business* 2.13 (September 1982), 1.
98. Tim Smith, 'Far-reaching implications of CBS-Fox decisions on prices and rental', *Video Business* 2.13 (September 1982), 26–8.
99. Anon., 'CBS to create a wholesale elite', *Video Business* 3.4 (21 March 1983), 4.
100. Steve Mandy, 'We must not be at the mercy of market forces', *Video Business* 3.8 (18 April 1983), 34.
101. Steve Mandy quoted in Anon., 'Policy change as CBS/Fox moves to broaden product', *Video Business* 2.17 (November 1982), 6.
102. Anon., 'UK Buyers Like "Nasty" Cassettes'.
103. Paul Campbell, 'Pyramid aiming to stand out on shelves', *Video Business* 3.12 (May 1983), 36.
104. For whom, for a short while, CBS/Fox also handled manufacturing, sales and distribution.
105. Maurice Claridge (of Pyramid Productions) quoted in Campbell, 'Pyramid aiming', 36.
106. Campbell, 'Pyramid aiming', 36.
107. Campbell, 'Pyramid aiming', 36.
108. Anon., 'CBS/Fox picks up Premier', *Video Business* 3.2 (28 February 1983), 11.
109. The cover is a reworking of the image used to promote the film in 1980 by its first British video distributor Home Video Supplies.
110. Premier Video (CBS/Fox), untitled consumer advertisement (*The Deadliest Season*), *Popular Video* (June 1983), 98–9.
111. Egan, *Trash or Treasure?*, 190.
112. *Vipco's Vaults of Horror*, quoted in Egan, *Trash or Treasure?*, 190.
113. Alun Rees, 'Violent videos are outlawed'.
114. On the popularity of *Zombie Flesh-Eaters* on video see Gordon Booker, 'Zombies – A day in the afterlife', *Popular Video* (November 1982), 76. *The Bogey Man* is also featured in this article, but as an anticipated new release. On the notoriety of the artwork used to promote *The Driller Killer*, see Peter Dean, 'Dressed to sell', *Video Retailer* 7 (23 June 1983), 21.

115. Egan, *Trash or Treasure?*, 54.
116. Barrie Gold, of S. Gold and Sons, confirmed with me that Adam Corporation was, in fact, a new venture established by VIPCO's founder, Mike Lee, and named after his son. I have been unable to locate any article from the trade press discussing Adam Corporation, or CBS/Fox reaching an agreement with Lee. I am therefore relying on the video releases I have been able to obtain bearing 'Adam Corporation', and the words of Gold, who worked closely with Lee up until the early 2000s. I am indebted to Mark McKenna for first alerting me to this information, and to Mr Gold for validating it.
117. *The Daily Mail* quoted in Martin, *Seduction of the Gullible*, 14.
118. Anon., 'Video violence', *Spare Rib* 120 (July 1982), 16.
119. On the 'Angry Women' episode, see Martin, *Seduction of the Gullible*, 17; on the ACTT conference, see Martin, *Seduction of the Gullible*, 18; and on the broadcast of *A Gentleman's Agreement?*, see Martin, *Seduction of the Gullible*, 19.
120. Anon., 'CBS/Fox pacts first deal', *Video Business* 2.16 (mid-October 1982), 2.
121. They are some of the same images use to promote the film during its theatrical release.
122. Egan, *Trash or Treasure?*, 47–8. Original emphases.
123. Justin Wyatt, *High Concept: Movies and Marketing in Hollywood* (Austin: University of Texas Press, 1994), 122.
124. Wyatt, *High Concept*, 6.
125. As Wyatt argues, 'high concept' is 'a striking, easily reducible narrative which also offers a high degree of marketability' (13). The print marketing for a film, he goes on to explain, is central to its reducibility in the eyes of consumers (112–33).
126. Egan, *Trash or Treasure?*, 52.
127. *The Sunday Times* quoted in Martin, *Seduction of the Gullible*, 16–17. On such contemporaneous reports see Martin, *Seduction of the Gullible*, 14–18.
128. On the popularity of such films see, for example, Graham Wade, 'Films that make more than profits jump', *The Guardian* (19 July 1983), 11. See also Egan, *Trash or Treasure?*, 59.
129. Jason Lee, 'The devil you don't know? The rise and fall and rise of Linda Blair', in Jane O'Connor and John Mercer (eds), *Childhood and Celebrity* (London: Routledge, 2017), 122–32.
130. Peter Kruger (operational head of Scotland Yard's Obscene Publications Squad) speaking with *The Sunday Times* in May 1982, cited in Martin, *Seduction of the Gullible*, 14.
131. R. T. Thomas, 'Insensitive Avatar?' [letter], *Video Retailer* (4 August 1983), 2.
132. Steve Mandy quoted in Anon., 'Avatar reassure retailers', *Video Retailer* (18 August 1983), 24.
133. Heikki Hellman and Martti Soramäki, 'Economic concentration in the videocassette industry: a cultural comparison', *Journal of Communication* 35.3 (September 1985), 122–34. Quotation at 130.

134. See, for example, 'Britain's Top 50', *Video Retailer* (25 August 1983); and also, 'Britain's Top 50', *Video Retailer* (26 January 1984).
135. Steve Mandy (of CBS/Fox) quoted in Anon., 'Show Report', *Video Retailer* (22 September 1983), 22–3. Quotation at 22.
136. On CBS/Fox profits see Anon., 'Off Screen', *Video Business* 3.31 (26 September 1983), 8; on CBs/Fox and film-buying see Anon., 'CBS-Fox UK enters buying market', *Video Business* 3.9 (12 November 1983), 4.
137. Hellman and Soramäki, 'Economic concentration in the videocassette industry', 128.
138. Anon., 'Astra in liquidation owing £200,000', *Video Retailer* 15 (25 August 1983), 1.
139. Egan, *Trash or Treasure?*, 71.
140. Egan, *Trash or Treasure?*, 71.
141. Bev Ripley quoted in Terry Ilott, 'Three years of waste in the video industry', *Screen International* 414 (4–8 October 1983), 24.
142. As practice companies such as Derann and Intervision had taken to doing.
143. Richard Larcombe, 'Please let us have more warning on these top titles', *Video Business* 3.16 (13 June 1983), 22. On Walton and World of Video 2000 see Anon., 'Receivers in at Walton & Fletcher Films', *Video Business* 3.18 (27 June 1983), 4.

CHAPTER 4

# Regulation and Adaptation

> [L]ife was so much easier when Joe Public gazed in awe at racks
> of films he'd never heard of but would queue up and rent anyway.
> Fil Adams-Mercer, 'The demise of leasing – and
> another welcome trend', *Video Business* (17 March 1986)

The above quotation, from a video journalist in 1986, embodies the plight of many of Britain's independent distributors in the mid-1980s. The previous chapter has shown how the emergence of the major companies, and many smaller distributors in 1982 and 1983, let to market saturation and, consequently, many companies going bankrupt. The period that followed was one of a rapid change for the video business, which saw new legislation brought in to police the video business in the wake of the video nasties panic, adaptive measures taken by distributors in attempts to assure their longevity in the business, and the emergence of new markets.

The chapter begins with a consideration of the oft-discussed Video Recordings Act 1984: new legislation bespoke to the video business. Second, it explores some of the strategies adopted by independent distributors that enabled them to outstep the fate of bankruptcy, which met so many of their competitors. Some companies, it is revealed, strove to shape their corporate identity at this time in a manner akin to major Hollywood studios and communications firms, while others saw longevity in power-selling budget releases. Third, it considers the development of the video sales – or 'sell-through' – market.

## Major changes

In scholarship and popular discourse, the mid-1980s are viewed as a turning point for the British video industry, as they witnessed the implementation of regulatory measures in response to growing concerns surrounding piracy and the video nasties scandal. As discussed in Chapter 2, pirated

**Figure 4.1** A sign of things to come: a haul of pirated cassettes seized by the Federation Against Copyright Theft (FACT) in 1983. Photographer unknown. Credit: Popular Film and Television Collection.

videocassettes were believed at the beginning of the 1980s to account for 80 per cent of material available. Within twelve months of the establishing of the Federation Against Copyright Theft (FACT), the organisation had seized 30,000 illegal tapes.[1] By the summer of 1984, rates of video piracy had reportedly dropped by two-thirds.[2]

For those working in the video business, FACT was an unprecedented success, and provided a down-trodden industry with much-needed good news, given that the press reports, on account of the video nasties panic, continued to be so damning.[3] For industry critics, there was more to come, with the passing of industry-wide legislation: the Video Recordings Act 1984. Proposed as a Private Member's Bill by Tory MP Graham Bright in May 1983 and making its way onto the statute books soon after, the Act made it a legal requirement for all videos released onto the British market to carry, at a cost, a certificate by the BBFC. The certificates – U (suitable for all), PG (parental guidance), 15 (not for sale or rent to persons under the age of 15), 18 (not for sale or rent to persons under the age of eighteen) and R18 (restricted sales of sexually explicit film and video works to adults in licensed sex shops) – were designed to help curb the alleged spread of obscene video nasties and offer consumer advice. Distributors were given until 1 September 1986 to submit their catalogues to the BBFC for certification, a period that was then extended to 1 September 1987, and then 1988.

The significance of the VRA cannot be understated.[4] As stated above, it demanded compliance from distributors, but also video stockists who, if caught trading in uncertified material, could face legal consequences, including time in prison. For these and other reasons, it was and remains widely controversial. Martin Barker, in his significant book from 1984, *Video Nasties: Freedom and Censorship in the Media*, decries the intentions behind the Act as disingenuous, remarking that the Video Recordings Bill (as it then was) 'holds out real threats of practical censorship – disguised, of course, as moral protection'.[5] Similar arguments were made at the time, including by then-journalist Julian Petley, who has since claimed – echoing the opinion of many others, including some working in the industry – that the Bill was 'hasty, ill-conceived and thoroughly authoritarian'.[6] Subsequent '[l]egal explorations' of the VRA, Sian Barber has argued in her work on the topic, have given legal credibility to these claims.[7]

However, there are two commonly held misconceptions about the VRA and its effect on the video business that require further scrutiny. First is the claim that the VRA led to the collapse of independent video distribution. The most recent iteration of this argument appears in Mark McKenna's *Nasty Business*, where the author claims that the VRA 'devastated the independent video industry in the United Kingdom', allowing major distributors to take control away from the multitude of smaller firms that, he argues, characterised the first few years of the boom.[8] The government, the NVLA, the BVA and the BBFC, McKenna claims, 'joined together in harmony to condemn the independent sector as a deviant and corrupting force in British society'.[9] Consequently, he argues, the VRA provides 'a clean break' between a period 'dominated by the independent sector' and one that 'was suddenly not'.[10]

It is in some respects reasonable to argue that the Act validated the concerns of certain industry watchers – that, in their view, video was indeed a 'deviant' industry, and that distributors and shopkeepers were trading in wares that were, at best, distasteful and, at worst, corrupting. The Act certainly compounded the negative stereotype that had plagued the industry since the late 1970s and, as McKenna rightly acknowledges, that the BVA wanted to quash (see Chapter 5 of this book). Yet the claim that the VRA 'devastated' independent distributors is questionable, as is the claim that it ensured that 'control' of the video industry 'remained in the hands' of major companies.[11]

The VRA did not signal a 'clean break', because the video market was not, contrary to what McKenna suggests, the 'sole domain' of independent companies prior to 1982 (the year he claims the majors joined the market).[12] While there was certainly a higher number of independent companies in operation than there were majors, this did not translate into a greater market share for the smaller distributors. In fact, major firms had dominated both video sales and rentals since entering the market two years earlier, in 1980. In the first ever video chart, published in *Video Business* in February 1981, major companies accounted for 60 per cent of video sales, with twenty-four titles of the 'Top 40' comprising releases from Warner, CIC (Paramount's British distributor), Rank and Twentieth Century Fox (trading as Magnetic Video).[13] Moreover, of the top twenty rentals, eighteen were popular Hollywood movies.[14] CIC's prominence in both charts with known – and fairly recent – titles such as *Jaws* (Steven Spielberg, 1975), *Saturday Night Fever* (John Badham, 1977) and *Grease* (Randal Kleiser, 1978) indicates how, even at this early stage in the business's history, the appeal of mainstream Hollywood product outweighed that of lesser-known (or, in many cases, unknown) titles that the independents were carrying.[15] Indeed, the video arm of CIC had been in operation a mere two months when the aforementioned charts were compiled – further attesting to the appeal of its catalogue in comparison to those of its independent counterparts. Given this information, it cannot reasonably be claimed that the VRA led to any *subsequent* domination of the market by major companies, when such companies were already dominant.

Indeed, at the end of 1984, some three years before the official deadline for all companies to have their stock certified by the BBFC, the fate of many independent companies was already apparent as 'majors *continue*[*d*] to dominate' the charts.[16] A multitude of factors, including a bout of warm weather (resulting in fewer people than usual seeking home entertainment), a decline in VCR purchases, a spike in time shifting, a nationwide slump in video rentals (down 50 per cent on the previous year), a preference among consumers for 'blockbuster titles' and a push by major companies to offer trade discounts reinforced what was clear in the summer of 1983.[17] Over-zealously promoted B movies by independents and majors alike (such as CBS/Fox through its MSDAs) were even less likely to compete in this climate against glossier, bigger-budgeted fare, especially when such cassettes tended to be priced the same as their blockbusting counterparts.[18] The end-of-year rental charts are illustrative of this, which see the 'six biggest shares' taken by majors.[19] In a rationalising market, where majors continued to show strength and resilience, the fate of independents, as companies lacking the resources to compete or withstand such market pressures, was inevitable.

The second misconception about the VRA is that it was unanimously opposed by the industry. Petley rightly acknowledges that many believed the Bill to be 'neither practicable or desirable', but there were nevertheless some influential figures in the business, including distributors and legitimate dealerships, who welcomed it.[20] Amid rationalisation and the video nasties panic, where uncertainty abounded, legal assurances that distributors, wholesalers and dealers knew where they stood was one factor that could, in the view of some, offer the business a sense of stability at an otherwise chaotic time. By the time the VRA was proposed as a Private Member's Bill, the notion of industry-wide regulation had been a discussion point across the trade for at least two years. Since the inception of the video business, wholesalers and retailers had been subjected to regular police raids, as officers searched for hardcore pornographic material to prosecute under the Obscene Publications Act.[21] Rarely was such material found. Nevertheless, raids caused tradespersons great financial and reputational worry. At the end of 1980, wholesalers S Gold and Sons and Video Unlimited had £40,000 worth of stock seized between them, from companies as diverse as Intervision, Hokushin, IFS, Scripglow and Videomedia: none of which traded in hardcore films.[22] 'The situation is getting worse', managing director Barrie Gold explained to the trade press in January 1982. '[W]e are hearing that at least one of our accounts is raided everyday [sic].'[23]

Raids were a cause of anxiety and frustration among tradespeople worried about having the majority of their stock removed (thus disabling them from renting the videos), prosecution and paying legal fees for operating what, to their minds, were wholly legal businesses. After all, there was, at present, nothing enshrined in law bespoke to the video medium. Writing for *Video Business* in response to legal questions surrounding the rental and sale of adult videos, journalist Tim Smith captures the mood:

> the whole situation has become increasingly worrying for those retailers who want to operate within the law and satisfy the demand that unquestionably exists for adult material.
> 
> But the guidelines that dealers need are simply not available when it comes to deciding what to stock and what to steer clear of.[24]

He goes on to describe how, 'at present the only place [sic] to which a video shop can look for guidance' are distributors and wholesalers who, 'by necessity, have each had to develop their own policies over what is handled and produced'.[25] When implemented, such policies were inconsistent, and typically consisted of a mix of the following: arbitrary box and/or catalogue labelling such as 'Adult Movies' and 'Family Viewing',[26] no such labelling at all,[27] the employment of certificates awarded by the BBFC to films when released theatrically in Britain,[28] the adoption of US ratings awarded to films by the Motion Picture Association of America (MPAA),[29] or in some cases ratings systems unique to individual companies.[30] As Smith tells it, 'some sort of guidelines for video retail and trade' and 'some predicable policy' from the Home Office and local magistrates, would be '[h]appily' welcomed by the video business. A single policy – or set of policies – it was agreed, would quell fears of prosecution and negate damages to livelihoods caused by legal fees and/or losses in stock.[31]

The Video Trade Association (VTA) supported changes in the law to protect the dealers it represented. It broadly endorsed ('[f]or want of anything better') proposals that were made by the BVA for a voluntary code – that the latter Association would manage, at a cost to distributors – in May 1983, though it remained sceptical of how such a code could be practically enforced and whether or not it would, in actuality, satisfy the public or the police in lieu of formal legislation.[32] Some distributors also supported, for the most part, the adoption of a BVA-style code to help guide the consumer – though again confusion and trepidation remained around the extent to which such a code would be effective if not enshrined in law. The main concern was that a code, if/when implemented, would not guarantee distributors and dealers protection from prosecution under the OPA, because a good number of the tapes being seized were carrying BBFC certificates (albeit certificates granted to the films for theatrical distribution).[33] Consequently, only a handful of distributors complied.[34]

A new law was the preferred option for many because of the assumed stability and protection it would bring them. The government, having initially supported the BVA's proposal to self-regulate,[35] changed tack in July 1983 in response to mounting pressure from outlets such as the *Daily Mail*, finally committing to legislation.[36] The BVA, while dissatisfied with the decision and proceeding to accuse the Bill of having 'not been carefully drafted', for being ambiguously worded, and for in fact failing to offer the industry guaranteed protection from prosecution as originally promised, found itself in an awkward position.[37] On the one hand, the Association had a moral duty to protect the interests of the business in the best way it saw fit. It was the opinion of the BVA's leadership team that the government and the BBFC did not know enough about the inner workings of the business to control it effectively. The BVA, comparatively, had unmatched experience. On the other hand, the Association had to think practically. As Petley explains, by the time 'the statutory control of video was included in the Tories' 1983 election manifesto', and the video nasties panic continued to be exacerbated by the press, the BVA had little choice but to accept that its continued efforts to campaign against the Bill were proving futile.[38]

For others in the trade, time was of the essence, and not all distributors agreed with the BVA that the BBFC was inadequately equipped to regulate. After all, a number of distributors already had working relationships with the Board given the fact some had backgrounds in theatrical distribution. For others, the notion that legislation, managed day to day by an historic and experienced body, was anticipated to grant the industry security and stability. 'I have faith in this long standing establishment', David Hodgins, of independent distributor Medusa Communications, told *Video Retailer* some months after the company's first title, *Absurd* (Joe D'Amato, 1981), was charged as an obscene publication.[39] Similarly, Mike Cole of VCL communicated to the trade press his view that '[t]he sooner legislation is brought to bear, the better it will be for us and the dealer.'[40] In this context, the BVA, unable to exert any influence on the government, U-turned, promising to focus its attention on 'making [the VRA] as workable, effective and reasonable as possible',[41] to ensure that it spoke to the wants of the trade, not the moralists denigrating the industry.

The public image of the video business in the wake of video nasty hysteria compounded the low performance of the rental market across 1984 and 1985. The summer of 1985 – during which videocassette manufacturer Scotch predicated that demand for blank media was destined to spike because video rentals were so low – saw the bankruptcy of no fewer than five distributors (Capricorn, Films Galore, Mountain, VideoSpace and VTC), and a decision by video pioneer Intervision to join forces with CBS/Fox, cease the operations of its distribution arm and concentrate its efforts on establishing its new 'video racking' division (see Chapter 5).[42] The reduction in companies during this period made it clear that video distribution was unsustainable on its present terms.

Three significant shifts would then occur, enabling those distributors still in business – and, indeed, new companies continuing to emerge against the odds – to sustain. First, there was a push by several companies to pursue 'outward growth' and diversify their business interests, by, for example, branching out into adjacent areas of media communication, and establishing offices overseas to make headway into comparatively thriving international video markets. Second, several companies experimented with price reductions. As discussed in the previous chapter, one of the main criticisms levelled at international film companies by distributors was that video rights for films remained very high, even in the case of the lower-budgeted B-list films that the independents tended to gravitate towards. Independents struggled to market such films at the same price as those being offered by their major equivalents, the latter of whom – as we have seen – were inevitably more popular with retailers and consumers. In 1983, however, the majors began experimenting with cheaper pricing, and a number of independents started making video rights available for B-list films that they believed were no longer commercially viable. This enabled competing independents to buy film rights very cheaply, set prices lower than the majors, and continue operating when many of their equals were facing hardship. Third, in 1985, the video sales market began in earnest. The remainder of this chapter considers these developments.

## Outward growth

The 1980s is regarded as the beginning of a period of 'accelerated intensification of international cultural flows' including 'much greater internationalisation on the part of cultural industry businesses'.[43] Related to this are shifts in the changing mediascape and resultant interest by video companies in adjacent forms of communications.[44] The cancellation of the majority of British video software tradeshows in 1984 evinced such shifts, as did the decision of the organisers of the industry's biggest sales event, Vidcom, to switch to a multi-media format, inviting for the first time companies from cable, satellite, and pay TV, '[s]o the opportunities for those holding the rights are much greater'.[45] With heightened competition from these rightsholders, some video distributors responded by expanding their business interests. Opportunities also presented themselves for video distributors to hone what Mario Alvesson terms the 'ideational dimensions' of an organisation: 'the crucial role played by corporate image, reputation and identity' in any organisation's market longevity.[46] Making inroads into foreign territories, incorporating broader commercial interests into one's portfolio, and foregrounding these endeavours in company marketing were hoped to result in numerous positive effects for British video companies in an otherwise fraught climate.

Prior to the mid-1980s, the efforts of UK companies to internationalise amounted to the enhancement of what economics scholars term the 'inward growth' of a company, to enhance, through capital gain, its market position in its domestic setting. This is the opposite of 'outward growth', which is signified by, for example, a company establishing offices overseas.[47] There were, of course, several exceptions, including Australasian subsidiaries of Intervision and Home Video Holdings and a number of foreign companies with British distribution, including Italy's Cinehollywood, in addition to several international firms with British divisions including Sweden's VTC and Dubai's GVC.[48] For the majority of home-grown indies, however, international agreements typically involved buying/selling video rights from/to independent agents (i.e. other video/film distributors) overseas, as in the case of, for example, Go Video's relationships with European firms, VPD's distribution connections in Scandinavia, South Africa, Australia and the US, and Guild's relationships with companies in the US, Australia and Europe.[49]

Of all the companies investing in outward growth, VCL was the most successful, and most other companies looking to expand took inspiration from it. The company was advertising heavily in trade periodicals, boasting of its international presence, as early as 1981. By 1982, while other

**Figure 4.2** Go Video was one of many independent distributors with international connections. Credit: Popular Film and Television Collection.

distributors suffered the effects of the crowded domestic market, VCL was expanding rapidly in foreign territories and thus benefited from lucrative income streams that the majority of its British competitors were lacking. By 1983 and into the latter half of the decade, the corporate reputation of VCL was secure among those working in the video business. Established in 1978, and occasionally (albeit incorrectly) identified as the oldest software distributor, the company's longevity was an indication of both its success and its credibility. Moreover, VCL went largely unscathed by the video nasties panic. Its only title targeted by the Director of Public Prosecutions, *Zombie Creeping Flesh* (Bruno Mattei, 1980), was distributed on behalf of another company (Merlin), and ultimately avoided prosecution.[50] These factors, coupled with the company's open support of the VRA, made VCL very much a team player in regard to the demands of the BVA and the government, negating subsequent claims by one scholar that 'respectability . . . elude[d] the company' in the mid-1980s.[51] Nevertheless, in spite of its good standing, and given the declining performance of video rental in the UK, VCL continued to hone its corporate image by projecting, in the trade press and at trade shows, a narrative of evolution, growth in the international arena and diversification into other non-video areas of media communications. A consideration of VCL's marketing and branding strategies during this time proves an illuminating case study, revealing an approach that allowed the company to sustain and achieve levels of success that ran counter to those of many of its British competitors.

Until 1982 the success of VCL was exceeded by that of Intervision, the company with which it shared the nascent video market in the late 1970s.[52] However, while Intervision struggled during rationalisation, VCL was able to survive as a distributor, and continued to thrive into the late 1980s and beyond. The outward growth of the company during this period was a consequence of strategic thinking by the company head, Alan Judd, and its managing director, Mike Cole. Rationalisation had certainly impacted VCL as it had its many competitors. Indeed, when Astra Video went bust, VCL lost one of its most lucrative cassette duplication contracts.[53] Yet by the time these events played out, VCL was operating international subsidiaries in Germany, the Netherlands, Australia, South Africa, Spain and the US, with distribution agreements in France and the Far East.[54] The success of these operations afforded Judd and Cole the luxury of being able to step away from the UK market and 'fall back' on the company's international revenue streams as things got tough at home.[55] Speaking with *Screen International* in October 1983, Judd relates VCL's international success to the business acumen of its executives, to the willingness of the firm to take risks at the right time, and to the corporate muscle the company was able to flex as a result of five years' profiteering in the video business. This combination of experience by strategising, risk taking and continued capital attainment (further evidence of its success) is what allowed the firm to remain buoyant, enabling Judd to present VCL as a major market force when the opposite was true for others. By waiting for the right moment and then spending 'an absolute fortune', Judd remarks, the company was able to establish an international presence 'properly', allowing the company to recoup its initial outlay, and proceed to expand its market reach.[56] Judd offers VCL's Australian subsidiary as an example of such success, claiming the label sold 50,000 videocassettes in less than twelve months, in turn making the company one of the country's leading distributors.[57] Such claims to the trade press reinforced VCL's reputation as a credible entity with historic and ongoing success, and worked to enhance its corporate image as a global-facing firm.

Executives at VCL responded to its growing international presence by rebranding the company, further enhancing its corporate identity. First, the company name was finessed. VCL Video Services Ltd, by which it had been known since the late 1970s, was changed to VCL Communications Ltd: a switch that more accurately reflected the new media interests of the company, including experimentation in feature film production and television distribution.[58] It also signalled to the trade the growth of the company from a firm offering 'services' to a single market area ('video') to one with clout across the gamut of global entertainment technology ('communications'). The strategy worked to distinguish VCL from its domestic competitors, who, by the very nature of their national operations appeared more parochial and less significant on a global stage by comparison. It also semantically aligned the organisation to bigger international players, such as Warner Communications: a decision that was likely taken to present VCL as a firm on par with, or at the very least operating within the same field as, historic corporate giants. Whereas smaller firms had historically striven to mimic the promotional strategies of major studios to mobilise an air of prestige (as in the case of IFS's allusions to Pinewood Studios, for example, discussed in Chapter 1), VCL conversely had the evidence to support the boldness of its claims.

The company logo was altered to complement its expansion. It is suggested by advertising scholars Jonathan Lufferelli, Mudra Mukesh and Ammara Mahmood that the main purpose of a logo is to '[trigger] memory associations of the target brand'.[59] Companies invariably opt for either a 'more' or 'less' *descriptive* logo; which is to say 'the extent to which the textual and/or visual design elements of a logo are indicative of the type of product' the brand in question 'markets'.[60] For example, in the present day, the logo for the high street coffee outlet Costa Coffee, which 'includes coffee beans and the word "coffee"', is more descriptive than that of its main rival, Starbucks, which contains no such 'indicative' components.[61] 'More (vs less) descriptive logos', Lufferelli et al. explain, 'are easier [for consumers] to process and thus elicit stronger impressions of [brand] authenticity.'[62] VCL's logo change is to be understood on the same terms, albeit with a caveat. As the analysis below reveals, the 'descriptiveness' of the new logo does not speak to the company's *product*, which, given the nature and audience of the film/video periodicals in which it appears, and the tendency for its ads to identify the areas of communication the firm specialises in, was obvious.[63] The new logo sought instead to describe the extent of VCL's *global penetration*, thereby anchoring people's 'memory associations' of the brand to its international expansion, on the knowing assumption that its prospective customers had knowledge of the goods in which it traded.[64]

In 1979 the company logo consisted of the letters 'VCL' in a bold geometric font.[65] At times, the image was housed within a truncated circle, resembling a television screen. The descriptive quality of the logo's latter presentation, thus, acknowledges video's functional dependency on a television set, and projects VCL as a telecommunications company. In October 1981, however, its cassettes and trade advertising began bearing a logo displaying the company name stretching across a map of the world.[66] McKenna offers commentary on the descriptiveness of the new logo in *Nasty Business*, arguing that it was a design choice intended to '*create the illusion* of a global presence'.[67] However, within a year of the logo's adoption, VCL was recognised by industry commentators as 'the most internationally oriented' independent distributor in Britain.[68] By 1983, it was boasting representation in thirty territories and, by 1984, was operating nine international sales offices.[69] Endorsement from the trade press, thus, validated what VCL was claiming via its own marketing speak, namely that it was a 'worldwide independent'.[70] The appearance of the logo on video sleeves and in film/video periodicals, where it appears alongside text acknowledging the firm's specialisation and countries of operation, therefore complements the descriptiveness of the new VCL logo as one that 'symbolises VCL's position as a leading worldwide video distributor', denoting an authentic corporate image of a global video brand.[71]

The influence of VCL, as a British distributor excelling amid a fraught period for the video business, is visible across other companies, which began expressing narratives of outward expansion and corporate muscle in their branding. Entertainment in Video, thus, began advertising as one strand of the Entertainment Group of Companies, including its respective

Figure 4.3 A leading worldwide distributor: VCL's 'descriptive' new logo. Credit: Popular Film and Television Collection.

theatrical and video arms (historically advertised as separate entities).[72] Merlin Video took a similar tack, rebranding as Miracle Communications and advertising as part of the new Miracle Group, which included its owners' long-established theatrical distribution arm, Miracle Films.[73] In both cases, the autonomous arms of these companies are promoted together to reflect, to quote a Miracle Communications ad, the 'multimedia' context of the video business in the mid-1980s, of which VCL was at the forefront.

The greatest indication of VCL's market presence and significance, however, came when the company was acquired by Richard Branson's Virgin Vision in 1985.[74] The Branson buyout was the second acquisition of a British distributor by a national conglomerate. The first was the acquisition of Videoform by the Heron Corporation (a company with interests in finance and real estate) in 1983.[75] The Heron-Videoform buyout made waves in the trade press. At the time, Heron was 'the largest privately owned corporation in Europe', and the purchasing of Videoform constituted its first forays into the entertainment sector.[76] From the perspective of Heron and Videoform's business interests, it meant considerable growth.[77] From the perspective of Videoform's corporate reputation, the buyout spoke of a reputable company whose success warranted the level of investment a company as big as Heron was willing to give. However, it meant little for Videoform's brand longevity. Within two years the 'Videoform' label was abandoned in favour of Heron Home, and all of Videoform's titles were deleted from its catalogue.[78] VCL fared somewhat differently.

The VCL buyout was far more beneficial to Virgin than Videoform was to Heron. Whereas Heron withdrew from the video business in 1990, Virgin Vision continued to expand its video operations internationally.[79] And while the VCL company name was eventually subsumed into the Virgin Vision brand in the UK and most other international territories, it remained a leading brand in Germany until it filed for bankruptcy in 2010.[80]

The trajectory of VCL is of great significance to the history of the British video industry. It was a company that challenged assumed logic about the fate of independent video distributors; one that expanded in spite of rationalisation, and in spite of the VRA on account of the strategic choices made by its managing directors to internationally orientate their company and brand. The history of VCL, thus, speaks to an alternative history of independent video distribution, and the success that could be attained by strategic companies at an otherwise fraught time for the video business.

## A niche at the bottom of the market

Other independents displayed flair and discernment during this period, though not all believed the key to market survival was international expansion or, indeed, projecting corporate muscle. On the contrary, many believed that the video business could continue as usual (or near enough) despite the VRA, and that there was still much to be gained from trading in strikingly illustrated low-budget horror and exploitation films.

The companies that shared this view, whether they were established operations who had survived rationalisation or the numerous others that emerged c.1985, present an additional challenge to the argument that the VRA 'devastated' the independent sector. On the contrary, there were at least forty such companies operating in the mid-to-late 1980s, trading in genre films of varying budgets, quality and national origin. Among those that had withstood the pressures of rationalisation were ABC, Ariel, Avatar, Delta, Electric, Entertainment in Video, Guild, Medusa, Odyssey, Precision, Pyramid, Palace and VPD.[81] Other companies emerged as breakaways from known entities. Thorn EMI Screen Entertainment, for instance, split up in 1985, resulting in the birth of a new B-movie distributor, Screen Entertainment Ltd.[82] Similarly, the Braveworld company, established by Warren Goldberg following his departure from Videoform (a company of which he was also co-founder), launched in 1985.[83]

Several companies underwent rebranding exercises or were vacated by staff hoping to establish successful ventures of their own. One of the many companies established in 1982, Cyclo Video, became Apex Distribution; Des Dolan retired the Go Video name and launched Mogul Communications; Maurice Lawson and David Finch, formerly of Cannon Video, established PACE; Peter Scott, formerly of Odyssey, established Sheer Entertainment; and Paul Donovan, formerly the marketing director for Avatar, launched Colourbox.[84] Finally there were those who were new to video, including Barry Jacobs, formerly a theatrical distributor, who established Elephant Video,[85] and Chris Maliphant, a property developer, who established Futuristic Video.[86] For these companies – and a plethora of others – low-budget exploitation films in popular genres, from horror to martial arts to sex comedy, constituted a large portion, and at times the bulk, of their output.[87]

The spike in independent companies of this nature was a situation born of opportunism. A number of firms established in the early 1980s and presently experiencing financial turmoil were sitting on a wealth of back catalogue material that their managing directors no longer believed to have any market value. Newly emergent independents were able to exploit this situation for their own ends by approaching such companies, negotiating cheap rights, and then remarketing them at prices considerably lower than those being asked for new releases by bigger companies. This strategy was distinct from those adopted by the first companies at the beginning of the video boom, which strove to capture as broad a cross-section of the market as possible (see Chapter 1). Indies emerging post-1985 were less ambitious, and deliberately so. No longer, the trade press reported, was there 'middle ground for rental product' in Britain. The marketplace was riven, with British renters drawn either to the 'bigger acquisitions' of major distributors, or the goods of 'small companies trying to create a niche at the bottom of the market'.[88] Rather than seeking to compete with major companies at 'the top', the choice to focus on discrete market areas, reducing prices so that the cost of their cassettes better reflected the quality of the material they offered, was a strategy anticipated to generate steady, if modest, cash flow.

Apex Distribution was the pioneer of post-VRA, budget B-movie reissues.[89] The value at which Apex held formerly issued films is telling across its portfolio of releases between 1985 and 1987, almost 70 per cent of which were repackaged editions of back catalogue fare acquired from independent distributors (Table 4.1).[90] An exploration of Apex's operation speaks broadly to the tactics adopted by other 'bottom of the market' independents. Little concerned with establishing a global presence, Apex

**Table 4.1** Videos on Apex Distribution's 'Apex' and 'Horror classics' labels, 1985–7. Thirty out of the forty-five titles were previously released by other companies (66.67 per cent). Table compiled using data from *Video Business, Screen International*, http://pre-cert.co.uk and http://videocollector.co.uk.

| Film title | Previous UK video rightsholders | Genre | Most recent video release year |
|---|---|---|---|
| **Apex (Dealer priced £13.50–£19.95)** | | | |
| *67 Days* (1974) | Merlin (VCL) | War | 1983 |
| *The Black Pirate* (aka *Rage of the Buccaneers*, 1961) | n/a | Drama | n/a |
| *Cathy's Curse* (1977) | Intervision | Horror | 1982 |
| *The Children of Ravensback* (1980) | Alpha (Intervision) | Horror | 1983 |
| *Conquest* (1983) | Merlin (CBS/Fox) | Sword and Sorcery | 1984 |
| *Cover Girl Models* (1975) | n/a | Erotic | n/a |
| *Crossbone Territory* (1986) | n/a | War | n/a |
| *Crypt of the Living Dead* (1973) | Intervision | Horror | 1981 |
| *Dawn of the Mummy* (1981) | Film Town (VideoSpace) | Horror | 1983 |
| *Death Dimension* (1978) | Intervision | Blaxploitation | 1979 |
| *The Devil within Her* (1974) | Arcade (VideoSpace) | Horror | 1984 |
| *Don't Go in the House* (1979) | Arcade (VideoSpace) | Horror | 1982 |
| *Escape* (aka *The Woman Hunt*, 1972) | n/a | Action/adventure | n/a |
| *Fireback* (1983) | n/a | Action | n/a |
| *Fly Me* (1973) | n/a | Comedy/adult | n/a |
| *Foolin' Around* (1979) | Merlin (VCL) | Romantic Comedy | 1983 |
| *For the Love of Betty* (unknown) | n/a | Erotic comedy | n/a |
| *Ghostkeeper* (1980) | Intervision | Horror | 1982 |
| *The Hitter* (1978) | Hello | Blaxploitation | 1982 |
| *House of Evil* (aka *The House on Sorority Row*, 1982) | Merlin (CBS/Fox) | Horror | 1984 |
| *Impulse* (1974) | Mega Films | Horror | 1983 |
| *Kingdom of the Spiders* (1977) | Intervision | Horror | 1981 |
| *The Love Pill* (1972) | n/a | Comedy | n/a |
| *The Marriage of Maria Braun* (1979) | VCL | Drama | 1982 |

Table 4.1 (continued)

| Film title | Previous UK video rightsholders | Genre | Most recent video release year |
|---|---|---|---|
| *Massacre at Central High* (1976) | Merlin (VCL) | Horror | 1982 |
| *My Therapist* (1983) | Arcade (VideoSpace) | Erotic | 1983 |
| *Nights of Terror* (1980) | CBS/Fox | Horror | 1984 |
| *Ninja Warrior* (aka *Ninja Warriors*, 1985) | n/a | Martial arts | n/a |
| *The Northville Cemetery Massacre* (1974) | Intervision | Biker | 1980 |
| *Out of the Blue* (1980) | Prime Time (CBS/Fox) | Drama | 1984 |
| *Run Like a Thief* (1967) | VRO (Video Network) | Crime/thriller | Unknown |
| *Seven Against the Sun* (1964) | n/a | War | n/a |
| *The Sex O'Clock News* (1983) | IVS | Comedy | 1985 |
| *Sexual Desires* (1983) | n/a | Drama/erotic | n/a |
| *Tales of Ordinary Madness* (1981) | Merlin (VCL) | Drama/erotic | 1983 |
| *Tales of the Third Dimension* (1984) | n/a | Comedy | n/a |
| *The Temptress* (1979) | n/a | Thriller/erotic | n/a |
| *Thor: The Conqueror* (1982) | VIP (Video Independent Productions) | Sword and Sandal | 1983 |
| *Up Your Ladder* (aka *Up Yours*, 1979) | n/a | Comedy/erotic | n/a |
| *Women in Cages* (1971) | n/a | Drama | n/a |
| **Horror Classics (Dealer priced £24.99)** | | | |
| *Alison's Birthday* (1979) | Inter-Light (Intervision) | Horror | 1983 |
| *Curtains* (1982) | Film Town (VideoSpace) | Horror | 1984 |
| *Evilspeak* (1981) | Film Town (VideoSpace) | Horror | 1983 |
| *Mausoleum* (1982) | Film Town (VideoSpace) | Horror | 1983 |
| *Zombie Creeping Flesh* (1980) – unreleased | Merin (VCL) | Horror | 1982 |

established a model that was easily replicated by new companies with less capital or ambition.

The business rationale of Apex, and those it inspired, was propelled by three factors. First, under the VRA, retailers were no longer permitted to trade in material that failed to carry a BBFC certificate. This generated panic among the trade when first announced, with retailers fearing imminent bankruptcy if a 'large proportion' of their 'existing stock' was to be outlawed.[91] Some distributors took it upon themselves to supply newly certified versions of pre-VRA cassettes to dealers at a discounted rate, though this was not a widespread practice.[92] In most cases, retailers found themselves having to sell off much uncertified stock ahead of the numerous VRA deadlines throughout 1986–8.[93] Apex, launching operations the same week as the BBFC's classifications timetable was announced, used this situation to its advantage: its editions of previously released material constituted the only legal versions of said titles available, and therefore the only means for retailers to formally (re)acquire them.[94]

Second, as Apex's new acquisitions were first released by other companies when the market was beginning to rationalise in the early 1980s, it was unlikely the films had realised their full market potential. Horror, for instance, remained a popular genre relative to the otherwise poor climate, so it was feasible that the company's releases in this area would generate consumer interest despite having been available from other companies in recent months/years.[95] That being said, Apex was aware that such films were unlikely to have as much appeal as the new, 'quality "exploitation"' released in the latter half of the 1980s by its 'deep-pocketed' rivals.[96] For example, its chief rival, Medusa, was acquiring newer B-list films produced by reputable US indies such as New World, and wowing the trade with both the quality of its releases and the marketing campaigns that accompanied them.[97] The Apex videos therefore needed to be marketed effectively alongside the output of Medusa and other high-profile indies of the period such as Entertainment and Guild. Drawing on the power-selling experience of the company's new managing director, Maurice Claridge (formerly of Pyramid), Apex proceeded to repackage its reissues, removing any evidence of each film's production year (which at times extended back as far as the late 1960s), and promoting them with 'strong sleeve[s]' in a style resonant with the design choices of its leading competitors.[98]

At the time, the aforementioned companies' video box art tended to comprise paintings in a bold, colourful, realist style, inspired by mainstream movie posters of the period by fine artists such as Drew Struzan.[99] So-called 'airbrush art' of this nature, identifiable by its technical, detailed, photorealistic qualities – including 'subtle gradations . . . and shadows',[100] emphasising colour and 'shiny' objects[101] – is visible across promotional materials for film and video in the 1980s, including in the UK by the likes of Entertainment, Guild and Medusa. The adoption of this style marked a contrast with the material used to promote videos in the first half of the 1980s, which tended to feature photographs, paint-brushed (as opposed to airbrushed) paintings, or a combination of both. Consequently, airbrushing signifies a moment in video history demarcated from an era characterised by the gory photograph adorning the cover of *The Driller Killer* or the flat painting on the sleeve of *Cannibal Holocaust*. Apex embraced airbrush art to reinforce the demarcation and present its older releases in a 'contemporary' style.

The artwork used on the sleeve of Intervision's 1982 release of *Cathy's Curse* (Eddy Matalon, 1977), for example, is comparatively rudimentary when considered alongside Apex's airbrush version from 1985. The Intervision cover (a version of the film's theatrical poster) comprises a monochromic illustration of the title character in a manner redolent of newsprint, set atop a black background. The remaining space is dedicated to white print, including a tagline ('She has the power . . . to terrorize') and a handwritten poem.[102] Intervision's blue logo, the green title and Cathy's green eyes, are the only flecks of colour present. The result is one of a simple image with a flat presentation. Comparatively, the collage adorning Apex's newly commissioned sleeve is awash with colour, depth and texture. An airbrushed image of Cathy, here depicted with vibrant orange hair, sits above the silhouette of a large gothic house engulfed in flames. An explosion of fire is seen to the bottom left of the image, and a white full moon is positioned in the top right corner appearing to light up the evening sky. One similarity across the two is that, as with the Intervision artwork, the Apex version renders Cathy's eyes the same shade of green as the title font. However, while the former example refrains from showing any technical detail, in the Apex version we see Cathy's pupils, her pigmentation and light reflecting on the surface of her eyeballs.

One finds similar disparities across the video box art of Apex's other re-releases. Its photorealistic cover used for Al Adamson's 1978 blaxploitation film *Death Dimension*, for example – initially distributed by Intervision in 1979 – captures the sheen of the protagonist's skin and other 'shiny' surfaces including a gun, as well as the smooth curvature of bodily features such as, for instance, a woman's legs and a man's muscular torso. This stands in contrast to Intervision's earlier version which, while also in full colour, lacks depth and definition. Similarly, Apex's re-release of the 1973 Spanish horror film *Crypt of the Living Dead* (Julio Salvador and Ray Danton), which, in contrast to the muted pastel drawing on

Intervision's 1981 release, depicts a wolf/woman creature with large, curvaceous breasts, laying across a tomb and baring its teeth, from which strings of glistening saliva hang.

In these examples and others, Apex's versions are more colourful and intricate that those of their previous distributor. Adopting a style routinely commended by industry watchers and video dealers as having 'original and eye-catching' qualities grants the Apex releases a sense of 'newness' familiar to video consumers, enabling the company to align its older releases with the marketing pull of its bigger independent competitors.[103]

The third factor to consider in regard to Apex's business model is its pricing strategy. While several majors were experimenting with lower pricing (discussed below) others continued to charge premium rates. During Apex's first twelve months of business, for example, CBS/Fox trade-priced its blockbuster releases at £50 per cassette.[104] Apex's releases, comparatively, were dealer-priced between £13.50 and £19.95 (Table 4.1). These prices, relative to the 'quality' of the material Apex was offering, proved enough of an incentive for dealers reluctant to trade exclusively in expensive releases during the market's stabilisation period. Unlike major releases, which for some dealers remained risky stock given their price and uncertainty as to their rentability, Apex's releases offered the dealer assurances via 'a price point which enables them to make some money'.[105] Claridge, speaking with *Video Business*, explained the situation:

> Frankly, the reason why we are selling cassettes is that dealers are buying these high-price Blockbusters, but they still need a new face on the wall. They are looking for well-sleeved 'B' pictures at affordable prices, rather than the second-line product from the major companies which could be as much as £15 more to the trader than my material.[106]

As a result, the visibility of Apex in the trade press, on contemporaneous wholesaler charts and on the shelves of video shops showed others that B-list films could still be profit generators if marketed appropriately and priced sensibly.[107]

Numerous companies followed Apex's lead. In the post-VRA marketplace, however, smaller firms could no longer rely on promises of 'strong uncut' material to lure consumers as the likes of VIPCO had done a couple of years ago (see Chapter 3). It was now widely accepted that British video censorship was among the strictest in the world.[108] Moreover, the establishment of a new regulatory board in 1987, the Video Packaging Review Committee (VPRC), sharply became an obstacle for those companies counting on adopting the kind of power-selling tactics that had birthed the notion of the 'video nasty' in the first place.

The logic guiding the formation of the VPRC was to account for the fact that the VRA was lacking in one key area: it only applied to the *programmes* contained on videocassettes, not artwork or other point-of-sale materials. As Petley explains, the committee comprised 'distributors, the Advertising Standards Authority (ASA) and senior officers of the BBFC', benefited from the government support and carried a logo recognised by trading standards officers as 'an indication of testing and approval by an authorised body'.[109] In years to come, a relaunched VIPCO was able to mobilise slogans such as 'banned since 1982!!', and a logo carrying the text 'previously banned!' when advertising heavily censored BBFC-certified reissues of video nasties such as *The Bogey Man* (Uli Lommel, 1980) and *Cannibal Ferox* (Umberto Lenzi, 1981) – all of which carried the VPRC logo.[110] Such a strategy, Kate Egan explains, enabled VIPCO and others in the 1990s to 'market a re-released nasty as both the ultimate extreme horror title *and* the ultimate historically significant horror title',[111] with the presence of the VPRC logo adding an additional layer of assurances for dealers.[112] In the mid-to-late 1980s, however, independent companies trading in exploitation films would be foolish to mobilise such a strategy given the temporal closeness of the video nasties panic. By the same token, because horror and exploitation films constituted the bulk of their offerings there was pressure to sell them in a way that was both 'striking' and convincing enough to assure customers that, for example, horror films remained horrifying in spite of their BBFC certificates.[113] As such, many of the smaller companies opted not to submit sleeves for VPRC approval. In some cases, this was a decision made so that companies could maximise gory and/or titillating imagery. Other companies were more measured in their approach, adopting methods that hinged on balancing established power-selling strategies with awareness of the new legislation and the ongoing sensitivity of moral campaigners regarding visceral horror fare. Regardless, independents found means to present the new certification system as one that still permitted affective pleasures akin to pre-VRA video releases, even when such films were, much of the time, heavily cut.

Quick Video's 1987 censored re-release of *The Blood of Dr Jekyll* (Walerian Borowczyk, 1981) – originally released by VTC in 1984 – is a good example of the extent to which independent video distributors pushed the envelope in their advertising post-VRA.[114] The painted image adorning the sleeve presents a bare-breasted woman, in knee-length socks and boots, lying back in ecstasy. Above her, a knife appears to slice through the upper half of the video cover, resulting in a red, vaginal 'V' pointing downwards to the woman's lower abdomen. The title at the bottom of the image, upon which the woman's buttocks appear to rest, foregrounds the word 'Blood' in a dripping red font. While a BBFC '18' certificate is clearly visible, the presence of such evocative imagery, conflating images of sexual pleasure and the threat of violence, suggests that the material contained on the cassette itself far outsteps that deemed permissible by British law in the post-VRA era. Avatar's release of the Italian horror film *Specters* (Marcello Avallone, 1987) is another example of this strategy at play. Despite the film containing very little in the way of violence and gore (reviews predicted that 'gorehounds will be sorely disappointed'), the promotional materials suggest the contrary.[115] The box art, depicting a creature rising from a blood-soaked coffin, is, by the standards of the mid-1980s, decidedly innocuous – and a far cry from that used to promote *The Blood of Dr Jekyll*. The tagline, however, alludes to illicit content: 'if you go down to the tombs today you're in for a NASTY surprise'. By riffing on the first verse of the nursery rhyme 'The Teddy Bear's Picnic' – 'if you go down to the woods today, you're in for a big surprise' – the tagline appears to conflate the innocence of childhood with the 'adult' pleasures of horror cinema, and thus evokes the concerns that initiated the video nasties in the first place. Rendering the word 'nasty' in yellow, in a jagged font larger than the other white serif text, also functions as a direct attempt at evoking the controversy in the minds of consumers. These allusions to the video nasty, in terms of both the panic's legacy and the videos' alleged 'nasty' content, suggests that *Specters*, despite having been approved for certification by the BBFC, retains the affective impulse of uncertified, and now illegal, horror videos.

The recent legacy of controversial videocassettes was mobilised by distributors in a host of other ways. Several companies re-released certified versions of titles pursued and/or eventually banned by the DPP. Elephant Video and European Creative Films, for example, issued cut, budget reissues of *The Beyond* (Lucio Fulci, 1981) and *The Living Dead* (Jorge Grau, 1974) respectively – both of which were featured on, then subsequently dropped from, the DPP list in 1983 – while Elephant was the first company to achieve certification for a censored version of an outlawed title: *The House by the Cemetery* (Lucio Fulci, 1981).[116] Others tried a different tack, promoting their releases' 18 certificates as symbols, not of films diluted by cuts, but rather of their boundary-pushing, adult-oriented content. For example, a trade advertisement for PACE's debut title, the 'savage thriller' *Nightmare on Alcatraz* (Philip Marcus, 1987),[117] declares it 'a *definite* 18' that is 'hard hitting', 'tough and brutal', and anticipated to generate 'good business' among 'BLOOD AND GORE MANIACS'.[118]

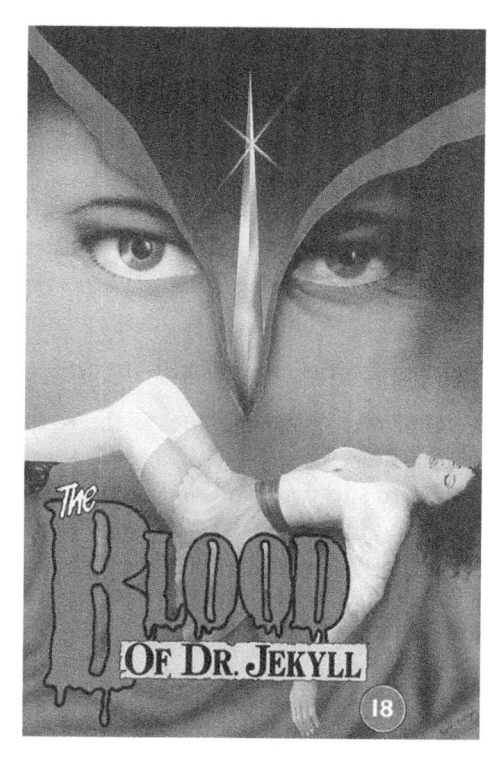

Figure 4.4 Pushing the envelope post-VRA: Quick Video advertises *The Blood of Dr Jekyll*. Credit: Martin Brooks.

Similarly, material promoting Braveworld's release of the horror anthology *Deadtime Stories* (Jeffrey Delman, 1986) quotes a *Video Trade Weekly* review claiming that the film is 'fully justifying an 18 certificate'.[119] In this context, distributors are attempting to mobilise controversy in a similar manner to those trading in 'borderline' nasties in 1983: working within the parameters of legal acceptability to create the aura of a freer recent past.

The foregoing examples represent efforts made by independent distributors to stay afloat within the floundering rental sector. However, the belief that 'old rules apply' when it came to power selling B-list films lacked the longevity that companies such as Apex had hoped for, in spite of their ambitious pricing strategy.[120] A growing black market emerged for uncut, uncertified versions of film now being traded legally in censored versions, suggesting that the presence of a BBFC certificate on the boxes of such films (which, at times, was accompanied by a disclaimer speaking to the edits made to the film to ensure compliance with the VRA), downplayed such films' transgressive potential.[121] Moreover, independents trading this sort of thing found it increasingly difficult to operate in the wake of the

VPRC given the refusal of some shops to trade in titles failing to carry the Committee logo. Added to this was an allegation made by distributors that the BBFC, at the discretion of its president James Ferman, delayed film certification until artwork had been submitted for the VPRC's consideration.[122] Some companies were able to change tack and move into other areas. Others, however, would soon no longer be operable, their fate the result of old school practices, trading in 'B or C quality rubbish', 'putting films into fantastic covers' and 'hyping them way out of all proportion'.[123]

## The rise and rise of sell-through

Eventually, Apex would meet an ironic fate, as the rights to many of its titles were eventually acquired by a Midlands wholesaler, who repackaged the cassettes in cardboard slip-cases and sold them in discount stores and petrol garages throughout the UK in the early 1990s for as low as £1.99.[124] What began life as a 'budget' initiative for the rental market was swept away by another current: that of the burgeoning sell-through market, which boomed throughout the latter half of the 1980s.[125]

As discussed in earlier chapters, videos were always available to consumers to purchase, though it was unusual for them to do so. Similar to the culture around Super 8 and 16mm, the high price of cassettes in the late 1970s and early 1980s has made buying videos a niche practice reserved for collectors or those with incomes permitting them to experiment with the latest gadgetry. Distributors themselves, on the whole, have also believed (rightly, it turned out) that the immediate future of the business was in renting, on the assumption that consumers would, in all likelihood, want to watch the same film once or twice – just as they would if a film were at the cinema. The logic propelling many of the exchange clubs at this time was guided by this assumption, in addition to the recognition that most films released onto video were not 'classics', and that consumers were already taking gambles on films they might not necessarily have been very familiar with.

VCL's failed attempt at making a fully fledged success of the UK's first 'budget' label in the early 1980s illustrates this. The '21st Century Video' range, as it was known, offered consumers an assortment of titles on Betamax for £14.95 and on VHS for £19.95.[126] At £15–20 cheaper than cassettes offered by Intervision and Warner Home Video (WHV), such prices constituted the lowest yet of any distributor.[127] 21st Century's catalogue was, however, lacking in one key area. While the company could boast that its 'reproduction standards' are 'as high as you'll find anywhere' (VCL oversaw the duplication of its own cassettes), the same could not be

# REGULATION AND ADAPTATION

## 21st Century Video presents
## 100 NEW MOVIES.

**FEATURE LENGTH FULL COLOUR**

Beta £14·95 Recommended retail price
VHS £19·95 Recommended retail price

2100 21st Century Video

## THE WORLD'S LOWEST PRICES.

Video cassettes have crashed right through the price barrier.

Now you can open up your 4th Channel for a whole lot less than the TV licence fee.

Our massive new range – at unbelievably low prices – really does mean you can enjoy the company of your favourite stars whenever you like.

In westerns, action, adventure, drama, thrillers and musicals.

Only 21st Century can give insomniacs new hope, entertain restless children on a rainy afternoon, and offer a welcome, low-cost alternative to network television.

Send today for a catalogue and enjoy a host of stars at low, low prices.

**2100**

**21st Century Video**
58 Parker Street, London WC2
Tel: 01-405 3732
Telex: 8814427 UNION G

To: 21st Century Video
58 Parker Street, London WC2

Please send me your catalogue together with the name and address of my nearest dealer.

Name _____
Address _____
_____
Town _____
Postcode _____ TV 12/80

**Figure 4.5** The world's lowest prices: an ad for 21st Century Video, VCL's failed budget label. Credit: Popular Film and Television Collection.

said about the 'standard' of films in its catalogue (per se). Included in the ad was a disclaimer of sorts, making clear that, while the films were 'carefully selected' for the consumer's enjoyment, 'we've avoided promises of "blockbusters" [sic] we can't deliver'.[128] Reading between the lines, the series of genre films on offer (westerns, horror films, 'spy thrillers', family films, etc.) were by the distributor's own admission not comparable to the higher-end (and, of course, higher-priced) productions available from the likes of Magnetic and WHV. From this perspective, a lower price also meant a compromise on films with big budgets and known actors. Subsequent 'budget' labels by Portland Video and others that launched in the early 1980s were marred by the same issue as those of 21st Century: the majority of releases were deemed by most consumers to be unworthy of the prices they carried.[129] Simply put, owning films was not as economically viable, or, indeed, as desirable, as renting one or two per week. If the sales market were to take off, prices would need to be lower, and the nature of the material on offer of a greater – which is to say, more recognisable – standard.

In the US, one major studio did proceed to toy with video sales with some success, by 'reducing prices' on a handful of fairly recent blockbuster films, in 1982.[130] Paramount Home Video marketed *Star Trek II: The Wrath of Khan* (Nicholas Meyer, 1982) at the price of $39.95 (some $40 cheaper than what it had sold copies of the first film for in 1980), eventually clearing 290,000 units (double what the first sold), and leading to a reduction in the price of several other titles.[131] UK distributors were incentivised.[132] By 1983, numerous companies were cutting prices, or introducing sublabels that were more competitively priced than their standard ranges. Yet while in the US rental continued to boom, in Britain price cuts were a necessity to encourage shop owners to purchase more stock, to see through the stagnation of the rental market, and to help struggling distributors in the process.[133]

For example, in July 1983 MGM/UA began offering tapes to retailers in its new 'Classic Collection' for £15.19 so that dealers could sell them, if they so desired, for £24.95 or less, making a minimum 30 per cent margin in the process.[134] In August, CBS/Fox's Neon label was launched with fifty titles at £9.99 each – the lowest price yet for any pre-recorded videotape.[135] Others, such as Rex and CIC (the latter of which remained the distributor of Paramount product, including *Star Trek II*), were offering releases priced at £19.50.[136] Crucially, these were trade prices, and were in some instances offered to dealers under specific conditions. For example, the Neon range was offered only to 1,000 dealers across the country, with minimum orders set at 100 cassettes.[137] Nevertheless, Neon and the other budget lines enabled the distributors to make an assessment of the current state of the market, initiating a 'long-term strategy . . . to see a sales market develop'.[138] With no sales or rental restrictions on the tapes, such series were conceived as cautionary measures for distributors operating in uncertain times, to give the distributor some indication as to whether or not the rental market would improve, or if a sales market was likely in the immediate future.

A crucial moment came in October 1983, when CIC offered Paramount blockbusters, *Raiders of the Lost Ark* (Steven Spielberg, 1981) and then *Flashdance* (Adrian Lyne, 1983), to retailers at £13, so that the cassettes could be sold on by dealers for £20 per copy.[139] This was the first legitimate attempt by any distributor in Britain to foreground the potential of a sales market awash with recent 'quality' Hollywood product. In demonstration of CIC's commitment to this initiative, both titles were supported by six-figure marketing spends.[140] Prior to this, only MGM/UA had pushed the notion of 'quality' in a comparable sense, promising the 'best prints' of 'known' titles. The strategies of the rest (and of course future labels such as Apex) echoed 21st Century's earlier model, with titles comprising lesser-known works, older films, TV pilots, or otherwise 'material, which, for one reason or another, we didn't feel entitled to charge dealers full price for'.[141] Releasing major releases *Raiders* and *Flashdance* at heavily reduced prices set a precedent: as long as consumers were convinced that videocassettes were of quality, and that they were not being over-charged, video sales was a viable proposition for fledgling dealerships and distributors to benefit from.[142]

However, the aforementioned examples were chiefly experiments designed to test the water, and did not evidence a full commitment to 'sell-through': a term yet to be coined. Despite the success of *Raiders* and *Flashdance*, sales figures were clearly not enough to incentivise the major studios to lower prices further, not least because such titles were renting at pleasing rates. While it represented an incredible price reduction, £20 remained a figure high enough to dissuade consumers from parting with their cash for most of the films CIC issued. So, while CIC managed to shift 80,000 units of *Raiders*, other A-list titles 'never came near to hitting that figure'.[143] For the sell-through market to take off, prices would have to come down further. And, as at the beginning of the video boom, it would take an independent with a radical vision to make the inroads required.

The company to do so was The Video Collection, which, on 1 October 1985, launched fifty titles in all 860 outlets of the major high-street department store Woolworths, priced at an unprecedented £6.99 each.[144] The new label was the brain child of Paul Levinson, co-founder of Videoform, who left the company following the Heron buyout, eventually to become chairman of the UK-based investment company and parent of The Video Collection, Prestwich Holdings.[145] Together with Steve Ayres, former MD of MGM/UA Home Video who had presided over the company's price reductions in 1983, Levinson negotiated a deal with Woolworths, convincing the company's entertainment buyer of video's potential to be the next 'impulse buy' in a manner comparable to records and music tapes.[146] The label's success was immediate, having, by the end of 1985, expanded into other high-street retailers and selling 'as many cassettes as the entire video industry achieved the previous year'.[147] Other companies were quick to follow suit, including Vestron and BBC Video, which within months of The Video Collection's launch were stocking titles retailing at between £6.99 and £9.99 in branches of Marks & Spencer.[148] By March 1986, a joint venture between Heron and Polygram, Channel 5, had launched throughout the W. H. Smith, HMV and Virgin Records chains, reportedly selling 100,000 units in its first week.[149] By September 1986 a flurry of new operations, as well as the majority of the majors, had launched sell-through lines, with some retailers expanding their videocassette shelving four-fold to cope with demand.[150]

The reasons why sell-through boomed when it did are numerous. Pricing was a key driver, helping to expand video's appeal to a larger consumer base by aligning it with similar-priced products on high-street shelves. This, in turn, made video attractive for both those on a budget and those with 'disposable incomes'.[151] Timing was another factor. Launching in October, The Video Collection was able to capitalise on the run-up to Christmas, as many bought videos as gifts.[152] The main reason for sell-through's success, however, can be attributed to the extent to which VCRs had now penetrated households throughout the country. By the end of 1984, the UK boasted 'the third largest population of video recorders in the world', amounting to some 7 million machines in all.[153] During the same period, around 50 per cent of VCRs were to be found in households with children, machines were used habitually by sixteen- to twenty-four-year-olds, and there was a growing number of users in their mid-forties and early fifties.[154] With a hardware bedrock well-established, there were many demographics ripe for exploitation with affordable video product.

This meant, however, that, as with the rental market in 1978–82, the core demographic for video *sales* was not yet established, and thus no one was sure as to what type of releases would prove most popular. One thing, however, was a given: feature films could not be the main driver. It was agreed across the business that blockbuster releases were better suited to the rental market and that, certainly, higher profits were to be accrued by upholding this standard. Moreover, rights for new films remained very high, negating the budget price that The Video Collection and its subsequent competitors wished to maintain (cassettes were trade-priced at around £5.00 per copy).[155] Levinson and Ayres, in their early discussions, predicted that a sales market could excel in areas where the rental sector had previously failed, and that The Video Collection could capitalise on the diverse tastes of those demographics aforementioned.

The men had recent history to learn from. The UK release of music video/documentary, *The Making of Michael Jackson's Thriller* (John Landis, 1984), on the Palace-Virgin-Gold label, became the fastest selling video in the UK in late 1984 – echoing the title's success in the US.[156] Wasser argues that Jason Peisinger, CEO of its US distributor Vestron, was of the view that the success of *Thriller* in north America was due to the celebrity status of Jackson rather than the 'repeatable popular music format'. In the US, music videos had been a tough sell to consumers from the outset of the business. Despite efforts by RCA/Columbia and Sony to launch successful lines of music videos in the early 1980s, music fans tended to gravitate towards cable television, where the Music Television (MTV) network cornered the market. The pre-recorded videocassette, Wasser argues, 'proved to be a less than ideal format for music video'.[157]

Things were slightly different in the UK. While music videocassettes had failed to take off in Britain in 1978–81 (despite the best efforts of companies such as VCL – see Chapter 1), in 1984–5 the genre became a viable option for video distributors pining for diversification. Moreover, UK video companies were better positioned to a make a success of music video than their US counterparts. In Britain, the rolling out of cable television was plagued by problems since it was first proposed as a national initiative by the government in 1981. By November 1985, most of the regional franchise operators – citing poor government resourcing no less – were 'about a year behind schedule', with many experiencing cash flow problems and some having already collapsed.[158] Any threat that cable may have posed to the video business was certainly not an immediate one. As such, most in the trade were either unphased by it or encouraged by the constant stalling. To this end, the British consumer response to *The Making of Michael Jackson's Thriller* indicated to Levinson and Ayres that the sale of music videocassettes could prove lucrative, for the majority of music fans had no other means of regularly accessing comparable music-related programming.

Something else for the business to consider was that, if music videocassettes had retail potential, so too might other forms of non-filmic programming. After all, *Thriller* was not only the first breakthrough *music* videocassette; it was also, by default, the first non-feature-film to enjoy mainstream retail success. In this context, other sorts of video programming experimented with at the business's beginning could make greater waves if priced appropriately.

Levinson and Ayres took a risk and it paid off: of the first fifty titles released, only twelve were older feature films, thirty were children's titles and the rest a mix of music and general interest.[159] By 1987, charts revealed that the general public spent more on children's, music, general interest and TV titles than on films.[160] Children's titles were also good sellers as year-round gifts and treats.[161] Crucially, whereas feature films were certainly present and did very well, their popularity was routinely matched or surpassed by non-film material.

Sell-through's success was abetted by the outlets from which cassettes were made available to the public. Independent video rental outlets did not, on the whole, gravitate towards video sales. At first, this was due to The Video Collection having exclusive contracts with multiples including Woolworths in the first instance, and then W. H. Smith.[162] The agreements were telling of the image Levinson and Ayres wished to project, pitching video sales against the prevailing downmarket image of rental outlets.[163] Its first competitor, the Channel 5 label, attempted to attract the rental sector by offering its cassettes only to those with VTA memberships.[164] But, for reasons ranging from concerns over price margins to inadequate shelf space to carry the stock required to make a satisfactory profit, many independent outlets did not believe video sales to be worth their time.[165] Sell-through, thus, was a high-street phenomenon in the beginning, its image wedded to the family-friendly environment of the sanitised department store and chains with wholesome images that hitherto had never experimented with video rental, such as mother and baby outlets and sporting retailers.[166] This served to communicate to the video business and the public that families were now the priority of video; or rather that 'video' as it once was, was now something wholly different. It projected an image of a business that had reached maturity. Budget exploitation titles in the rental sector had given way to budget Hollywood classics, well-known cartoons and so on in the retail sector: material that, to all intents and purposes, was either known to consumers ahead of a purchase as being quality entertainment or less of a gamble than renting an unknown title. This was sell-through's greatest achievement as far as the industry was concerned. Amid the chaos of the fluctuating rental market, sell-through granted wary consumers or those new to video level footing: a consistent, sanitised experience that was free from stigma.

The VRA and the emergence of the sell-through aided greatly in shaping the 'image' of video from an industry of vice to a resolutely normal consumer experience. VCL attempted to shape the rental business in its own image, which proved successful for the company in overseas territories, but the main domestic successes as far as video distribution was concerned were embodied by The Video Collection as affordable, family focused, wholesome entertainment.

On the fringes of the sell-through explosion, the rental sector began taking stock of its own position. The decline in rentals dictated that something had to change, and it was agreed that 'image' would play a significant role in the future of the business, as Woolworths and its competitors began drawing new people to video as well as mopping up those videophiles jaded by the perceived slump in product and standards as show in media reportage. Industry watchers lambasted the rental trade, and called on it to spruce up the experience it afforded its customers, out of respect for the industry and for itself. However, as the next chapter reveals, notions of 'respect' were soon challenged when the industry bore witness to the arrival of ruthless corporate giants, the directors of which saw rental's decline as a business opportunity prime for exploitation.

## Notes

1. Anthony Hayward, 'FACT seizes 30,000 tapes in first year', *Screen International* 432 (11–18 February 1983), 59.
2. Anon., 'FACT reports sharp drop in British video piracy', *Screen International* 457 (4–11 August 1984), 18.
3. See for example: Steve Bernard, 'Looking back to video's watershed year', *Screen International* 483 (9–16 February 1985), 27–8.
4. See, for example, Julian Petley, *Film and Video Censorship in Modern Britain* (Edinburgh: Edinburgh University Press, 2011); and Sian Barber, 'Power Struggles, Regulation and Responsibility: Reappraising the Video Recordings Act', *Media History* 24.1 (2016), 99–114.
5. Barker quoted in Barber, 'Power Struggles', 99.
6. Petley, *Film and Video Censorship*, 33.
7. Barber, 'Power struggles', 112.
8. Mark McKenna, *Nasty Business: The Marketing and Distribution of the Video Nasties* (Edinburgh: Edinburgh University Press, 2020), 51–2. Similar claims are made by various interviewees in Marc Morris and Jake West's documentary *Video Nasties: Moral Panic, Censorship and Videotape* (2010).
9. McKenna, *Nasty Business*, 24–5.
10. McKenna, *Nasty Business*, 52.
11. McKenna, *Nasty Business*, 21.
12. McKenna, *Nasty Business*, 22.
13. 'Video Top 40', *Video Business* (February 1981), 12–13.
14. 'Video Business Rental Chart', *Video Business* (February 1981), 21. Of the twenty, eleven titles were distributed by CIC and seven by Intervision through its agreement with United Artists.

15. Some of these issues are raised in a contemporaneous interview between journalist Tim Smith and Intervision MD Bev Ripley. See Tim Smith, 'Intervision – making progress but problems remain', *Video Business* (May 1981), 8, 10.
16. John Hazelton, 'Distributors with major backing dominate market', *Screen International* 479 (12–19 January 1985), 26. Added emphasis.
17. See Anon., 'Long hot summer hits Intervision', *Video Business* 3.39 (21 November 1983), 12. See also Anon., 'More majors ponder file discounts', *Video Business* 3.27 (29 August 1983), 4.
18. Stuart Warrener, '1985 – year of video marketing campaign', *Screen International* 483 (9–16 February 1985), 31–2.
19. Hazelton, 'Distributors with major backing', 26.
20. Petley, *Film and Video Censorship*, 34.
21. See Tim Smith, 'Adult video or porn? Need to clarify the law', *Video Business* 1.12 (January 1982), 33.
22. Smith, 'Adult video or porn?', 33.
23. Gold quoted in Smith, 'Adult video or porn?', 33.
24. Smith, 'Adult video or porn?', 33.
25. Smith, 'Adult video or porn?', 33.
26. See, for example, catalogues for Intervision (1980), Go Video (1981) and Fletcher (1982).
27. See, for example, catalogues for the distributors Hokushin (1980), Precision (1981), Astra (1982) and Replay (1982).
28. See, for example, the first catalogue for the distributors, Magnetic (Fox, 1979), Warner Home Video (1980), Rank (1980) and Derann (1982).
29. See, for example, catalogues for the wholesaler, Carnaby (1981), and the distributor, Guild (1982).
30. The wholesaler PMA employed its own ratings system as 'a guide for the consumer', including, for instance, 'VAA', indicating that a specific title is 'suitable for mature older teenagers'. Anon., 'PMA claims a better classification scheme', *Video Business* 3.14 (30 May 1983), 10. On issues pertaining to 'mock-legal' video ratings during the early 1980s, see Egan, *Trash or Treasure?*, 61–5.
31. Smith, 'Adult video or porn?', 33.
32. Tony Tyler, 'The industry has the first responsibility', *Video Business* 3.12 (16 May 1983), 28. See also Colin Antrobus, 'VTA a failure? Not on your life!', *Video Business* 3.12 (16 May 1983), 18.
33. Anon., 'Skeletons in the cupboard?', *Video Retailer* (8 December 1983), 6.
34. This is discussed in some detail in the documentary *Video Nasties: Moral Panic, Censorship and Videotape* (Marc Morris and Jake West, 2010).
35. Petley, *Film and Video Censorship*, 72.
36. Anon., 'Government gets ahead on nasties', *Screen International* 3.20 (11 July 1983), 4.
37. Anon., 'Bright Brill "naïve and stupid"', *Video Retailer* (15 December 1983), 20. Alex Sutherland, 'Industry outcry over video Bill', *Screen International*

(7–14 April 1984), 1–2. For another example of criticism see Nigel Andrews, 'Taking stock of the Video Bill', *Screen International* 440 (7–14 April 1984), 25.
38. Norman Abbott quoted in Petley, *Film and Video Censorship*, 72.
39. Dave Hodgins (MD of Medusa Communications) quoted in Ian White, 'Medusa hits the road', *Video Retailer* (10 November 1983), 24–5. Quotation at 25.
40. Mike Cole (of VCL) quoted in Richard Gray, 'Declaration of independents', Video Retailer (8 September 1983), 36–7. Quotation at 36.
41. Abbott quoted in Petley, *Film and Video Censorship*, 72.
42. On Films Galore see Anon., 'Films Galore liquidation', *Screen International* 502 (22–9 June 1985), 25; on Mountain see Anon., 'Video distributor Mountain collapses', *Screen International* 503 (29 June–6 July 1985), on Capricorn see 34; Anon., 'UK independent collapses', *Screen International* 506 (20–7 July 1985), 21; on VideoSpace see John Hazleton, 'VideoSpace latest victim of UK's quiet summer spell', *Screen International* 509 (10–17 August 1985), 30; on Intervision see Maggie Brown, 'Intervision runs for cover by merging with CBS/Fox', *The Guardian* (25 January 1984), 18 and Anon., 'Video co drops UK sales', *Screen International* 509 (10–17 August 1985), 27, and Chapter 5 of this book; on VTC see Anon., 'VTC goes into liquidation', *Screen International* 510 (17–24 August 1985), 35; and on Scotch see Anon., 'Scotch estimates UK annual sales', *Screen International* 504 (6–13 July 1985), 26.
43. David Hesmondhalgh, *The Cultural Industries* (3rd edition, London: Sage, 2021), 270.
44. Hesmondhalgh, *The Cultural Industries*, 270.
45. Peter Rhodes (sales director at Vidcom) cited in John Hazleton, 'Tenth Vidcom switches to multi-media format', *Screen International* 467 (13–20 October 1984), 17–18. Citation at 17.
46. Alvesson paraphrased in Ralph Tench and Liz Yeomans, *Exploring Public Relations: Global Strategic Communication*, 4th edition (Harlow: Pearson, 2017), 214.
47. Lawrence S. Welch and Reijo Luostarinen, 'Internationalization: Evolution of a Concept', *Journal of General Management* 14.2 (December 1988), 35–55. Citation at 36. See also Otto Anderson, 'On the internationalization process of firms: a critical analysis', *Journal of International Business Studies* (Second Quarter, 1993), 209–31.
48. On the history of VTC see (the misleadingly titled) Anon., 'VTC – the all-British video indie aiming for the top', *Video Business* 3.10 (2 May, 1983), 2. On the origins of GVC (as a company working in video piracy), see Chapter 2 of this book. On Cinehollywood's Italian operation, see Hank Werber, 'Export a priority for Milan homevid co.; Italy comes later', *Variety* 305.11 (13 January 1982), 242; and on the establishment of its UK iteration (which was owned and operated by the British-based company, VPD), see Anon., 'VPD expand in Wembley', *Screen International* 312 (3 October, 1981), 49. Intervision's Australasian label was run by the Australian company Video

Classics. See, for example, Intervision's Australasian catalogue (Chatswood: Video Classics, 1981). On Home Video Holdings' Australian Video label, see Anon., 'The Australian video label launched through Home Video Holdings at a reception at Australia House', *Screen International* 449 (9–16 June, 1984), 11.
49. See, for example, Go Video, untitled trade advertisement, *Variety* 305.11 (13 January 1982), 238; Anon., 'Double aim for VPD in Milan', *Screen International* 418 (29 October – 5 November, 1983), 94; and Guild Home Video, untitled trade advertisement, *Screen International* 410 (3–10 September 1983), 1.
50. Anon., 'DPP "let-off" for UK horror titles', *Screen International* 506 (20 July 1985), 21.
51. Julian Upton, 'Electric Blues: The Rise and Fall of Britain's First Prerecorded Videocassette Distributors', *Journal of British Cinema and Television* 13.1 (2016), 19–41. Quotation at 35.
52. Upton, 'Electric Blues'. See also Chapter 1 of this book.
53. Gray, 'Declaration of independents'.
54. Anon., 'VCL turns distrib eye to global mkt; strong in Scandia', *Variety* 308.12 (20 October 1982), 277.
55. Anon., 'Leading independent VCL stands the test of time with step into the US market', *Screen International* 414 (1 October 1983), 50, 52. Citation at 52.
56. Anon., 'Leading independent VCL stands the test of time', 50.
57. Anon., 'Leading independent VCL stands the test of time', 50.
58. On film production see Tom Bierbaum, 'UK's VCL seeks outlet to stir action on sluggish US vid mart', *Variety* 306.12 (21 April 1982), 32. On television see VCL, untitled trade advertisement, *Screen International* 355 (7 August 1982), 1.
59. Michael F. Walsh, Karen Page Winterich and Vikas Mittal, 'Do logo redesigns help or hurt your brand? The role of brand commitment', *Journal of Product and Brand Management* 19.2 (2010), 76–84. Quotation at 76.
60. Jonathan Lufferelli, Mudra Mukesh and Ammara Mahmood, 'Let the logo do the talking: the influence of logo descriptiveness of brand equity', *Journal of Marketing Research* 56.5 (2019), 862–78. Quotation at 862.
61. Lufferelli et al., 'Let the logo do the talking', 862.
62. Lufferelli et al., 'Let the logo do the talking', 862–3.
63. VCL was not competing with as broad a host of services as coffee chains on the high street do, and was therefore not under pressure to foreground its products in its logo (in a manner similar to other companies operable at the same time, such as Warner Communications, the logo for which was, simply, the letter 'W' in a truncated circle). In other words, VCL's advertisements were always seen in context alongside those of other companies operating within the same area, e.g. in the pages of *Variety* or *Screen International*.
64. Walsh et al., 'Do logo redesigns help or hurt your brand?', 76.

65. See, for example, VCL, untitled consumer advertisement, *Television & Home Video* (March 1979), 62.
66. VCL, untitled trade advertisement, *Variety* 304.10 (7 October 1981), 88–9.
67. McKenna also directs this allegation at Go Video and VIPCO. However, as the present chapter acknowledges, Go Video was an established player in the international buying and selling of video rights in the early 1980s. McKenna, *Nasty Business*, 99–100. Quotation at 100. Added emphasis.
68. Anon., 'VCL turns distrib eye to global mkt', 277.
69. See also Gray, 'Declaration of independents'; and VCL, untitled trade advertisement, *Variety* (7 March 1984), 235.
70. VCL, untitled trade advertisement, *Screen International* 355 (7 August 1982), 1.
71. VCL, untitled trade advertisement, *Variety* 304.10 (7 October 1981), 89.
72. The Entertainment Group of Companies, untitled trade advertisement, *Screen International* 487 (9 March 1985), 1.
73. The Miracle Group, untitled trade advertisement, *Screen International* 484 (16 February 1985), 59.
74. Alex Sutherland, 'Virgin Vision buys VCL Communications', *Screen International* 520 (26 October–2 November, 1985), 1–2.
75. Anon., 'Heron into Videoform', *Variety* 311.4 (25 May 1983), 39. Heron would also proceed to purchase the US distributor Media Home Entertainment in 1983. On the latter, see Wasser, *Veni, Vidi, Video: The Hollywood Empire and the VCR* (Austin: University of Texas Press, 2001), 180.
76. Basil Comely, 'Mega $s come to UK – Millionaire buys massive share in British video', *Broadcast* (23 May 1983), 35. See also: Anon., 'Nothing less than the best', *Video Week* (7 May 1984), 6–12.
77. Videoform had by this point established autonomous video rental, music and film production divisions, which appealed to Heron. See also: Anon., 'Nothing less than the best', 6.
78. See, for example, Anon., 'Heron Home to delete titles', *Screen International* 529 (4 January 1986), 13.
79. Anon., 'Virgin Restructuring', *Billboard* 98.8 (22 February 1986), 64.
80. See Virgin Vision – Incorporating VCL (supplementary brochure), *Screen International* 675 (22 October 1988), 89–91. Citation at 89.
81. Anon., 'Stark & Richmond in adult label boom', *Video Business* 6.41 (13 October 1986), 12.
82. See Alex Sutherland, 'Dartnall jubilant as £110m deal secures Screen Entertainment', *Screen International* 527 (14–21 December 1985), 1, 2. See also Anon., 'From centre-folds to Friends of the Earth Screen Entertainment reveals all . . .', *Network Video* 7 (1–15 March 1989), 12. Carey Budnick, formerly of VTC and IVS would eventually work for Screen Entertainment in late 1980s (see Anon., 'From centre-folds', 12).
83. Anon., 'Braveworld launched', *Screen International* 497 (18 May 1985), 6.
84. On Apex see Anon., 'Apex ready to cash in on back catalogue rights', *Screen International* 499 (1–8 June 1985), 58; on Mogul see Anon., 'Mogul to

market second US label', *Variety* 319.7 (12 June 1985), 33; on PACE see Anon., 'Nightmare Sets the Pace', *Video Week* (15 June 1987), 3.; on Colourbox see Anon., 'Donovan's own label', *Video Business* (19 October 1987), 1.
85. Anon., 'Notes', *Screen International* 546–7 (3 May 1986), 10.
86. Anon., 'Futuristic launches into video area', *Screen International* 626 (5–12 September 1987), 20.
87. Others included, for example: Bronx Video Company, Cineplex, European Creative Films, HBL Video, Horror Theatre, Independent Video Services (IVS), In-House Video, Motion Pictures on Video (MPV), Network Channel, Pegasus Home Video, Senator, Screen In Doors (SID), Shades of Blue, SK Productions, Stablecane, Stateside, Turbophase, Videoline, Warad and Xstacy.
88. Jeremy Coopman, 'Gap grows in Brit HV between big deals and small potatoes', *Variety* 330.5 (24 February 1988), 17, 424.
89. Anon., 'Apex ready to cash in'.
90. Eventually Apex would establish full-price labels, Academy and Aries, retailing to dealers at £29.99.
91. Anon., 'UK dealers in uproar over Home Office proposals for classification timetable', *Screen International* 499 (1–8 June 1985), 58.
92. CBS/Fox, Medusa, Embassy and Warner agreed to replace newly censored versions of stock for the cost of £6.00 (plus VAT) per cassette on receipt of the original tape(s). Information obtained from: CBS/Fox, 'Certification status bulletin' (21 August 1986), and Nigel Edward Few (Warner Home Video, Sales Service Manager), 'Re: Video Recordings Acts Phase III – 1st September 1987' (letter sent out to dealers, August 1987). Author's personal collection.
93. After each respective deadline, it became illegal to trade in such films. Video wholesalers at this point supplied shopkeepers with lists of un/certified films, or, as in the case of Land of Video Victoria, compiled and then sold the *Certification Handbook* (retailing for £100), detailing all videocassettes released in Britain, their ex-rental value (in £) and the date each title would cease to be legal if the BBFC failed to grant it a certificate. See Land of Video Victoria, *Certification Handbook: A Guide to the Shelf-life of the 12,500 Film Titles Available within the UK Video Industry* (London: Land of Video Victoria, c. 1985).
94. Anon., 'Apex ready to cash in', 58. See also John Hazelton, 'Date set for implementation of UK Video Recordings Act', *Screen International* 501 (15–22 June 1985), 2.
95. Indicative of the popularity of horror video, the consumer press continued to run features on the genre, including the monthly 'Armchair Chamber of Horrors' column in *Video – The Magazine*. See, for example, Anon., 'Nibblers in the night', *Video – The Magazine* (June 1985), 35–6.
96. Coopman, 'Gap grows in Brit HV between big deals and small potatoes', 17.
97. Anon., 'Tough Medusa is still smiling', *Video Business* 5.21 (22 July 1985), 20–1. Anon., 'Medusa scoops up the cream of the crop at record AFM', *Video Business* 6.9 (March 1983), 1, 4.

98. Maurice Claridge, quoted in John Hayward, 'How Claridge wears a profit on his sleeve', *Video Business* 5.39 (25 November 1985), 24. The oldest film released on the Apex label between 1985 and 1987 is *The Black Pirate* (Mario Costa, 1961).
99. Struzan painted some of the most iconic film posters of the 1980s, from John Carpenter's *The Thing* (1982) to those advertising the *Back to the Future* (1985–90) franchise. See Drew Struzan and David J. Schow, *The Art of Drew Struzan* (London: Titan, 2010).
100. Bill Jonas cited in Ursula-Helen Kassaveti, '"Sharp Sybaritic" Retrofuturistic Deco Realism: Some Preliminary Notes on the 1980s Airbrush Art', *Imaginations – Journal of Cross-Cultural Image Studies* 10.2 (December 2019), 89–117. Available at: http://dx.doi.org/10.17742/IMAGE.OI.10.2.4. Quotation at 90.
101. On technical detail see Kassaveti, '" Sharp Sybaritic"', 95, and on colour and shininess, see 96.
102. The poem reads: 'I sent mommy to the mad house/The butler's scared to death/I threw nanny out the window/Now three of us are left/My daddy, my dolly and me . . . me . . . ME.'
103. Fil Adams-Mercer, 'Who cut it in '85 – for films, packs &back-up', *Video Business* 6.2 (13 January 1986), 10. See also Fil Adams-Mercer, 'How Fred covered a market and competed with the best', *Video Business* (1 December 1986), 18.
104. Anon., 'Blockbusters on CBS/Fox nearly £50', *Video Business* 6.48 (1 December 1986), 1, 4.
105. Maurice Claridge, quoted in Hayward, 'How Claridge wears a profit', 24.
106. Claridge quoted in Hayward, 'How Claridge wears a profit', 24.
107. Heron Relay, untitled trade advertisement (Apex/Aries), *Video Week* (22 June, 1987), 35.
108. Petley, *Film and Video Censorship*, 1. See also Robert Starks (of Colourbox video) quoted in Petley, *Film and Video Censorship*, 77.
109. Petley, *Film and Video Censorship*, 73–4. See also Anon., 'Sleeve designs for vetting before cert', *Video Business* (30 November 1987), 6.
110. See Egan, *Trash or Treasure? Censorship and the Changing Meanings of the Video Nasties* (Manchester: Manchester University Press, 2007), 185–228. See also McKenna, *Nasty Business*, 121–43.
111. Egan, *Trash or Treasure?*, 194. Other distributors adopting variations of the 'previously banned' legends in the 1990s include Cornerstone Media, Screen Entertainment, Stonevision and Warrior.
112. Egan, *Trash or Treasure?*, 195.
113. Anon., 'Ninja out for grabs', *Video Week* (22 June 1987), 18.
114. The Quick Video version was trimmed by forty-four seconds by the BBFC. Information regarding BBFC cuts obtained from BBFC, 'Video Recordings Act 1984' status update (May 1987–August 1987), 3. Author's personal collection.

115. Carolyn Krumins, '"Specters" – put a ghost in your machines', *Video – The Magazine* (May 1988), 33. See also Anon., 'Specters', *Video – The Magazine* (May 1988), 23.
116. Anon., 'Nasty gets certificate for Elephant', *Video Business* (22 February 1988), 4. See also Elephant Video, untitled trade advertisement, *Video Business* 8.37 (14 September 1987), 33. Such releases were budget releases, trade priced at either £19.95 or £9.95.
117. Anon., 'Nightmare Sets the Pace', 3.
118. PACE, untitled trade advertisement (*Nightmare on Alcatraz*), *Video Business* 8.26 (29 June 1987), 36. Added emphasis.
119. IVS/Braveworld, untitled trade advertisement (*Deadtime Stories*), *Video Week* (15 June 1987), 37.
120. Claridge quoted in Hayward, 'How Claridge wears a profit', 24.
121. For example, the box art for *Evilspeak* (Eric Weston, 1981) – a banned 'video nasty' subsequently reissued on Apex's Horror Classics label – features the legend 'EDITED TO CONFORM WITH THE VIDEO RECORDINGS ACT 1984'. For a discussion about the video black market in the wake of the VRA, see David Kerekes and David Slater, *See No Evil: Banned Films and Video Controversy* (Manchester: Critical Vision/Headpress, 2000), 287–313.
122. Petley, *Film and Video Censorship*, 73–4.
123. Fil Adams-Mercer, 'Dealers see wisdom of all pulling together', *Video Business* 5.8 (22 April 1985), 22.
124. This was something never covered by the trade press, but has been discussed at length on various fan forums by individuals who remember purchasing the videos at the time. See, for example, http://pre-cert.co.uk.
125. Tony Greenwood, 'The rise and rise of sell-through', *Video 89 Showguide* (British Video Association 1989), 26.
126. 21st Century Video, untitled consumer advertisement, *Video World* 2.11 (November 1980), 22–3. See also Anon., 'Tapes cut by VCL', *Television & Home Video* (December 1980), 17.
127. Both Intervision and Warner's recommended retail price for videocassettes was £39.95. See, for example, Intervision, untitled consumer advertisement, *Video Review* (January 1981), 39; and Warner Home Video, untitled consumer advertisement, *Video Review* (January 1981), 27.
128. 21st Century Video, untitled consumer advertisement, *Video World* 2.11 (November 1980), 22–3.
129. Portland's budget titles retailed at £29.95 – £10 less than their top-price range. Information obtained from Portland trade ephemera, c.1980 (author's collection).
130. Paul McDonald, *Video and DVD Industries* (London: BFI, 2007), 120.
131. McDonald, *Video and DVD Industries*, 120. See also Wasser, *Veni, Vidi, Video*, 132.
132. McDonald, *Video and DVD Industries*, 120.

133. See, for example, Jim McCullaugh, '1980–1990: The Video Decade', *Billboard* 102.1 (6 January 1990), V8, V40, V42, V48, V52, V54, V56, V58, V60, V62, V64.
134. Anon., 'Sell, sell, sell is MGM/UA pitch in classics launch', *Video Business* 3.16 (13 July 1983), 1.
135. Anon., 'Debut for the £9.99 title', *Video Business* 3.23 (1 August 1983), 1.
136. Tony Tyler, 'Get set for the retail market', *Video Business* 3.24 (8 August 1983), 20.
137. Anon., 'Debut for the £9.99 title', 1.
138. Anon., 'Sell, sell, sell', 1.
139. Alex Sutherland and Terry Ilcott, 'All eyes on CIC's cut-price "Raiders"', *Screen International* 416 (15–22 October 1983), 21; Alex Sutherland, '"Flashdance" is new CIC cut-price title', *Screen International* 429 (21–8 January 1984), 21.
140. Sutherland, '"Flashdance" is new CIC cut-price title', 21.
141. Laurie Hall (of CIC) quoted in Tyler, 'Get set for the retail market', 20.
142. Anthony Hayward, 'CIC, CBS/Fox set to follow cut-price video policy', *Screen International* 449 (9–16 June 1984), 27.
143. Anon., 'Wide title and price range is key to success', Channel 5 supplement, *Video Business* 8.16 (20 April 1987), n.p.
144. Anon., 'The Video Collection', *Screen International* 516 (28 September–5 October 1985), n.p.
145. Following Levinson's departure from Videoform, he established the Palan Entertainment Corporation, a rights broker for TV and video. After the injection of the company into Prestwich in 1984, Levinson became company chairman. See Anon., 'A far cry from 1984 situation', *Video Business* 8.33 (17 August 1987), 2–3, 5. Levinson eventually sold his remaining shares in Heron back to the company in 1986. See John Hazelton, 'Levinson makes £1.25m settlement with Heron', *Screen International* 534 (8 February 1986), 51.
146. Anon., 'A far cry from 1984 situation', 2.
147. Anon., 'A far cry from 1984 situation', 2. See also, Anon., 'Prestwich almost doubles its profits', *Video Business* 6.12 (12 March 1986), 8.
148. John Hazelton, 'The stormy growth of UK home video', *Screen International* 524 (23–30 November 1985), 122–4. Citation at 124.
149. For citation see Anon., 'Three companies in talks on under £10 joint venture', *Video Business* (17 March 1986), 1. For more information about the launch of Channel 5 see Anon., 'Far more high street sales on the horizon', *Video Business* 6.2 (3 March 1986), 4.
150. On Video Gems see Anon., 'Gems an immediate success!', *Video Business* 6.38 (8 September 1986), 28, 31. See also: Anon., 'Disney titles to sell for over a tenner', *Video Business* 6.36 (8 September 1986), 1, 4; Anon., 'MGM/UA announces first sales', *Video Business* 6.37 (15 September 1986), 1, 4; Anon., 'CIC goes under-a-tenner', *Video Business* 6.45 (10 November

1986), 1, 4; Anon., 'Stablecane to put Warner titles into Virgin at £14.99', *Video Business* 6.47 (24 November 1986), 1, 4. CBS/Fox waited a further year, 'sitting back . . . and watching how the majors handled sell-through.' See Anon., 'CBS/Fox sell-through', *Video Business* 8.34 (24 August 1987), 1, 4. Quotation at 1. Warner Bros entered sell-through in 1988. See Anon., 'Warner to invest £1.5m into sell-thru', *Video Business* 8.27 (4 July, 1988), 4.
151. Anon., 'Wide title and price range is key to success', n.p. See also Adam Sweeting, 'The Media: Rack and roll/Sale of video cassettes', *The Guardian* (16 June 1986); and Patrick Stoddart, 'Video tapes: the chain store massacre', *The Sunday Times* (6 October 1985).
152. John Hayward, 'What a good year', *Video Business* 8.6 (5 January 1987), 22.
153. Hazleton, 'The stormy growth of UK home video', 122.
154. Mark Levy and Barry Gunter, *Home Video and the Changing Nature of the Television Audience* (London: John Libbey, 1988), 6.
155. Mike Gower, 'A reverse structure to rental', *Video Business* 8.33 (17 August 1987), 5.
156. Anon., '"Thriller" video sets UK record', *Screen International* 441 (14–21 April 1984), 1. Palace Virgin Gold was a venture that saw the collaboration of Palace Films, Virgin Communications and the wholesaler S. Gold and Sons.
157. Wasser, *Veni, Vidi, Video*, 126.
158. Alex Sutherland, 'Lack of subsidy blamed for slow starts in new cable franchise areas', *Screen International* 524 (23–30 November, 1985), 137, 140. Citation at 137.
159. Anon., 'A far cry from 1984 situation', 2.
160. See, for example, Anon., 'Sell-through chart share', Video Collection supplement (*Video Business*, 17 August, 1987), 3.
161. Charles Robinson, '"Thomas" and friends attract interest of growing "tot" market', *Video Business* 6.45 (10 November, 1987), 42.
162. Anon., 'Video Collection force to sell to the independent dealer', *Video Business* 6.8 (24 February 1986), 1, 4.
163. Stoddart, 'Video tapes: the chain store massacre'.
164. On the beginnings of the Channel 5 label see Anon., 'Heron, Polygram launch joint venture low-price scheme in UK', *Screen International* 529 (4–11 January 1986), 14; on its VTA policy see Anon., 'Video Collection force to sell to the independent dealer', 4.
165. See, for example, John Bickley, 'An incitement to the indies', *Video Business* 8.2 (12 January 1987), 37.
166. Greenwood, 'The rise and rise of sell-through'. On the latter see Alison Bridge, 'On the right track: video goes for gold', *VST – The Video Sell-through Magazine* 8 (June 1989), 14–15.

CHAPTER 5

# Independent Spirit vs Corporate Muscle

In 1985, the chairman of the Video Trade Association (VRA), Derek Mann, wrote an opinion piece that was published in the trade periodical *Screen International*, addressing the negative public image of video rental outlets in Britain. He argued:

> the video industry has no one to blame but itself. The retailers are in many cases apathetic and unconcerned about the need to give the industry a sound and acceptable base. Many of them are frighteningly naïve, particularly in the knowledge of how to run reputable and professional business.[1]

Unfortunately for shop owners, Mann's article reflected the mood of the period. More pervasive than ever was the caricature of independent dealers as cowboys or fly-by-nights, unable to sustain the levels of professionalism required to keep the video business buoyant.

Mann's assertion that the proprietors of said outlets were wholly responsible for the image of video lacks nuance, though his comment about the naivety of (some) shop owners rings true. The opportunities that video had given those new to business earlier in the decade had by the mid-1980s all but dissipated. Many shops were facing financial hardship, with many others already bankrupt. In the wake of the video nasties and the Video Recordings Act (VRA), it was deemed imperative more than ever for shops to reinvent themselves and present video as an attractive consumer activity.

The irony could not have been more self-evident. According to a survey carried out by the British Video Association (BVA) in late 1985, 'less than 3% of consumers had a spontaneously negative impression of their local video shop'.[2] However, over half of those interviewed admitted to renting less frequently than in 1984. Analysis at the time suggested that the main issues were that the 'novelty' of video had worn off for consumers, and that the standard of material being released was not as appealing as it could be.[3] According to BVA chairman David Rozella, the solution to this was for the business to 'present video as a much more vibrant and exciting industry'.[4]

Video shops, it was agreed, would play a pivotal role. It is the purpose of this chapter to examine how.

As discussed in Chapter 2, at the beginning of the 1980s small-time video shop owners triumphed over the multiples. High-street shops such as Rediffusion carried limited stock and tended to serve inner-city locations, while independent outlets flowered in suburbia and beyond. This situation had changed by all measures by 1985, as an increasing number of mainstream outlets began aggressively renting video cassettes as a sidestream to their main business. By the end of the decade, the industry was flooded by the first national video chain stores: a smattering of companies, each striving to be market leader.

## 'Dealer of the Month'

Before the emergence of national chains, several tactics were employed by the video industry to aid the independent dealer in helping improve their image. One such example, and to which this chapter now turns its attention, is the 'Dealer of the Month' column published in the trade periodical *Video Business*.

The column was a mainstay of the magazine following its first issue in 1981 and covered a range of dealers of different size and scope. Its purpose was to showcase alternative business approaches and membership models, shop layouts, how different businesses went about generating custom, their preferred wholesalers, their most popular genres and so on. The column at one time addressed the broadest church of video dealers, from the glossy and professional to those more frugal and less resourced. By 1985, however, it began prioritising dealers from the former category, often those with multiple outlets, wide-ranging stock and established reputations with local clientele.

As a rule, the column refrained from platforming shops such as newsagents, greengrocers and petrol garages; the type of establishment that was supplied with 'racks' of videocassettes by so-called 'rack-leasers'. Typically (but not exclusively), rack-leasers were divisions of distributors or wholesalers, and would lease batches of around 100 videocassettes, for a weekly fee, to so-called 'secondary outlets' for which video rental was not the primary means of income.[5] Their clientele included independently operated businesses, but also a host of multiples, such as major supermarkets, department stores and chemists. In 1985, such operations – the highest profile of which were Videoform and a new company established by Intervision and CBS/Fox, Videoserve – were deemed one of the biggest threats to independently owned specialist outlets. There were three principal reasons for this. First, the stock discounts such companies offered their clients enabled secondary outlets to charge considerably less per rental than conventional video shops. This risked pricing specialists out of the market. Second, there was concern that racking stood to stall the trade bodies' plan to improve video's public image, as it was assumed staff working in such places would inevitably lack the specialist knowledge of those with experience running a bespoke video club.[6] Third, concerns over racking were exacerbated by the rate at which secondary outlets were opening rack-leasing accounts. In late 1984 Videoserve was adding to its list of 600 high street chains and 300 independents at a rate of fifty to sixty per week, with the company predicting that, by the end of the following year, 'racking will account for 75 per cent of video tape sales'.[7] From the BVA's perspective, as representatives of the distributors, this did not matter, as its members were racking's chief profiteers. Moreover, several of the Association's executive committee were involved in that side of the business, not least its then-chairman, Iain Muspratt, who stood down in mid-1985 to dedicate his time to one such company, Video Box Office.[8] But for *Video Business* and the VTA it was a moral issue that they could not ignore. The entire concept of racking set out to discriminate against the industry bedrock and was therefore not in the best interests of the business – their members/readers – as a whole. In response, the VTA with the support of *Video Business* and other trade magazines encouraged its members to boycott purchasing stock from the likes of Videoform and CBS/Fox, and open accounts with anti-racking wholesalers instead.[9]

The 'Dealer of the Month' column was a platform on which *Video Business* helped set the agenda. The focus was now on shops that were excelling *as specialists*; as outlets that were demonstrably successful in fending off the advances made by Videoserve and its ilk. The column strived to make specialist retailers as distinct from secondary outlets as possible. On occasion, this meant featuring shops whose owners were vocal about their stance against racking companies. Much of the time, featured shops tended to operate multiple outlets, utilise the latest retail technology, and, crucially, foreground a pleasurable consumer experience (precisely that said to be lacking from secondary outlets). In all cases, featured dealers in any given month were shown to be doing the industry a service by maintaining high standards.

For example, Vidi Vidio [sic] of Luton, the reader learns, while it is 'Tucked rather out of the way', offers a professional and 'streamlined' operation across both of its branches, with prices that either match, or beat by 50p, those of its nearest racked competitor, the Co-op supermarket.

The £10 lifetime membership fee is waived for workers from the local Vauxhall car factory.[10] Pitching an independent against a racker as this article does embodies the strategy of the magazine to great effect. It presents an independent dealer as one that is worth seeking out ahead of a more conveniently located shop, due to the former prioritising a consumer experience unlikely to be found in the latter. Its arrangement with local workers projects an image of a company on the side of the people, with local interests at heart. Racking, the article intimates, is a threat to this. The price cuts that Vidi Vidio has made are framed as an undesirable yet necessary means of ensuring longevity: not simply for the shop itself, but also the personable, quality experience from which customers stand to benefit if they continue opting for specialists over secondary outlets. The implication is that more shops modelling themselves on outlets like Vidi Vidio will ensure that such custom is not lost to the racker who, while possessing high-street visibility, locations convenient for the public and all the advantages of corporate muscle, fundamentally lacks the knowledge and personality that *Video Business* deems so intrinsic to the future of the rental trade.

Another example is Anglia Video of Norwich which, the reader learns, has five branches, is 'neat and organised' and offers consumers 'endless attention to detail' and 'colossal' choice.[11] As above, a customer-focused experience ('neat and organised', 'attention') is foregrounded and championed. The threat of racking is again made apparent – the owners describe themselves as 'very anti-racking' – and suggestions are made as to how to combat it.[12] The onus in this example is on not reducing prices, but rather maintaining them and carrying greater depth and breadth of stock. Given that secondary outlets would routinely stock fifty to a hundred titles, the vast range offered by Anglia, the column suggests, guarantees that '*something*' will most certainly appeal to customers.[13] Indeed, its owners' disapproval of racking firms suggests that, while its prices are invariably higher than those of rackers – outlets ranging from 'newsagents to Chinese takeaways to bicycle shops' charging '50p–£1' – the experience it offers consumers results in excellent value for money.

The decision of the magazine's editorial team to focus on shops of this nature was, unquestionably, strategic. By foregrounding examples of video outlets that reflected the side of the video rental industry that *Video Business* and the VTA were keen to promote, the magazine might shepherd its readership to make changes to their own shop premises and, in the process, help contribute to improving the image of video in the public eye. Such coverage, in other words, communicated to other retailers that the *potential* of the video business was in the hands of reputable specialists, not opportunistic rackers. It was the responsibility of independent dealers, thus, to learn from their peers, and step up to the plate.

It is impossible to quantify the extent to which 'Dealer of the Month' had any demonstrable impact. What is undeniable is the fact that emerging reports about a generally 'improved' image began running parallel to its publication. In January 1986, Peter Lee, of the successful regional chain Bogarts Video, wrote in the trade press that 'Dealers are becoming more professional in their approach'. He cites the emergence of several regional video shop chains as indicative of a changing culture, one that is encouraging 'single dealers . . . to stay right on top of things to ensure their share of the marketplace'.[14] The BVA agreed, blaring to journalists in March that 'rental outlets are cleaning up'.[15] By the end of the year, video rental was in its best health. The BVA reported that the public had spent some £375 million on renting cassettes, representing a 25 per cent increase on the previous year.[16] Further encouragement came in the form of emergent data showing that rental numbers were unfettered by the runaway success of sell-through (see previous chapter).[17] It was conceivable, for the first time in two years, that video rental was projecting longevity.

From the sidelines, entrepreneurs looking to stake a claim in the renewed marketplace observed these developments with interest. A gap in the current landscape was apparent. For all that many a high-street multiple had jumped on the racking bandwagon, there was yet a bespoke rental chain – a brand that could channel the slickness of the 'best' specialists and the product expertise lacking from the rackers. Woolworths had shown how much money could be made – thanks to appropriate resourcing and PR – from *selling* videos within the slick environment of a mainstream store. This begged the question: could something similar be done for rental?

## 'The best business opportunity I have seen': the first national chains

One individual with a keen eye on the future of the rental business was entrepreneur David Quayle. Quayle had made his name as a 'retail pioneer', when he co-founded, with business partner Richard Block, the UK's first DIY and home improvements chain, B&Q, in 1969.[18] In 1986, having sold his share in B&Q a few years earlier, Quayle was serving as the Deputy Chairman of one of ITV's franchise networks, Television South, when he and two of his colleagues injected £400,000 into Intervision: a line to return the financiers to the stock market after almost five years away.[19]

As previously acknowledged, Intervision was by this point co-running Videoserve with CBS/Fox. However, while the operation proved very successful in its first few months, its executives' projections about the future of racking had not come to fruition.[20] It was now largely agreed in the trade that Intervision was 'ailing',[21] and 'little more than a shell'.[22] When Quayle joined the company he stripped it back, restructured it and changed its name. Its new moniker, Cityvision, communicated the firm's status as a Public Limited Company ('The City' was and remains the moniker of London's financial district), and made the nature of the business opaquer, creating an image of a firm with interests that were not solely anchored to video racking – or indeed video in any general sense.[23] By early 1987, it was clearer than ever that rack-leasing was not the success story that earlier figures had intimated, with three-quarters of all video rental transactions being made at specialist outlets.[24] This data, collected by the BVA, suggested that the ongoing industry 'clean-up' was proving a success for specialists, and that Videoserve's market position, while steady, was ultimately peripheral to the main goings-on. For Quayle, this change in video culture proffered an opportunity for Cityvision's expansion – 'the best business opportunity I have seen since I founded B&Q' – and he immediately set to work on planning what, over the course of the next twelve months, would become the UK's first national video chain.[25]

Though Quayle didn't come out and say it, he no doubt took inspiration from happenings overseas, specifically America, where a handful of national chains were well established. Dallas-based Blockbuster Video was once such example, having launched in 1985 and which proceeded to expand its 'clean and bright' video superstores into the late 1980s and beyond.[26] However, when Cityvision declared its intentions to establish a British chain, Blockbuster was not yet the global behemoth it would later become.[27] A more immediate source of inspiration was the US's then 'fastest growing' chain, Philadelphia-based West Coast Video.[28]

The West Coast story was impressive. In 1986, the chain's president, Elliot Stone, claimed to have rented 5 million videocassettes since opening his flagship store three years earlier.[29] A major factor in his firm's success, he believed, was its glossy corporate image: a response to his disillusionment 'with stores [where] I was shopping'.[30] In the US, the video business was marred by a similar stigma in the early-to-mid 1980s (albeit to a much lesser extent) to that of the UK, due to the pervasiveness of pornography, with the resultant caricature of 'mom and pop' shops being, as Blockbuster CEO Wayne Huizenga later articulated, 'sleazy joints in bad neighbourhoods'.[31] Stone looked to corporate America for a model to quash – or at least distinguish his own operation from – this stereotype, specifically the McDonald's fast-food chain. I acknowledge in the introduction to this book how Blockbuster also looked to McDonald's for inspiration, going so far as to appoint the fast-food restaurant's marketing executive, Thomas Gruber, in 1988. West Coast, however, was the first to express its allegiance to the McDonald's approach. Stone's aim, he told the trade paper *Billboard* in 1986, was to strive for the same levels of consistency at West Coast that diners at McDonald's had come to expect.[32]

In this way, West Coast is one of the earliest examples of 'McDonaldisation': 'the process by which the principles of the fast-food restaurant – efficiency, calculability, predictability and control – are coming to dominate more and more sectors of American society as well as of the rest of the world'.[33] From the outside looking in, West Coast, via McDonald's, offered a model that was, in theory, easily replicable. The video chain strove for *efficiency* in its promise to offer customers 'a fast, in-and-out, transaction'.[34] With some outlets stocking up to 15,000 titles and oftentimes multiple copies of the same film,[35] it was propelled by *calculability*, of offering 'quantity' as evidence of 'quality',[36] and mounted signs on its storefronts displaying its countrywide rental figures to the public, as McDonald's did with its burger sales data.[37] As with the 'Golden Arches' of McDonald's, the video chain had a recognisable logo that bore a similar colour palette: a 'golden' yellow sun and the company name in an embossed, white, font (again, similar to the fast food chain). West Coast sites, like McDonald's, had a consistent colour scheme (the red/yellow/white of its logo), a design that was 'essentially the same' from store to store, and a corresponding uniform for its workers, to 'enhance its 'corporate image' and ensure *predictability*.[38] New employees were required to complete the 'West Coast Video College' training scheme, itself modelled on McDonald's 'Hamburger University' employee programme, whereby they participated in role-playing 'behind the counter' scenarios, checked stock, stacked shelves and so on.[39] In so doing, West Coast was able to exert *control* over its staff, by offering its employees basic knowledge 'to do a limited number of tasks in precisely the way they are told to do them'.[40] The same was also true of its customers. In West Coast stores, contra UK shops at the time, 'There is no such thing as a "Film on Hire" sticker'. Instead, 'Covers are handed in to be stored behind the counter . . . while cassettes are on rental', meaning that 'everything out on the shelves is available and a customer never has to resort to second or third choice of title'.[41] This, when coupled with its shopfloor designs and spacious aisles to create 'smooth traffic flow', resulted in environments where, as in the case of McDonald's, consumers could enter and leave quickly so that the store was able to maximise turn over in the most efficient way possible.[42]

Figure 5.1 Two variations of the West Coast Video logo, seen here in a US television commercial, c.1987. Source: Classic TV Ads (YouTube).

Quayle's track record with B&Q suggested to some that he would simply carry over his established home-grown business model into the video industry.[43] However, just as Cityvision was gearing up to launch its first outlets, West Coast announced its plans to establish a British subsidiary, and Quayle's approach was routinely bundled with Stone's and US-style business practices.[44] *Screen International*, for example, referred to both West Coast and Cityvision as 'the Ronald McDonalds of video', in reference to the fast-food giant's clown mascot. *The Guardian*, following the same tack, referred to both as 'Video's Big Macs', in reference to McDonald's most famous hamburger.[45] Lumping both companies together in this way, despite their distinct national origins and the fact that Quayle had established a leading retail chain of his own, speaks to the influence US companies were thought to wield and, indeed, the mileage Cityvision was to gain by taking heed of Stone's model. There is evidence to suggest that Quayle viewed West Coast, even ahead of the US company's decision to penetrate the UK, as a standard to replicate, given the latter's rapid success within the business in which he himself was attempting to make waves.

Quayle intended to expand his operation at a rate that appears from news coverage to be comparable to that of Stone in the US. He began in earnest in May 1987, buying up four regional chains to the tune of £2.6 million and acquiring forty shops in the process. They comprised Bogarts, Mega Movies, Potters Video and Ritz Video Film Hire, the latter of which became the chosen trading name for the nationwide venture.[46] With these outlets acquired, Quayle's short-term goal was to establish a total of 100 Ritz stores by the end of 1988, all bearing hallmarks similar to those of West Coast, including 'a generic shop-front and in-store design scheme and a standardised rental price structure for tapes'.[47] Furthermore, Ritz's new logo, and the accompanying in-store design scheme, replicated the

INDEPENDENT SPIRIT VS CORPORATE MUSCLE     181

basic components of West Coast. Typically, on posters and shop signage, the word 'RITZ' appeared in red across a yellow background – the West Coast scheme in reverse – and a colour scheme that filtered through Ritz stores as it did those of its US contemporary. Ritz exteriors were adorned with yellow facias with red writing stretching across the top of the shop front, and red window trims bearing red and yellow vinyl stickers. Inside, hefty signage directed consumers to different sections of the store that, as

Figure 5.2  The logo of Ritz Video Film Hire.
Credit: Popular Film and Television Collection.

Figure 5.3  The exterior and interior of a Ritz shop, c.1990. Source: The Duke Mitchell Film Club (YouTube).

in West Coast's US sites, were also dominated by red, from the walls and shelves (complemented by a yellow trim) to the shop counter at the rear.[48] To all intents and purposes Ritz appeared to be striving to offer its consumers a streamlined retail experience of on par with that of an American giant.

The comparisons made between Ritz and West Coast indicates more than Quayle's apparent indebtedness to West Coast's basic principles and aesthetic. It also speaks to Quayle's determination to 'dominate' the market and in the process adopt what one British dealer described, in reference to West Coast, as a 'bully boy American' attitude.[49] Indeed, in the months that followed, Ritz was targeted by the trade for the mercilessness of its rapid expansion, specifically its apparent strategy to open new outlets in close proximity to independent shops. As an 'Offscreen' editorial for *Video Business* argued in relation to one specific case, in June 1988:

> SO WE know that all's fair in the cut-throat commercial world of video, but we at *Offscreen* reckon the *Ritz* move to open one of its superstores right next door to Peter Blakemore's established (but much smaller) library in Carshalton smacks of dirty pool. Quite apart from the obvious suspicions that Ritz looked all over Carshalton – a prosperous Surrey berg – and just happened to light upon a nice location in the middle of a housing estate as opposed to the High Street, Mr Blakemore will be up against a chain that has enough muscle to buy its product cheaply and attack hard with discounts.[50]

By this point, Cityvision was emboldened. West Coast, in spite of the bluster of its British executives, had ultimately failed to penetrate.[51] Its UK managing director, Kenneth Taylor, resigned suddenly – for reasons later rumoured to relate to financial mismanagement in an earlier business – in July 1987.[52] By the time the US chain opened its first shop in Britain – a site in Greater Manchester in February of the following year – Ritz was operating sixty countrywide.[53] By October, West Coast, now with three shops to its name but plagued by financial issues, had cut its plan for expansion down to a mere twenty-four outlets in total – a far cry from the 500 it had initially projected.[54]

The rapid demise of West Coast was fortuitous for Cityvision for it enabled company executives to spin a narrative of defiance over a powerful international competitor. Thus, in response to the *Offscreen* piece about the video shop in Carshalton, South London, Cityvision's deputy, Peter Lee (recruited following Cityvision's acquisition of his Bogarts chain) was nonchalant and unsympathetic, not solely to the plight of Mr Blakemore (the dealer acknowledged in the previous quotation), but to independent dealers everywhere. 'I make no apologies', he wrote. 'Mr Blakemore appears to be under the misapprehension that as a public company director I have a duty to watch out for the smaller dealer.'[55] The following month, he continued his rhetorical offensive, brashly declaring that Cityvision's 'aim is 400 shops and we have no intention of stopping there'.[56]

The narrative was clear; the intention behind it deliberate. By foregrounding the status of Ritz as a 'public' company versus Blakemore's status as a 'smaller dealer', coupled with Lee's disinterest in taking any responsibility for the fate of independent shops, Lee was appropriating on behalf of the company the 'bully boy' stereotype of its one-time US competitor. In so doing, Lee was mobilising the ruthless machismo with which West Coast had launched its campaign to render the fate of Cityvision's competition inevitable and emerge victorious, having surpassed its North American adversary.

Flourishes of resilience were shown to Cityvision (and, initially, West Coast). An increasing number of regional dealers were opening multiple outlets at this time, at times expressing defiance to the nationals. For example, speaking with *Video Business* in 1987, the owners of The Video House in Sheffield, South Yorkshire, spoke confidently of their plans to expand from nine outlets to twenty-six, expressing a vision redolent of their major competitors. As co-owner Fred Oldfield explained:

> ... the image I want to create in my shops is similar to the Wimpy Bar, the Little Chef, Top Shop, Tie Rack; so as soon as you see a Video House shop, you're automatically aware of both the quality and product you'll find there ... I believe we've got something equally as good as CityVision [sic] or West Coast.[57]

Oldfield's bravado notwithstanding, his remarks reflect an effort among pockets of the community to play the nationals at their own game, by aping the strategies of well-known high-street brands (and in the case of Oldfield, specifically *British* brands at that). Other individuals were more callous in their approach. For example, Alex Nell, company chairman of the Video Shuttle chain, adopted a tone similar to that of Peter Lee. Upon announcing his intention to 'set-up 30 video megastores in London', Nell declared to the trade press that 'We will be able to open in the same street as a good video trader and he will not last, we have economies of scale on our side'.[58]

For many, however, a complete rebrand to capture a fresh, clean image akin to Ritz was not a viable option. The imminency of Cityvision and the regionals' domination was exacerbated by the outward support of high street multiples by the major distributors – one of which stated frankly in June 1987, that 'as a major distributor ... I see the future lying in the domination of the retail scene by major chains'[59] – and a damning appraisal of the industry by a US marketing executive who, speaking at an industry conference in the following year, 'berated his audience' for the pervasiveness of 'run-down' shops that he had experienced in London.⁶⁰ In this climate many dealers believed the odds to be stacked against them.

This major industrial turn placed the trade press in a precarious position. *Video Business*'s 'Dealer of the Month' column had shown some defiance of the corporate insurgency, but its emphasis on racking was, it turned out, misplaced. It became apparent by 1988 that the role the publication should be playing in the industry clean-up was a more active one, if it were to truly help boost morale amongst its readership.

## 'The most deserving independent'

To this end, on 6 June 1988, *Video Business* launched the 'Superstore 88' campaign, a competition that was open to all independent retailers in Britain. The prize was a shop refit worth £20,000 featuring contributions from known companies and the support of the VTA, which concurrently launched a new Family Code 'to promote better standards' among its membership by having them agree not to carry 'offensive, uncertified, or illegal material'.⁶¹ Winners would receive a full stock update from Heron, a new shop front funded by Vestron, a computer system developed by Custom Video, a new shop interior by Maxirun and free VTA membership.⁶² To be eligible to win, dealers were asked to write a letter outlining why they believed themselves to be the deserving winner.

The campaign was, at its core, an extension of the 'Dealer of the Month' column: a symbolic PR exercise. It was a move taken to align *Video Business* with corporatisation by offering the winner access to what multiples like Ritz had at their disposal: a contemporary look and credibility in the eyes of industry watchers and trade bodies. It also offered a beacon of hope for struggling independents, who believed they were already operating at a comparable standard. Throughout the campaign, the public image of video shops – and by extension the entire video trade – remained paramount.

As a campaign riding a wave of change, the transformative aims of its outcome were pushed heavily in campaign discourse. Superstore 88, the promotional bumph claimed, would help remedy the 'dingy, seedy looking premises that is the abiding image of the corner store'. The name of the campaign itself pointed to this desire explicitly. Transforming a tired 'corner store' into a modern 'superstore' was a process that hinged on the cutting of ties between a 'dingy', unregulated past and a policy-driven, more accountable present. By offering the winner the resources to supe-up

> **The Family Code**
>
> 1. We do not trade in uncertified films
>
> 2. We will not supply films to young persons who have not attained the required age.
>
> 3. We will not deal in any illegal films of any sort.
>
> 4. We care about our reputation and we believe in offering the highest standards of service.
>
> 5. We will ensure that you will not be exposed to any material that a reasonable person may consider offensive.
>
> 6. We operate in accordance with a registered Code of Practice which provides additional safeguards for the rights of our customers.
>
> Your safeguard for all the family!

Figure 5.4 The Video Trade Association's Family Code, launched in 1988.

their operation, the campaign promised to 'bring their shop into line with the squeaky-clean image that organisations like the BVA and VTA are promoting'.[63]

The charitable nature of the campaign, as one might expect, was pushed very hard. Superstore 88 was promoted as a helping hand for 'the most deserving owner operated video library' and, as 'the biggest prize ever offered to the video trade', a generous one at that.[64] The campaign was a gesture likely cultivated to win the trust of smaller dealers, in the face of rapid change, by helping them adapt with the times. The written features that accompanied the weekly coverage of the campaign's progress all featured encouragement from the leading industry figures supporting the operation, creating an image of an industry set on working together to help, rather than wipe out, smaller retailers. Such support included weekly in-progress features and follow-up stories: unmatchable trade visibility for fledgling stores with the most limited means of PR generation. In another respect, it was a declaration to the trade organisations, media and government that the industry was able to come together and play an active role in shaping a much grander, profitable vision of video's continuing role in the British economy.

The timing was deliberate. Earlier statistics, as discussed above, spoke to the revived popularity of video rental. But there were concerns coming from Westminster, amid reports of dealers continuing to contravene the law, that the VRA had failed. With the assistance of the BVA, the government threatened to 'step up' prosecutions on noncompliant shopkeepers.[65] Independent shops – or rather sketchily drawn images of such – remained at the centre of this discourse, and reportage continued to cast the video industry in a negative light. There were also rejuvenated worries about the effect violent videos were having on children when teenager Michael Ryan, said by the press to be inspired by the Rambo film series, shot and killed sixteen people in the market town of Hungerford, Berkshire, in August 1987.[66] The Superstore 88 campaign, as *Video Business*'s 'contribution to improving the image of the video trade' looked to jump in and quash such negativity, and help 'the independent video dealer survive' ongoing media stigma (and, of course, the Cityvision juggernaut).[67]

Central to the campaign were relatable, 'human' narratives, of individuals striving to achieve the best for themselves, their family and their industry. This 'human' component – one wedded to the Thatcherite enterprise ideology of the moment – was paramount to *Video Business*'s plan to convey to those beyond the industry that the business was comprised of decent, hard-working people (in all cases men): precisely those endorsed by the government.[68] These were, Thatcherite discourse had it, people 'standing on [their] own two feet', who were 'looking out for [themselves] and [their] famil[ies]'.[69] Promoting the competition entrants in this manner was integral to the campaign, given how hard the government had come down on video. There was therefore pressure on the industry to show compliance: that it was listening, but also that there were many dealers already toeing the line.

The magazine projected this image by printing some of the entrant's letters as they were received. Across the piece similar experiences, ethics and goals are apparent, suggesting the editorial decision dictating their inclusion was strategic, to reinforce claims that the industry was for the most part cohesive and working towards a uniform set of ideals. One dealer writes that he acquired an established, albeit 'rundown', video library after taking voluntary redundancy from the Royal Air Force following twenty-three years of service. His decision to enter the video business, the letter reads, was taken to 'provide me with an exciting future in civilian life'.[70] The shop refit, he writes, would enable him to acquire a better selection of films, having already disposed of the older and 'illegal' titles that made up the stock he inherited when he took the shop over. The fact that the editors have chosen to print this handwritten letter in full (others are typeset and abridged) speaks broadly to the goals of the industry clean-up as whole. He is a relatable video dealer, having faced hard times, using his initiative to shape video's future away from the stigma of the video nasty. Video is mobilised as a dynamic and forward-facing industry with longevity, that normal people ('civilians') will continue to carry forward. The business becomes an extension of the man's military service (of note given Britain's victory in the Falklands earlier in the decade); his letter implying unreserved commitment to the video cause, to protect the interests of the business in its fight for respectability. In this way, the man is presented as an upstanding British citizen, who has paid his dues both to the country and the video industry he loves.

References to 'family' life and a commitment to 'family-friendly' in-store experiences pervade the letters. In the aforementioned example, the dealer explains how his business is a joint venture with his wife, while another explains that he 'relies on his wife and son for help'.[71] The resulting image is one of wholesomeness; of a family-friendly industry that campaigners were looking to achieve, whereby families come together not solely as consumers of 'family entertainment', but as the bedrock of the entire rental sector. In all of the examples given, the shops are decidedly 'normal', run by everyday, decent folk, who want the best for their business and the customers they serve.

Unsurprisingly, the winners of the competition, the owners of Silver Screen Video in Nottingham, fit the mould. The shop is a family venture run by husband-and-wife team Liam and Rita Corkery, who have customer experience at the forefront of their business philosophy. Their relatability to the readership of *Video Business* is conveyed via their unassumingness and honesty, their intention to succeed while recognising their own limitations, and their need for guidance in some areas (Liam, the reader discovers, is a 'modest man, . . . pleased to have some expert advice').[72] Their strengths in offering a tailored customer experience – by for example, having open floorspace so that their wheel-chair-using customers have easy access – is balanced by, for instance, their inexperience with modern technology, which has resulted in them not yet having installed a computerised cataloguing system.[73] (Corkery, the reader learns, has 'never handled a computer in [his] life'.[74]) One of the key takeaways from this sketch, through the normalcy the Corkerys convey, is that Silver Screen is not in any way atypical. Rather, it is a representative example of independent specialists everywhere: a little 'grotty', but its owners, with the right support, are keen to bring their operation in line with the 'superstore' environment of Cityvision and the growing regional chains.[75]

The campaign was a success. Silver Screen saw a rapid increase in footfall in the two weeks following its renovation. Within three months it had increased its membership by 30 per cent and doubled its weekly turnover.[76] The message was clear to all dealers: 'Brightening up your shop certainly improves the public image of what a video library is all about', stated one follow-up article. '[I]mproving your image improves your business.'[77] This communicated to the trade that a rebrand could be a lifeline for struggling dealers.

Superstore 88 showed the potential of video and offered inspiration; but its effect beyond this was negligible. The following year, when the magazine launched 'Superstore 89',[78] trumpeting the same rhetoric before announcing its winners as yet another hard-working husband-and-wife team, the same publication was reporting that Ritz had opened its five hundredth store.[79] Not only that, but it was opening new outlets 'at the rate of seven per week'.[80] The disparity was increasingly apparent. If independents were to survive this onslaught, the playing field needed to be levelled.

## 'The spirit of an independent, the muscle of a multiple'

Some industry watchers were not convinced that the buck was destined to stop with Ritz. Some were of the belief that the national chain, for all its increasing visibility and the positive role it was playing in the 'clean-up', had not in fact fully exploited the potential of the opportunity that befell it. Paul Feldmann of Parkfield – a company that made inroads into the sell-through market with great success – recognised that independent rental outlets were not dispensable and that the video industry could continue to benefit from the operations of smaller shops. Key to this, as Feldmann saw it, was for rental outlets to integrate sell-through more forcibly in their businesses (something that the Superstore 88 and 89 campaigns had also encouraged). According to a Parkfield promotional film from 1989, high-street multiples such as Woolworths and others controlled 80 per cent of the sell-through market, but were not, due to issues pertaining to space, location and other such factors, adequately prepared to 'handle the expected growth'.[81] Moreover, Ritz shops – given Cityvision's vested interest in rental – did not yet stock sell-through cassettes. There was, therefore, a gap waiting to be filled.

When Feldmann, formerly of Videoform, moved into wholesaling in 1985, his eyes were on sell-through and its cross-over potential with other media forms, such as music cassettes, CDs and computers. He was among the first to see the potential in, and wanted to develop, in his own words, 'the first true, complete home entertainment centre'.[82] The dominance of Ritz, and the faltering position of independent specialists a few years later, provided him with the opportunity he needed to realise his vision. In 1988, Feldmann set about forming an alliance with independent retailers: to marry their 'spirit' with his corporate 'muscle', and take on Cityvision in a more aggressive way than the Superstore 88 campaign ever could. The form this alliance took was that of the video business's first 'symbol group': Hollywood Nites.

The practice of symbol groups has decades-long history within British retail, namely within the convenience shop sector. Historically, independent shopkeepers, when faced with increasing competition from high street multiples, were granted opportunities by grocery chains such as Spar and others to adopt the bigger companies' corporate identity, trade on their terms and, in most cases, agree to purchase a named percentage of stock from them or one of their affiliated suppliers. In exchange for doing so, retailers were the receiver of 'a range of benefits', including a shop fascia bearing the Group's branding (while retaining the store's original business name), exclusive discounts on stock, access to ranges of products unique to the Group, 'professional guidance and advice' and, perhaps most crucially for the present discussion, access to 'marketing and promotional programmes'.[83] Parkfield promised all of this to its prospective membership as 'protection' from ruthless multiples. As a promotional leaflet for Hollywood Nites read:

> A symbol group uses the collective 'muscle' of the dealers to obtain more competitive discounts and provide better levels of advertising support.
>
> By virtue of it's [sic] national identity, the Symbol Group can use it's [sic] massive advertising strength to bring more customers into your shop and provide you with the means to keep their custom; it means you can compete with the multiples on their own terms.[84]

In exchange for £1, up to 1,000 members of the VTA (which charged £150 per annum in membership fees) would, if their application were successful, receive a free illuminated shop fascia, be given access to discounts from Parkfield's wholesale division (it had recently bought out London-based wholesaler, Lightning), be given branded membership cards, category signage and carrier bags, and benefit from an expansive nationwide television campaign worth £500,000.[85]

Up until this point nationwide campaigns of this sort had always been distributor-facing. For example, in the summer of 1988, CBS/Fox launched what was then the 'biggest-ever TV campaign', comprising twenty-second ads on networks throughout the UK, supplemented by 'the usual point-of-sale, trailering and press and PR coverage'.[86] Neither this campaign, nor several others like it, were tailored to the specific shops participating in the scheme.[87] The Parkfield campaign, comparatively, was retailer-facing, and promised to target individual shops within each region.[88] The Group also promised that store owners would be able to 'safeguard the market around their own outlets', ensuring that 'once accepted for a particular area, [they] will never find another symbol retailer directly competing with him [sic].'[89]

The scheme was set to benefit retailers, but the benefits to both Parkfield and the VTA were mammoth. For Parkfield, it was another guaranteed income stream to help further its expansion, from its distribution and wholesaling operations, into the retail the sector, like Cityvision – its main competitor. For the VTA, the initiative meant more members and more money, and stood to help the Association in its role in the industry 'clean-up'. Indeed, Hollywood Nites anticipated 1,000 members which, at the time, amounted to around 15 per cent of video retail outlets across the country, all of which were obliged to agree to, and to display a poster promoting, the VTA's Family Code, in addition to complying with an industry-wide 'Code of Practice' launched by the newly formed, government-endorsed, Video Standards Council (VSC) in 1989.[90]

As an initiative to compete with the high-street multiples, Parkfield wrote into its promotional materials an attitude of defiance to the likes of Ritz, and sympathy to the plight of the everyday tradesperson. While Cityvision made 'no apologies' to those independent businesses it was affecting, Hollywood Nites was presented as a helping hand to those small retailers that were either feeling the strain or living in fear of imminent closure. Bearing 'the spirit of an independent' and 'the muscle of a multiple', Parkfield intended, through an 'alliance of video shops', to counter the ruthlessness of those hoping to run many a business out of town.[91]

An examination of the initial campaign to attract members to the Hollywood Nites symbol group reveals much of Parkfield and the VTA's intentions. The campaign was put together hurriedly, beginning in earnest following the appointment of CBS/Fox's Steve Mandy to the role of commercial director in November 1988, continuing the following month with the opening of its pilot store, in Golders Green in London, with a view to hitting its target of 1,000 members for a national launch in spring of the following year.[92] Having revealed the Golders Green shop to much fanfare, including a positive two-page write up in *Video Business*, Parkfield began placing ads in the trade press and issuing informational leaflets to video outlets throughout the country.[93]

The main thrust of the campaign, as with the idea behind the symbol group in the first place, was to place the *bigness* of corporate retail within the comparatively 'small' hands of the independent retailer. Central to this narrative of 'bigness' was drawing on the mythology of Hollywood as the home of quality films. Rental chains overseas were already doing this to great effect, as the success of the Blockbuster, West Coast and Hollywood Video chains in the US attested, but the employment of 'Hollywood' in the British context was especially significant given the video industry's contemporaneous associations with extreme (i.e. non-Hollywood) horror film.[94] Film historian Richard Maltby argues that 'Hollywood is a state of mind, not a geographical entity'; one found 'in the familiar surroundings of the neighbourhood movie theatre, the back seat of the family car at the local drive-in, and now most often in your living room, on television, video or . . . "home cinema"'.[95] Parkfield was reliant on evoking this mythology in its campaign to attract dealers, capitalising on the 'familiarity' of Hollywood to offset the pervasively 'alien' image of what independent retailers – by virtue of the video nasties they were alleged to be trading in – had now become.[96] Equally as important to the campaign was Parkfield's attempts to equate video with a cherished British pastime, a 'night out at the pictures'.[97] Chapter 1 of this book explores how the first distributors capitalised on cinema going to sell video as a cheaper and more convenient alternative. Parkfield's focus in 1988 was not on the convenience of video per se – something that by this point was well-established – but rather on how the experience of cinema going may be instilled into the video shop experience, to rekindle consumer interest in video as a tenet of film culture proper. Christine Geraghty, writing in the context of 1950s cinema going, argues that, while 'going to the pictures was an ordinary and natural event for all kinds of people', 'entering into the cinema's space could also be exciting, since a physical sense of the cinema's glamour had been retained from the pre-war days'.[98] Parkfield wished to draw on this characterisation to encourage in video a sense of glamour that frankly was never there, to dispel the associations video had with unseemly goings-on behind closed doors.[99]

This augmentation of the video shop experience echoed the inroads being made into the rejuvenation of cinema-going culture epitomised by the opening of the first multiplex cinema, The Point, in Milton Keynes in 1985.[100] As Stuart Hanson explains, cinemas and cinema going had been in decline since the 1970s, with 'cutbacks in staffing, heating, lighting, and a failure to refurbish', meaning that cinemas once revered as '[picture] palace[s]' were now regarded as dingy 'fleapit[s]'.[101] One of the main purposes of the multiplex, thus, was to 'elevate the experience of cinema'.[102] In the British context, this involved retuning audiences to the notion of going to the pictures as a regular, family occurrence.[103] Parkfield was primed to exploit the excitement surrounding this 'revolutionary step forward in cinema',[104] by presenting its video symbol group as one in part wedded to the corporate image and ethos that the multiplex – as a 'one-stop entertainment centre' – signified, while also retaining nostalgia for the picture palaces of old.[105] It is telling that the symbol group's name deviated from its competitors by not referencing 'video' at all. Instead, 'Hollywood' and by extension its experiential associations, were at the front and centre of its corporate image, at a time when 'cinema' itself was being folded into a swathe of other activities befitting the broad offerings of the leisure complexes where multiplex cinemas were housed.[106] The Symbol Group was designed to enable independent retailers to play a role in helping alter the public's 'state of mind' regarding video in the 1980s: to make it a credible and attractive entertainment source once more.[107]

An affinity with idealistic notions of cinema and cinema going's glorious past, while simultaneously acknowledging the contemporary moment, was stressed from the outset of the campaign proper. The company logo bridged the past and present to great effect. A 'fantail cartouche' evocative of the art-deco period, it recalled the lighting and signage of opulent picture palaces of years gone by.[108] A lightning bolt finishes off the motif, connoting power and excitement and complementing the vibrancy of the logo's magenta/blue 'neon' colour palette. The company's striking shop facias were back-lit cinema marquee-style facades, with removable black lettering, to enable shopkeepers to 'highlight' their 'hottest new attractions' in the same fashion as theatrical exhibitors.[109] Clichés from the history of film advertising were abundant in the campaign's marketing-speak, too. The first full-page ad for the Group, for example, is a 'teaser' poster that, as with print materials designed to generate curiosity and excitement ahead of the launch of a films' marketing campaign, gave very little away, encouraging the inquisitive to 'phone us now' for 'the inside track'. On the poster there is a photograph of signage bearing the symbol group's logo and a marquee blaring a legend typical of film trailers:

HOLLYWOOD NITES
COMING SOON TO A HIGH STREET NEAR YOU

Drawing from established practices and iconography of theatrical exhibition in this way, Parkfield was aligning the present of the video

**Figure 5.5** Coming soon to a high street near you: Hollywood Nites.
Credit: Popular Film and Television Collection.

business with the pre-video age, overstepping the years of the industry blighted by the stigma of pornography and video nasties. Subsequent adverts were more befitting the age of the multiplex, and included an image of a glass shop front on a typical high street in the evening, neon lights and spotlights highlighting the shop's contents as crowds of families gather below its marquee.[110] The image chimes with the emerging multiplex as an outlet for family entertainment, while the uses of 'bright lights' and flashes of colour evoke their building exteriors, the aesthetic of which 'promised a place of entertainment that was in tune with its contents – namely the glamour and excitement of the ... Hollywood feature film'.[111] By straddling the past and the present, Parkfield projected an image of a company committed to selling consumers an experience wedded to the security of a familiar past and the excitement of a promising future.

Evoking American culture in these ways was beneficial to Parkfield, but it also brought with it some risks. In Britain, as elsewhere in Europe, America was considered 'both a model and a menace'.[112] For Ritz, as discussed above, it provided a model; for independents it posed a 'threat'.[113] For example, in the summer of 1987, shop proprietors were reportedly 'terrified' at the thought of West Coast's expansion and demanded 'protection' from the industry.[114] Similarly, when Blockbuster eventually opened its pilot store it was met with a protest by demonstrators spearheading a 'RENT BRITISH' campaign.[115] Parkfield, as a British company proposing to serve independent British businesses – many of which had been built from the ground up by individuals and families – therefore had to walk the line between positive and negative connotations of American culture very carefully. The Group approached this in two ways. First, it made clear to the trade press that, unlike West Coast, Hollywood Nites was 'not a franchise'.[116] While a symbol group fascia would sit above the door of its members' shops, the dealer would retain their business name, their staff and the reputation they established among their local 'customer base'.[117] Promotional materials thus presented the Group as a means of assistance, of something to aid in enhancement, of working together; antithetical to the narrative of domination and avariciousness being spun by those leading the expansion of Ritz. Second, Parkfield looked to promote, albeit cautiously, 'cultural' elements of the Group as perceivably unique to Britain, thereby assuaging 'the paradigm of the traditionless' and one-size-fits-all standardisation so central to critical discourse about Americanisation.[118]

Proclamations regarding nationhood or national belonging were rarely prominent in the Hollywood Nites campaign. When they were,

Figure 5.6 The Hollywood Nites symbol group permitted shopkeepers to retain their original business name. Photographer unknown. Credit: Popular Film and Television Collection.

they tended to serve pragmatic purposes. One campaign material, for example, refers to 'nationwide standards' and 'nationwide advertising', and features an illustration of a map of the British Isles to symbolise the anticipated countrywide penetration of the Group.[119] Another refers to a 'nationally known identity'.[120] Aside from these examples, however, Parkfield promoted its national interests in a manner that can be understood on the same terms as what sociologist Michael Billig would later theorise as 'banal nationalism'. That is to say, national belonging was 'flagged discursively', with references couched within 'routinely familiar habits of language' and 'small' and 'prosaic' words that 'take nationhood for granted, and which, in so doing, inhabit them'.[121]

A case in point is the promotional film that Parkfield released onto videocassette to promote the symbol group initiative, *My Beautiful Video Shop* (Bonnie Molnar, 1989). Advertising in the trade press in April 1989 and directed at interested parties, it encouraged them to send away for their free copy, and 'change [their] life' in the process.[122] The seven-minute film summarised the current state of play of the video business in the UK. Statistics are narrated across an array of infographics including graphs and stock footage of crowds gathering to convey the popularity of video, Parkfield's extant business success in non-connected areas such as manufacturing, and the untapped sell-through market where the company was making strides. The voiceover narration is peppered with allusions to the Group's national interests, primarily through the employment of inclusive wordage. Billig argues that, in media and political discourse, words such as 'we' are used to remind 'us' that '"we" live in nations'.[123] In *My Beautiful Video Shop*, similar turns of phrase are found. The narrator, for example, employs the phrases 'we all' and 'our industry' to evoke a sense of belonging that is implicitly national. Similarly, the viewer is reminded of the national context through allusions to relatable challenges that independent video shopkeepers were facing. These include references to, for example, 'fragmented' supplier networks and, perhaps most crucially, 'the media' and 'its sensationalist approach to the teething pains of the industry'. Using terms such as 'we' and 'our industry' in this context thus suggests a collective purpose, in this instance to strengthen the national video business through partnership and to prove the British media wrong about the video business that 'we all' play a crucial role in. Together, the narrator states, 'we'll give the public an image to look out for', and in so doing, make an impactful contribution to the national reimaging of video and the British economy.

Another way that *My Beautiful Video Shop* implicitly invoked discourse of the national was through its allusions to a recent British film, *My Beautiful Laundrette* (Stephen Frears, 1984), which, when released in cinemas in 1985 and onto video the following year, became a surprise hit.[124] The commercial success of the film provides one explanation as to why Parkfield may have wished to anchor its campaign video to it, as video retailers would most certainly have been aware of it.[125] Yet the film's content – or at least, part of it – was also ripe for exploitation. The film, which is chiefly concerned with the developing romantic relationship between Johnny (Daniel Day-Lewis), a white neo-Nazi, and Omar (Gordon Warnecke), an Asian entrepreneur, is widely celebrated for its razor-sharp critique of Thatcherite economics and engagement with 'contemporary issues' hitherto peripheral to much narrative cinema of the time (not least queer sexuality and racial politics).[126] But it is also, on the surface, a film about two unlikely business partners who successfully renovate a dilapidated laundrette in contemporary London and make a huge success of it. In short, despite its radical political statements, the basic premise was at the time widely relatable, reflecting as it did the aims of many working within the video business. *Video Shop* drew on this reductive element, what David Bordwell and Kristin Thompson might describe as the 'referential meaning' of *Laundrette*, using its 'bare bones plot' to sell Parkfield's symbol group concept to struggling dealers.[127] By

Figure 5.7 *My Beautiful Video Shop* (R) homages *My Beautiful Laundrette* (L).
Credit: The Duke Mitchell Film Club/Film4.

erasing the potent subtext of *Laundrette* from the *Video Shop* campaign, the company was able to riff on the film's reputation as a successful film set in the 1980s about a successful business venture, without alienating members who may have been dissuaded by its 'eye-opening' social commentary.[128]

Homage to *Laundrette*, therefore, is useful but tokenistic. In the *Video Shop* film, following the narrator's allusions to the industry challenges discussed above, the film cuts to a team of workman on scaffolding hanging 'Hollywood Nites' signage. The camera then pulls back to reveal a plush shop front. This sequence references the 'reveal' scene in *Laundrette*, where Johnny and Moose climb a ladder and hang the 'LAUNDRETTE' sign, signalling Powders' completion.[129] Geraghty, in her book about the film, writes that the scene's final shot, showing the audience for the first time a 'view of the whole façade', has 'no narrative function except to show the spectacle' of the sign's 'neon lights'. She characterises the shot as a 'moment of magic', where 'mundane reality' is transcended.[130] The homage in *Video Shop* serves the same purpose, with one caveat. The unveiling of the Hollywood Nites fascia is a moment of magic too, a slow zoom out revealing the storefront in all its grandeur. It is also, given that the reveal follows narration about the media's negative portrayal of the business, designed to transcend the 'mundane reality' of the British video retailer. But herein lies a crucial difference. *Laundrette* is 'about' much more than that suggested by its title. The 'beautiful' laundrette transcends and indeed subverts enterprise culture: it is a 'metaphor for hope', within which Johnny and Omar can live freely without fear of persecution.[131] The 'beautiful' video shop of *My Beautiful Video Shop*, however, is all the film amounts to. It embraces the Thatcherite culture that *Laundrette* seeks to critique.[132]

**Figure 5.8** Parkfield apes the video artwork of *My Beautiful Laundrette*. (The Hollywood Nites logo shown here was soon replaced with the refined 'fantail cartouche'.) Credit: Popular Film and Television Collection/Film4.

The promotional strategies for Frears's film at the time drew squarely on the romantic relationship that develops between Omar and Johnny. The widely distributed poster, used to promote both the theatrical and subsequent video release of the film, depict the couple standing in front of the refurbished laundrette. For Duncan Petrie, the film 'made such an impact *precisely because* of its tale of the love affair' between Omar and Johnny.[133] The *Video Shop* campaign borrows this element, showing two individuals standing in front of a newly renovated video shop – set against an evocative slogan that chimes with *Laundrette*'s key themes, 'Power in Partnership' – but with several key differences. First, signifiers pertaining to the film's social commentary are abandoned, including those relating to race, sexuality, and working-classness. On the film poster and video cover for *Laundrette*, the class disparity between Omar and Johnny is evident: Johnny wears a hooded sweatshirt and a ragged, plaid, sleeveless jacket, while Omar wears a business suit. Their distinct racial backgrounds are also apparent: Johnny is clearly Caucasian, Omar is clearly Asian. On the Parkfield poster, however, both individuals are white, one is male and the other female, they appear to be in their mid-to-late forties, and, from their appearance (him in a shirt and tie, her in a blouse), are coded as middle class. Such 'changes' are strategic, of course. The presence of a white, older couple projects an image of heteronormative, middle-class family friendliness. This mature couple, the image suggests, know what they are doing. The video business, the image suggests, is safe in their hands – and those of people like them – as they have the life and work experience to draw from. It is an image that, ultimately, conveys respectability, and belies the racist rhetoric of deceitful South Asian immigrants and East End cowboys that continued to pervade industry discourse.[134] Thus if the interior of the laundrette thus is a 'metaphor for hope' for the socially maligned, then the image adorning the front cover of *Video Shop* represents the hegemonic ideals mobilised to suppress said transgressions in Thatcherite Britain. It is the image of a corporation striving to instil in the video business an image of compliance, of adherence to the status quo. As such, *Laundrette* functions in the most basic of ways as a point of reference exploited by Parkfield to situate Hollywood Nites within a national context: textually, as an initiative to enable to the transformation of staid video shops into (to quote the video box of *Laundrette*), 'veritable palace[s]', and paratextually, as a firm projecting commitment to the success of the British film and video industries.

The campaign worked, in the short term at least. By the end of April 1989, Nites was the second largest chain, having secured over 200 members (approximately fifty-seven premises shy of Ritz's outlets), over 1,000 dealers having made enquiries, and with fifty contracts being sent out per week to dealers throughout the country.[135] Within the year, 600 dealers were operating as part of the symbol group.[136]

However, Parkfield's fate would rapidly change. By the summer of 1990, it became apparent that the company was fraught with financial difficulties – despite the company's best efforts to disguise the fact – and had been for at least twelve months.[137] The deals it made with various major distributors to carry a set number of units of sell-through cassettes, in some cases 'running into the millions', were, it turned out, overambitious.[138] The establishing of Hollywood Nites – hoped to provide the company with the dealer base it needed to fulfil its commitment to the distributors – compounded the problem. The company was overspending, and now, with a slew of exclusive distributor contracts – about 10 million cassettes, but not enough shelf space to stock them – it faced a bottleneck of its own creation.[139] Once news of the company's 'major overstock nightmare' finally broke, Parkfield's share value plummeted, distributors walked away and the company collapsed.[140]

Much of Parkfield's surplus stock was sold off – at times back to its original distributors at a reduced price – eventually materialising on the market, retailing per unit at £4.99 or lower (50 per cent less than its initially projected market value).[141] The outcome for Hollywood Nites members was cruelly ironic. Here was a company quashed by the Thatcherite ambition it championed, and its effect on the self-starters it recruited was damaging. There were no longer any deals that members of the Group stood to benefit from, or the resources to support its promotion at a national level.[142] Members were simply left with a shop facia, their existing stock, in-store signage and a depleting supply of branded carrier bags. Without the clout of major backing, without access to major films and exclusive deals, the entire purpose of the Group was compromised, and there were now hundreds of retailers, once protected by the Group, in the same situation as they were prior to having joined it.[143] And while the VTA initially urged Hollywood Nites members to continue supporting the symbol group, without the infrastructure that Parkfield had provided, the suggestion, while well-intentioned, was futile. Hollywood Nites, for all intents and purposes, was over.[144]

While the Parkfield collapse generated much anger and frustration within the trade itself, the impact it had on the video business's 'public image' was negligible.[145] By this point, chains were legion throughout the country, including Azad Video and Global Video in Scotland, Homerun Video, Titles, Video Magic and The Video Store in England, and Xtra-Vision in Ireland and Northern Ireland, all of which were courting corporate legitimacy.[146] Meanwhile, Cityvision continued to buy up shops and entire regional chains at a rate compared in the press to the videogame character Pac-man: 'computerised creatures obsessively eating everything in their path'.[147] While independents continued to feel the brunt of such rapid proliferation – including a 'price war' in early 1990, which saw the chains lower their prices further in a move to undercut one another – as far as the consumer was concerned, video renting was at its most affordable (as low as 50p for two videos in some Ritz outlets), and there was now an abundance of glossy video shops, oftentimes within close proximity to each other and offering free membership, to choose from.[148] A failed attempt by the tabloids to restoke the video nasties panic later in the year, during which it was reported that a gun-toting murderer in the north east of England took inspiration from the recent horror film *Halloween 4: The Return of Michael Myers* (Dwight H. Little, 1988), showed the extent to which public perception had shifted.[149] The 'image' of video rental in Britain in 1990 was, simply, more respectable.

## The way to Blockbuster

Over the next two years, the respectable image of video would be best embodied by the Blockbuster chain, which had cautiously expanded its UK outlets to a total of twenty-six by 1991.[150] While it was far from the market leader – Ritz had 800 shops to its name – it displayed elements that proved popular with the general public and impressed industry watchers.[151] It was operating a formula known to work in the US, where it had by this point established itself as the nation's biggest chain.[152] It was agreed that, ahead of video or anything else, Blockbuster was simply 'professional', and that its approach to renting and selling videocassettes evidenced a clear understanding of 'the basic principles of *retailing*'. This was a belief shared throughout the industry, including by bosses of other chains.[153] Blockbuster's UK managing director, Mike Toll, explained the principles as such:

> One, focussing on satisfying the family that comes into store to rent or buy product; two, having people capable of running the business; three, buy in depth to satisfy the consumer; four, create an environment that people can enjoy and look forward to; and five, advertise – let people know what's going on.[154]

Other chains were also striving for all of the above, of course (albeit to varying degrees). Ritz, in fact, advocated a similar list in an industrial film

**Figure 5.9** One of Blockbuster's first British stores, Clapham Junction, London. Photographer unknown. Credit: Popular Film and Television Collection.

made in association with CBS/Fox in 1990, entitled 'Who Cares Wins'.[155] Yet Blockbuster, so rang the consensus, seemed to do things *better*.

Blockbuster's approach was favoured by the public and industry alike because it showed a greater degree of innovation in its embracing and promotion of family friendliness than its rival chains. For example, like its US outlets, the chain's British shops did not trade in adult-related material. Contentious genres such as a horror and other 18-certificated videos were stocked sparingly.[156] Moreover, its outlets tended to be thought of as more accommodating of families than those of, say, Ritz. Whereas Ritz's locations tended to be dictated by the established premises of the chains its parent acquired – not in the high street, but rather, to use David Quayle's words, in 'just round the corner places' – Blockbusters were often strategically located in areas frequented by families on days out, such as shopping arcades.[157] Video renting could, therefore, be more easily folded into a family's 'regular shopping routine'.[158] At 7,000–8,000 square feet, its stores were also much bigger than what video consumers were used to; Ritz outlets, by comparison, were smaller, measuring between 500 and 1,500 square feet.[159] Blockbuster stores were therefore more spacious, easier to navigate and could accommodate greater numbers of people. They carried more stock (including, in an industry first, a section for the deaf and hard-of-hearing), had ample parking, three nights rental as standard, later opening hours (Ritz closed at 21.00, Blockbuster at 23.00 or midnight in some locations), and a special box for twenty-four-hour cassette return (later badged 'the Quikdrop') so that customers could fit shop visits around their work/family lives.[160] When a customer arrived at a Blockbuster shop, they could expect unrivalled customer service that, according to contemporary reports, was remarkably consistent from store to store.[161] 'Everywhere staff, however briefly met', one commentator wrote, 'are genuinely friendly.'[162] 'We want people to feel real comfortable in our stores', explained Mike Toll.[163] Lastly, each of its stores (as further testament to their size) had a creche, the 'Kids Corner', 'where children can watch cartoons or play'.[164] The idea was that, if needs be, all members of a family could visit the shop, with adults being able to relax knowing that, when they were making choices for themselves, their kids had something to occupy themselves with. Making video rental an 'event' for 'the whole family' had long been a goal of the British video rental chains. Blockbuster, as far as the public and industry were concerned, came closest to achieving this.[165] Indeed, Blockbuster's membership data told an encouraging story. In 1990 members averaged between 4,000 and 8,000 per store,[166] with the firm's pilot reaching 8,000 within thirty days – then a company record.[167]

Blockbuster proved popular among the trade, too – a rare feat, given the negative press Ritz endured when launching its operation in 1986. Unlike its chief competitor, Blockbuster was widely regarded as measured, strategic – a 'professional' operation, guided by 'a well-honed corporate formula', as opposed to brash opportunism.[168] Of course, as discussed in the introduction to this book, Blockbuster would also garner a reputation for ruthlessness in coming years. But, in the context of late-1980s Britain, there was none of the bluster or shameless declarations of ruthless expansion coming out of Blockbuster HQ that one had come to expect from Ritz. Indeed, across the six-month period spanning late 1989 and mid-1990, Ritz opened seventy shops, while Blockbuster was more restrained, opening twenty-three. Offering 'at least' 10,000 cassettes per store, which included 5,000–6,000 titles and fifty to a hundred copies of major releases, it was inevitable that Blockbuster's impact on independent dealers would be detrimental.[169] But the cautiousness of company executives and the excellent consumer experiences the stores were reported as offering enamoured industry watchers and proved fruitful for the company in each location it launched. Tellingly, in 1990, one of its first UK stores, in Clapham Junction, London, was featured as 'Dealer of the Month' in *Video Business*.[170] The same year, the chain won the BVA award for 'Multiple Retailer of the Year'.[171] In short, Blockbuster, through the layout of its stores, its approach to stock, the customer service it promoted and the family values it espoused, was regarded as a company that was striving to get it right for the business as a whole. Ritz could claim no such vindication.

Blockbuster's well-honed family image and reputation, coupled with its judicious approach to expansion, enabled the company to maintain a steady hand throughout 1991, while many of its contemporaries – Ritz included – fell on hard times. High interest rates, falling house prices and 'an overvalued exchange rate' contributed to a drop in consumer spending throughout the UK.[172] As consumers 'cut back on video rentals', the industry suffered immeasurably, leading to numerous bankruptcies across the gamut of dealers.[173] Xtra-Vision – which operated some forty-nine shops in England, seventy in Northern Ireland and 170 in the Republic of Ireland – was sold to a financial company in early 1991, following an 'over-zealous' plan to secure 1,000 retail sites.[174] A number of other chains facing financial hardship in 1991, such as Azad, The Video Store, Acadia and Video Magic – amounting to 279 shops in all – were all in the hands of receivers by the end of the year.[175]

In times gone by, multiples were able to cope with the 'peaks and troughs' of the business better than smaller outlets,[176] but the industry-wide decline in rentals in the lead up to and throughout the recession meant that Ritz, as the most aggressive domestic spender – and by this point 'Europe's largest video chain' – suffered more.[177] By October 1990, having opened shops at a rate of six per week at the beginning of the year,[178] shares in Cityvision had nosedived.[179] The company had recently expanded into Austria during this time, in a bid to make headway into German-speaking territories; perhaps to help it withstand the economic downturn at home by reaping the benefits of launching in a buoyant foreign market.[180] But with greater overheads in Britain than Blockbuster, it had more to lose. By August 1991, its pre-tax profits had more than halved.[181]

News of Cityvision's misfortunes encouraged Blockbuster executives to take stock of their position in the British market. Elsewhere, the company was expanding at some pace, having established footholds in Australia, Chile, Japan and Venezuela by late 1991.[182] By the end of the year, it was operating 2,000 stores globally, and the company's restrained approach to the British market eventually gave way.[183] When Cityvision started to ail, and rumours began to swell about a possible takeover,[184] Blockbuster executives wasted no time making an offer to the company which, in February 1992, was accepted.[185]

Blockbuster's acquiring of Cityvision enabled the company to penetrate Europe, and increase its global presence by a third. For the British video industry, it marked a turning point. Daniel Herbert argues that Blockbuster's US expansion 'entailed a standardisation of the video rental space throughout many parts of the country; just as Blockbusters became ubiquitous, so was the vision for the video rental store they projected'.[186] In the UK context, the same is true. Since 1985, video dealers had striven for legitimacy by incorporating elements from major high-street retailers. Blockbuster's purchase of Ritz enabled both Blockbuster and the industry as a whole to realise its ambition. While many chains fell afoul of the recession, their greed exposed, Blockbuster was able to harness its desires to monopolise the industry, and project an image of decency that appeared to put the families it served ahead of corporate ruthlessness. Beyond this, some argued that Blockbuster's bid was an essential boost – the UK video business's saving grace.[187] This image was intrinsic to Blockbuster's success in Britain. As the world-leading video chain, Blockbuster offered the British video industry the symbol of decent family entertainment, of video as a 'reputable and professional business', that it had yearned for so long.[188]

This chapter has charted attempts made by various parties in the British rental sector to help improve the video business's public image. From the 'Dealer of the Month' and Superstore 88/89 initiatives to the Hollywood

Nites symbol group, attempts were made to help enable independent storeowners to reclaim their stake in the business and help re-energise the rental sector in the face of rapid change. However, when these independents were challenged by competition from aggressive multiples, including, mostly notably, Ritz, it was clear that independent spirit was never destined to be a match for corporate muscle. The emergence of Blockbuster, and its eventual purchase of Ritz, underscored this truism and signalled changes that had considerable impact on the business as a whole. The following chapter, by way of conclusion, reflects on these changes.

## Notes

1. Derek Mann, 'Year of the Consumer aims to win back customer', *Screen International* 483 (9–16 February 1985), 28.
2. Anon., 'UK's BVA "consumer attitudes" survey detail announced', *Screen International* 516 (28 September 1985), 53.
3. Anon., 'UK's BVA "consumer attitudes"', 53.
4. Rozella quoted in Anon., 'UK's BVA "consumer attitudes", 53.
5. Several of the independent distributors hit hard by the slump in video renting and the rise of the majors reinvented themselves as rack-leasers in 1984, including Berkeley Leisure (formerly distributor Video Brokers), Maybury (formerly Atlantis), Guild and Intervision. New racking operations also emerged in the form of Entertainment Production Services (EPS), the Video Racking Company and the wholesaler, Tredegars. For a brief discussion about racking in the US context, see Joshua M. Greenberg, *From Betamax to Blockbuster: Video Stores and the Invention of Movies on Video* (Cambridge, MA: MIT Press, 2008), 70.
6. Anon., 'Dealers triumph over rackers', *Video Retailer* (14 January 1985), 4.
7. Ripley quoted in John Hazelton, 'Intervision thrives in rack leasing business', *Screen International* 469 (27 October 1984), 278.
8. Anon., 'New BVA council sets July Agenda', *Screen International* 503 (29 June 1985), 34.
9. See, for example, Anon., 'VTA encourages its members to boycott rack leasing companies', *Screen International* 489 (23–30 March 1985), 38. Wholesalers abstaining from racking at the time include S. Gold and Sons and Relay.
10. Charles Robinson, 'Computerised in car city', *Video Business* 4.51 (25 February 1985), 24–5. Quotations at 24.
11. Charles Robinson, 'They've geared up for growth in East Anglia', *Video Business* 5.4 (25 March 1985), 22–3. Quotations at 22 and 23.
12. Colin Staden (owner of Anglia Video) quoted in Robinson, 'They've geared up for growth', 22.
13. Robinson, 'They've geared up for growth', 22. Original emphasis.

14. Peter Lee, 'I believe that the video industry is shaking down', *Video Business* 6.4 (27 January 1986), 18.
15. Anon., 'Rental outlets are cleaning up, says BVA', *Video Business* 6.12 (24 March 1986), 1, 2.
16. Anon., 'Figures go zoom in video boom', *Video Business* 8.10 (9 March 1987), 1, 4. Citation at 1.
17. Anon., 'Figures go zoom in video boom', 1.
18. Jeremy Coopman, 'Cityvision Targets Vid Specialty Chain For British Debut', *Variety* (20 May 1987), 84.
19. Quayle sold his shares in B&Q to F. W. Woolworth in 1981. On his moving into Intervision see Anon., 'Quayle in joint plan for Intervision', *Billboard* (30 May 1986), 4. For an overview of the man himself and his various operations contemporaneous to the late 1980s/early 1990s see Peter Goodwin, 'David Quayle', *Broadcast* (9 March 1990), 10.
20. Hazleton, 'Intervision thrives in rack leasing', 270.
21. Anon., 'Quayle in joint plan', 4.
22. Warren Phillips, 'Peacock's leaks help ITV shares', *Broadcast* (6 June 1986), 7.
23. Anon., 'New name, line up for UK's Intervision', *Screen International* 561 (16 August 1986), 4.
24. Anon., 'Libraries in the pink, says survey', *Video Business* 8.15 (13 April 1987), 1, 4. Citation at 4.
25. John Hazelton, 'Video "supermarkets" prepare to launch in the UK', *Screen International* 605 (20 June 1987), 33.
26. Greenberg, *From Betamax to Blockbuster*, 127. On Blockbuster's founding see Lisa Lilenthal, 'New Dallas Operation Aims To Be Biggest and Best', *Billboard* 97.42 (19 October 1985), 30, 33; on its expansion see Anon., 'Blockbuster Stores on Expansion Route', *Variety* 323.12 (16 July 1986), 31.
27. Anon., '£ millions sought for video chain', *Video Business* 8.7 (11 February 1987), 1.
28. Hazelton, 'Video "supermarkets"', 33.
29. On the West Coast's success in the US see Debbie Rosenblum, 'West Coast is Expanding: Chain Learns from McDonald's', *Billboard* 98.21 (24 May 1986), 53–4. Citation at 53.
30. Stone cited in Rosenblum, 'West Coast is Expanding', 53.
31. Huizenga cited in Greenburg, *From Betamax to Blockbuster*, 127. See also Raiford Guins, *Edited Clean Version: Technology and the Culture of Control* (Minneapolis: University of Minnesota Press, 2009), 102–3.
32. Stone cited in Rosenblum, 'West Coast is Expanding', 53.
33. George Ritzer, *The McDonaldization of Society: Into the Digital Age* (9th edition, Thousand Oaks: Sage, 2019), 19.
34. Stone cited in Rosenblum, 'West Coast is Expanding', 54.
35. Tony Barrow, 'US muscle ready for the retail hustle', *Video Business* 8.23 (8 June 1987), 22.

36. Ritzer, *The McDonaldization of Society*, 20.
37. Rosenblum, 'West Coast is Expanding', 53–4.
38. Rosenblum, 'West Coast is Expanding', 54.
39. Rosenblum, 'West Coast is Expanding', 54.
40. Ritzer, *The McDonaldization of Society*, 22.
41. Barrow, 'US muscle', 21.
42. Stone cited in Rosenblum, 'West Coast is Expanding', 54. On McDonald's and 'control', see Ritzer, *The McDonaldization of Society*, 22 and, specifically, chapters 4 and 6.
43. Abbott cited in Hazelton, 'Video "supermarkets"', 33.
44. Hazelton, 'Video "supermarkets"', 33.
45. See Hazelton, 'Video "supermarkets"', 33; and Peter Dean, 'Video's Big Macs set to clean up', *The Guardian* (1 June 1987), 9.
46. Anon., 'Cityvision to control 100 chainstores', *Video Business* 8.29 (11 May 1987), 1.
47. Anon., 'Cityvision to control 100', 1.
48. Rosenblum, 'West Coast is Expanding', 54.
49. On McDonaldisation and market domination see Ritzer, *The McDonaldization of Society*, 22. On West Coast as a 'bully boy American company' see Anonymous video dealer quoted in Hazelton, 'Video "supermarkets"', 33.
50. Anon., 'Offscreen' reprinted in *Video Business* 8.23 (6 June 1988), 13. Capitalisation in original.
51. Anon., 'Cityvision Paving Way for National Vid Library Chain', *Variety* 229.13 (20 January 1988), 110.
52. On Taylor's resignation see Anon., 'Taylor says goodbye to West Coast', *Video Business* 8.30 (27 July 1987), 1, 4. On the alleged reasons behind said resignation see Anon., 'UK plan cut to 24 outlets', *Video Business* 8.39 (3 October 1988), 6.
53. On West Coast see Anon., 'Up-market debut for West Coast', *Video Business* 8.6 (8 February 1988), 18; on Ritz see Anon., 'Cityvision promotion', *Video Business* 8.7 (15 February 1988), 1.
54. Anon., 'UK plan cut to 24 outlets'.
55. Peter Lee, 'Expansion: no apologies' (letter), *Video Business* 8.23 (6 June 1988), 13.
56. Lee quoted in Anon., 'Watch out for a chain reaction', *Video Business* 8.28 (11 July 1988), 1.
57. Fred Oldfield cited in Charles Robinson, 'Tykes taking on West Coast', *Video Business* 8.31 (3 August 1987), 20.
58. Neel quoted in Anon., 'Watch out for a chain reaction', 1.
59. Chris Windle (of CBS/Fox) quoted in Anon., 'Windle criticises UK video dealers', *Video Business* 8.22 (1 June 1987), 4.
60. Anon., 'Glen from US slams poor shops he's seen', *Video Business* 8.24 (13 June 1988), 27. An article printed in *Variety* includes some choice quotes from the marketing executive in question, Peter Glen, taken from

the conference at which he spoke, 'Video 88'. Pointing to a slide image of one shop, he reportedly said to the crowd (comprising dealers from across the country), 'Look at this store. It's one great big awful yawn. It could be anywhere. It could be in Africa, it could be in hell. You have the luck of being an independent, so why not do something instead of just sitting there hoping that one of these days God will be good to you and take out a few rentals . . . Nobody gives a damn . . . It's as if the industry just had [sic] no respect for itself.' Glen quoted in Anon., 'Glen Slams Brit Vid Twits', *Variety* 100.27 (2 July 1988), 56, 58. Quotation at 58.

61. Nick Robertshaw, 'UK Tape Industry Overcomes the "Video Nasties"', *Billboard* 100.27 (2 July 1988), 56.
62. Anon., 'Dealers! Win a refit!', *Video Business* 8.23 (6 June 1988), 1.
63. Anon., 'Win a £20,000 shop refit', *Video Business* 8.23 (6 June 1988), 25.
64. Anon., 'Dealers! Win a refit!', 1.
65. Anon., 'Trade alert: VRA crackdown close', *Video Business* (26 October 1987), 1, 4. See also Anon., 'VRA must be seen to be enforced', *Video Business* (30 November 1987), 4.
66. Julian Petley argues in Petley, *Film and Video Censorship*, that the 'Rambo' connection was made '[s]imply because [Ryan] wore a bandana' (70, n.3). And, as David Buckingham explains, 'it later transpired' that Ryan 'had never seen' any of the films in the series. See Buckingham, 'Electronic child abuse? Rethinking the media's effects on children', in Martin Barker and Julian Petley (eds), *Ill Effects: The Media/Violence Debate* (2nd edition, London: Routledge, 2001), 63–77. Quotation at 76, n.15.
67. Anon., 'Dealers! Win a refit!', 1.
68. John Corner and Sylvia Harvey, 'Introduction: Great Britain Limited', in John Corner and Sylvia Harvey (eds), *Enterprise and Heritage: Crosscurrents of National Culture* (London: Routledge, 1991), 1–20.
69. John Corner and Sylvia Harvey, 'Mediating tradition and modernity: the heritage/enterprise couplet', in Corner and Harvey (eds), *Enterprise and Heritage: Crosscurrents of National Culture* (London: Routledge, 1991), 45–73. Quotations at 64.
70. Anon., 'A sneak preview of your entries', *Video Business* 8.28 (11 July 1988), 18.
71. Anon., 'A sneak preview of your entries', 18.
72. Anon., 'Operating on a tight budget', *Video Business* 8.39 (3 October 1988), 20–1. Quotation at 20.
73. Anon., 'Operating on a tight budget', 20.
74. Anon., 'The computer challenge', *Video Business* 8.45 (14 November 1988), 26.
75. Anon., 'Superstore "88"', *Video Business* 8.49 (12 December 1988), 22–3. Quotation at 22.
76. Rex Anderson, 'Getting a screen silvered', *Video Business* 9.9 (27 February 1989), 28–9.

77. Anderson, 'Getting a screen silvered', 28.
78. Anon., 'Could it be you in 1989?', *Video Business* 9.25 (19 June 1989), 32–3.
79. Rex Anderson, 'A third chance', *Video Business* 9.38 (18 September 1989), 28.
80. Anon., 'Cityvision seeks full listing as 500th store opens', *Video Business* 9.48 (28 November 1989), 1.
81. The film in question, *My Beautiful Video Shop*, is discussed in detail below, and can be watched, in full, online: http://www.drjohnnywalker.co.uk/rewind-replay-resources.html.
82. Feldman quoted in Anon., 'Feldman buys into Hollywood Nites', *Screen International* 503 (29 June – 6 July, 1985), 34.
83. The definition of 'symbol group' employed here is that of the Institute of Grocery Distribution (IGD), available at: https://www.igd.com/articles/article-viewer/t/symbol-groups-market-overview/i/15516 (accessed 21 April 2021). See also: Bob Mersey, 'What's happening to the GROCERY SYMBOL GROUPS?', *Retail and Distribution management* 1.2 (1 February 1973), 44–8.
84. Hollywood Nites promotional leaflet (c.1988), n.p.
85. See Anon., 'Hollywood Nites goes TV route on retail', *Video Business* 8.49 (12 December 1988), 4; and Anon., 'Protection promised for a thousand Nites', *Video Business* 8.50 (19 December 1988), 4.
86. Anon., 'Summertime blues are banished by biggest-ever TV campaign', *Video Business* 8.23 (6 June 1988), 1.
87. See also, for example, Anon., '£700,000 consumer campaign', *Video Business* 8.46 (16 November 1987), 1, 4. Quotation at 1.
88. Anon., 'Hollywood Nites on target for 500 stores', *Video Business* 9.2 (9 January 1989), 1.
89. Paul Feldman cited in Anon., 'Protection promised for a thousand Nites', 4. In the interest of clarity, prior to Hollywood Nites, one unsuccessful attempt was made to launch a *regional* symbol group: the East Midlands-based Imagination group of 'family entertainment centres'. However, this was a very small operation in comparison to Parkfield. It was promoted a few times in the trade press, but, in its attempt to attract retailers just as the Hollywood Nites initiative was starting up, it was rapidly eclipsed. See Anon., 'Symbol chain logo', *Video Business* 8.46 (21 November 1988), 14.
90. See *My Beautiful Video Shop*. On the VSC's 'Code of Practice' – including the Code in its entirety – see Anon., 'The good VSC guide to the galaxy', *Video Business* 10.14 (2 April 1990), 28–9. The VSC was headed by former Home Secretary, Merlyn Rees, and supported by then Home Secretary, David Mellor. It was conceived as the main association for both dealers and distributors and as a bridge between their operations and the government. While it was not a legal requirement, Mellor demanded all dealers become members. See Anon., 'Mellor warns: join VSC or else', *Video Business* 10.27 (2 July 1990), 1.

91. Sean Whelan, 'Video chain sets the pace', *Marketing* (8 June 1989).
92. See Anon., 'Mandy moves', *Video Business* 8.46 (21 November 1988), 11.
93. Charles Robinson, 'THIS NITES A SYMBOL OF FUTURE?', *Video Business* 9.8 (20 February 1989), 34–5.
94. Daniel Herbert argues that the Blockbuster chain specifically 'crystalized the idea that the video store was a *movie* store.' See Daniel Herbert, *Videoland: Move Culture at the American Video Store* (Berkeley: University of California Press, 2014), 34.
95. Richard Maltby, *Hollywood Cinema: An Introduction* (2nd edition, Oxford: Wiley-Blackwell, 2002), 6.
96. Kate Egan explores the 'alien' qualities of video nasties, and how their distributors capitalised on this, in *Trash or Treasure? Censorship and the Changing Meanings of the Video Nasties* (Manchester: Manchester University Press, 2007), 50–61.
97. Anon., cited in Christine Geraghty, *British Cinema in the Fifties: Gender, Genre and the 'New Look'* (London: Routledge, 2000), 7.
98. Geraghty, *British Cinema in the Fifties*, 6.
99. Geraghty, *British Cinema in the Fifties*, 6.
100. Stuart Hanson, *Screening the World: Global Development of the Multiplex Cinema* (Cham: Palgrave Macmillan, 2019), 100–5.
101. Hanson, *Screening the World*, 90–1.
102. Paul Ladensack (architect) quoted in Hanson, *Screening the World*, 40.
103. Mark Batey, CEO of the Film Distributors' Association, remarked that, until the opening of The Point, '[c]onsumers had forgotten about cinema'. Quoted in Hanson, *Screening the World*, 102. On the multiplex and the family audience, including children, in the British context, see p. 103 of the same volume.
104. Charles Wesoky (of AMC) quoted in Hanson, *Screening the World*, 102.
105. Floyd quoted in Hanson, *Screening the World*, 102.
106. Hanson, *Screening the World*, 117.
107. Maltby, *Hollywood Cinema*, 6.
108. Thank you to Sarah Thomas and Phyll Smith for alerting me to the correct terminology regarding the 'fantail cartouche'.
109. Parkfield (Hollywood Nites), untitled trade advertisement, *BVA Video 89 Show Guide* (May 1989), 27.
110. Parkfield (Hollywood Nites), untitled trade advertisement, *BVA Video 89 Show Guide* (May 1989), 27.
111. Hanson, *Screening the World*, 154. On 'family' appeal see 68.
112. Richard Kuisel quoted in George Ritzer, *The McDonaldization Thesis* (London: Sage, 1998), 71. Kuisel (and others) is writing specifically in the French context where, Ritzer summarises, 'American colonization' – symbolised by the presence of major US brands such as a Coca Cola – threatens the 'loss of traditional European spirit; of a "tainting" of the European "soul" . . .' (73).

113. Anon., 'US convenience store threat to the UK', *Video Business* 7.51 (22 December 1986), 1.
114. Anon., 'Windle criticises UK video dealers'.
115. Anon., 'Keep video British, say angry dealers', *Video Business* 9.9 (27 February 1989), 4.
116. Robinson, 'THIS NITES', 34.
117. See *My Beautiful Video Shop*.
118. Webster cited in Egan, *Trash or Treasure?*, 31.
119. See Hollywood Nites promotional leaflet and the reverse video sleeve of *My Beautiful Video Shop*.
120. Parkfield (Hollywood Nites), untitled trade advertisement, *BVA Video 89 Show Guide* (May 1989), 27.
121. Michael Billig, *Banal Nationalism* (London: Sage, 1995), 93.
122. Parkfield (Hollywood Nites), untitled trade advertisement, *Video Business* 9.16 (17 April 1989), 7.
123. Billig, *Banal Nationalism*, 93.
124. *My Beautiful Laundrette* was originally conceived as a modest made-for-television production for the nascent Channel 4, but subsequently achieved a theatrical release in the UK, and secured distribution overseas. On the film's production history see Christine Geraghty, *My Beautiful Laundrette* (London: I. B. Tauris, 2005), 6–26.
125. The film was in-and-out of the top twenty most-rented videos for three months between April and June 1986. See, for example, 'Video Top 20: Rentals', *Screen International* (7 June 1986), 25.
126. Geraghty, *My Beautiful Laundrette*, 13. Sukhdev Sandhu argues further that, at the time of the film's release, British cinema 'had been widely regarded as moribund by cultural critics. Its biggest successes – such as the Oscar-winning *Chariots of Fire* (1981) or the work of Merchant and Ivory – were set in the past, preoccupied with the mores of the upper- or upper-middle classes, and formally rather unadventurous.' By comparison, *Laundrette* 'grappled with contemporary social and racial issues that were widely seen as divisive'. Sukhdev Sandu, 'An introduction to *My Beautiful Laundrette*', British Library, available at: https://www.bl.uk/20th-century-literature/articles/an-introduction-to-my-beautiful-laundrette#.
127. David Bordwell, Kristin Thompson and Jeff Smith, *Film Art: An Introduction*, 11th edition (New York: McGraw Hill, 2017), 58.
128. Sandu, 'An introduction to *My Beautiful Laundrette*'.
129. Geraghty, *My Beautiful Laundrette*, 53.
130. Geraghty, *My Beautiful Laundrette*, 53.
131. Jorge Berástegui Wood, 'The Analysis of Hybridity in *My Beautiful Laundrette*', *Revista Canaria de Estudios Ingleses* Año 54 (2007), 137–47. Citation at 147.
132. Sandu, 'An introduction to *My Beautiful Laundrette*'.

133. Duncan J. Petrie, *Creativity and Constraint in the British Film Industry* (New York: Palgrave Macmillan, 1991), 210. Added emphasis. Geraghty notes in her book on the film that the film was knowingly 'operating in controversial waters', yet 'those critics who liked the film felt that the relationship was at the joyous heart of the story'. See Geraghty, *My Beautiful Laundrette*, 23.
134. See, for example, Rob Wait, 'Turning over the Indian clubs', *Video Business* 8.26 (27 June 1988), 12.
135. Anon., 'Nites poised to be largest', *Video Business* 9.11 (13 March 1989), 1; Anon., 'A rush to join Nites', *Video Business* 9.12 (20 March 1989), 8; Anon., 'Gathering Nites in May', *Video Business* 9.17 (24 April 1989), 1, 4.
136. John Hayward, 'A case of big plans and over ambition', *Video Business* 10.31 (30 July 1990), 12–13.
137. Tony May, 'Parkfield calls in administrators', *The Guardian* (20 July 1990), 15; Dan Atkinson, 'Parkfield "window dressed books to avoid bankruptcy"', *The Guardian* (27 April 1991).
138. Hayward, 'A case of big plans and over ambition', 12.
139. Anon., 'Parkfield puts video at risk', *Video Business* 10.30 (23 July 1990), 1, 4. See also, Hayward, 'A case of big plans and over ambition', 13.
140. Hayward, 'A case of big plans and over ambition', 13. Anon., 'Companies drop Parkfield', *Video Business* 10.30 (23 July 1990), 8; Anon., 'Parkfield peddle parts', *Video Business* 10.32 (6 August 1990), 1.
141. Anon., 'Low price flood threat', *Video Business* 10.31 (30 July 1990), 1.
142. Anon., 'Parkfield crash hits all parts of video industry', *Video Business* 10.31 (30 July 1990), 1.
143. Hayward, 'A case of big plans and over ambition', 13; Anon., 'Legal question over Hollywood Nites', *Video Business* 10.31 (30 July 1990), 1.
144. Anon., 'Parkfield peddle parts', 1.
145. Harvey Lee, 'World's No. 3 video market feels the big chill', *Variety* (25 January 1991), 70.
146. On Global Video see Ian McFadden, 'The other chain's face', *Video Business* 10.13 (26 March 1990), 23; on Azad see Ian McFadden, 'Competition essential for healthy business', *Video Business* 10.44 (10 November 1990), 10; on Homerun see Charles Robinson, 'Prototype for national superstore network', *Video Business* 10.20 (11 June 1990), 20; on Video Magic see Boyd Farrow, 'Meaty & Magical', *Video Business* 10.6 (5 February 1990), 6; on Titles see Anon., 'Kingfisher swoops for £3.3m Titles', *Video Business* 9.20 (15 May 1989), 1, 4; on The Video Store see Anon., 'Video Store's £5 million', *Video Business* 10.8 (19 February 1990), 1; and on Xtra-Vision see Anon., 'Chain trebles profit', *Video Business* 10.20 (11 June 1990), 4.
147. Reg Thompson, 'But will it buy me love?' *Video Business* 10.8 (19 February 1990), 19. On Ritz's acquisitions in 1990, including its purchasing of the 44-shop strong Superflicks chain, see Anon., 'In Brief', *Marketing* (22 February 1990).

148. Anon., 'High Streets hit by price war plague', *Video Business* 10.3 (15 January 1990), 1. Once again, Peter Lee of Ritz stood defiant, telling the trade press that 'we can go cheaper than anybody if we have to'. Lee quoted in Anon., 'High Streets hit', 1. See also: Boyd Farrow, 'Price wars: Portsmouth is a lesson to us all', *Video Business* 10.15 (9 April 1990), 16; and Anon., '"Diabolical" Azad sparks price war', *Video Business* 10.7 (12 February 1990), 4.
149. Anon., 'BVA braced for tabloid attack', *Video Business* 10.19 (7 May 1990), 1.
150. Lee, 'World's No. 3', 70.
151. Lee, 'World's No. 3', 70.
152. Richard Westlund, 'The Blockbuster Philosophy: Dominate the Marketplace, Serve the Customer', *Billboard* 103.43 (26 October 1991), B-4, B-15.
153. Stephen Moore (MD of Nottingham-based chain, FoxVideo) quoted in Sean King, 'Retailer's winning formula', *Video Business* 11.46 (16 November 1991), 21. Added emphasis.
154. Toll quoted in King, 'Retailer's winning formula', 21.
155. Reg Thompson, 'Good staff: a priority asset', *Video Business* 10.19 (7 May 1990), 19. The entire video is available to stream at http://drjohnnywalker.co.uk/rewind-replay-resources.
156. Anon., 'US superchain opens up in Welling', *Video Business* 9.50 (11 December 1989), 8.
157. Quayle quoted in Lisa Buckingham, 'Video booms as it improves its image', *The Guardian* (11 March 1989), 11.
158. Toll quoted in King, 'Retailer's winning formula', 21.
159. Peter Dean, 'Gap between stores to widen', *Video Business* 10.24 (11 June 1990), 14–15. Citation at 15. See also Buckingham, 'Video booms as it improves its image', 11.
160. Charles Robinson, 'Blockbuster keeps it in the family', *Video Business* 10.23 (4 June 1990), 14–15. Quotation at 14. On the company's 'deaf and hard-of-hearing' initiative, see Anon., 'B'buster opens special section', *Video Business* 10.46 (3 November 1990), 6.
161. King, 'Retailer's winning formula', 21.
162. Robinson, 'Blockbuster keeps it in the family', 15.
163. Toll quoted in King, 'Retailer's winning formula', 21.
164. Anon., 'US superchain opens up in Welling', 8.
165. The British chain Homerun also had a kids' play area (itself modelled on Blockbuster), but, following press buzz around the opening of its flagship store, the chain failed to penetrate the market. See Robinson, 'Prototype for national superstore network', 20–1.
166. Robinson, 'Blockbuster keeps it in the family', 15.
167. Peter Dean, 'Ritz Buys Vid House, As UK's Big Chains Get Bigger', *Billboard* 102.21 (26 May 1990), 61, 67. Citation at 61.
168. Robinson, 'Blockbuster keeps it in the family', 14.
169. Robinson, 'Blockbuster keeps it in the family', 15.

170. Robinson, 'Blockbuster keeps it in the family', 14–15.
171. Anon., 'Industry acknowledges the best campaigns and dealers of 1990', *Video Business* 10.28 (9 July 1990), 4.
172. Tejvan Pettinger, 'UK Recession of 1991–92', *Economics Help* (28 November 2017), available at: https://www.economicshelp.org/macroeconomics/economic-growth/uk-recession-1991/.
173. Rich Zahradnik, 'Cityvision See Plunge in Pretax Earnings', *Billboard* (3 August 1991).
174. Paul Verna, 'Irish Video Chain Xtra-vision Sold After Disappointing Year', *Billboard* (26 January 1991).
175. On Azad, see Anon., 'Azad brothers bid to buy own firm from liquidator', *The Sunday Times* (24 March 1991); on the other chains see Peter Dean, 'UK Face Vid-Chain Fallout on High Street; Blame Laid on Banks, High Rentals, Bad Economy', *Billboard* (14 December 1991).
176. Dean, 'Gap between stores to widen', 14.
177. See Peter Dean, 'Ritz, UK Vid Giant, Expanding To Continent; Chain's Parent Buying Austrian Web As First Step', *Billboard* (15 June 1990).
178. Dean, 'UK Face Vid-Chain Fallout'.
179. Gillian Bowditch, 'Cityvision plunges on broker's revision', *The Times* (20 October 1990).
180. Dean, 'Ritz, UK Vid Giant, Expanding to Continent'.
181. Zahradnik, 'Cityvision Sees Plunge in its Pretax Earnings', (3 August 1991); Peter Dean, 'Cityvision May Be Takeover Target After Stock Plunges', *Billboard* (10 August 1991).
182. Charles Flowers, 'Blockbuster Around the World', Blockbuster advertising supplement, *Billboard* 103.43 (26 October 1991), B-17.
183. Anon., 'A Blockbuster Timeline: 1985–1991', Blockbuster advertising supplement, *Billboard* 103.43 (26 October 1991), B-13–B-14.
184. Dean, 'Cityvision May Be Takeover Target After Stock Plunges'.
185. Paul Verna, 'Blockbuster Wraps Buy of UK Chain Cityvision', Billboard (15 February 1992), 6.
186. Herbert, *Videoland*, 35.
187. Terry Ilott, 'Blockbuster's bid could boost UK vid biz', *Variety* 345.8 (2 December 1991), 66.
188. Mann, 'Year of the Consumer aims to win back customer', 28.

CONCLUSION

# Video Legacies

*Rewind, Replay* has mapped the evolution of video distribution and retail in Britain, from its beginnings in 1978 up to Blockbuster's acquisition of the Ritz Video chain in 1992. This chapter considers the post-Ritz video business in Britain and the legacy of the Britain's video boom in popular culture today.

My decision to draw things to a close in 1992, has, when I've presented parts of this research at conferences and the like, led to probing questions and comments from audience members. 'Surely, it doesn't just end with Blockbuster?' '1992 strikes me as somewhat of an arbitrary year.' 'What about DVD and Blu Ray? While we're at it, what about *Netflix*?' These questions are all valid, of course. And yes, as I remarked in the previous chapter, the story doesn't 'just end' with Blockbuster: the coming of DVD and subsequent technological developments – from rental-by-mail to Video on Demand – all impacted both distribution and retail in distinctive ways. Britain has stories to tell about all of this.

But one needs to end somewhere, and there is, in fact, good reason for wrapping things up (as much as one can) in the early 1990s. While I am wary to speak of any 'clean breaks' in British video history, Blockbuster's acquisition of Ritz does signal a turning point for the domestic video business. I discuss in the introduction to this book how Blockbuster is regarded – as scholarly interventions by the likes of Guins, Herbert and Greenberg, and the film *The Last Blockbuster*, show – as an aggressive corporate force that had a dramatic and largely negative impact on the operations of the entire video business.[1] Indeed, in Britain, by the mid-1990s, there were half the number of rental outlets in the UK as there had been in the late 1980s, with Blockbuster operating 10 per cent of these.[2]

The success of Blockbuster in Britain represented somewhat of a double-edged sword. As Chapter 5 shows, the British video business *needed* a respectable face to quell the onslaught of negative publicity following the video nasties panic and the ensuing slump in video rentals, with Blockbuster's squeaky-clean image helping to appease the government, suggest that there was in fact a future for video shops, and afford the BVA some relief in the process. By the early 1990s it was even more apparent that the industry's image had much to gain from Blockbuster's expansion, perverse through it seemed given the rapidity with which it was opening new stores to the despair of independent retailers.[3] In 1993, public concern around violent videos and their effect on children swelled once more, when Merseyside toddler, James Bulger, was murdered by two older children who the press falsely claimed had taken inspiration from the horror video *Child's Play 3* (Jack Bender, 1991). The media response was volatile, there were several headlines akin to those of the 1980s, a dubious report published projecting direct correlation between violent videos and violence in reality, and stricter censorship brought in.[4] A number of video chains came out in support of the spurious claims. These included Global Video, which promptly removed all copies of the three films in the *Child's Play* franchise from its shelves.[5] The Azad chain went a step further, reportedly burning 300 copies (an act that led to a now infamous front page from *The Sun* showing a stack of *Childs Play 3* cassettes aflame, the headline bellowing 'For the sake of ALL our kids . . . BURN YOUR VIDEO NASTY').[6] Blockbuster, however, chose to buck the trend. Rather than bow to the pressure as its main competitors were doing, the company's spokesperson expressed defiance, taking the opportunity to claim confidence in video's regulatory system, and thus signal to industry observers that the measures in place to protect children were adequate and that the video business was now equipped to protect its own interests and those of the consumers it served. 'We strictly adhere to [British Board of Film Classification] guidelines. The video has got an 18 certificate, which we strictly enforce . . . It is ultimately down to parents.'[7] Blockbuster's entire reputation hinged on its public 'family' image, of trading in reputable entertainment, of being especially selective when it came to stocking horror films and 'protecting' families and children from the alleged threats of pornography and so on.[8] In continuing to trade in *Child's Play 3*, and placing the responsibility in the hands of the families it served, Blockbuster showed solidarity with the industry as a whole, defending its rights, its reputation and, by extension, its independent contemporaries.

Its actions proved good PR for the video business, helping it weather the storms caused by subsequent film/video controversies as with *Natural Born Killers* (Oliver Stone, 1994), *Crash* (David Cronenberg, 1996) and others.[9] But whatever support for the industry Blockbuster's show of

## Shifts

defiance intimated, it was ultimately disingenuous, hinging more on protecting its own interests than the independents it continued to buy – and/or price – out.

This situation was compounded by the onslaught of video rackers which, having failed to have the impact many feared in the mid-1980s (discussed in Chapter 5), by the 1990s were pricing many competitors out of the game. As briefly alluded to in the previous chapter, one such example was Video Box Office, a racker established in 1984 by the Guild video distribution company and acquired the following year by Guild's former MD – and a former Chair of the BVA – Iain Muspratt.[10] With several of his ex-Guild colleagues, Muspratt turned Video Box Office into a formidable force in the 1990s, supplying around 6,000 retail outlets throughout the country, including convenience store multiples such as the SPAR symbol group. With capital gained from Video Box Office, Muspratt's company, Home Entertainment, was then able to establish the Choices video chain, a minor rival to the likes of Blockbuster, but one that nevertheless added to the pressures independent operators were enduring. It was, for example, the first British chain to experiment with online DVD 'rental-by-mail', a model that the LoveFilm and Netflix companies would refine and then dominate the market with in the mid-2000s.[11] Choices, along with other chains such as Global, squeezed the independent sector on account of their corporate muscle alone, with their smaller competitors unable to compete with latter-day postal schemes, or indeed the 'revenue sharing' arrangements the multiples had had with major Hollywood studios since the early 1990s, which enabled them to buy more copies of the top titles at a considerable discount.[12] And, while some of the better-resourced independents were able to keep their head above water in other ways by, for example, buying into Blockbuster and becoming a franchise store, or by renting video games (which had remained 'a vibrant business' since the beginning of the 1990s), the losses made on films through revenue sharing, and the rise of the internet and illegal downloading, proved impossible for many to withstand.[13]

Such pressures would eventually catch up with Blockbuster and Choices, too, of course. As discussed in the introduction to this book, Blockbuster filed for bankruptcy in 2010, and presently has one store remaining, in Oregon. Choices went a few years earlier, in 2007, citing the internet and the rise in 'on demand' services as principal reasons.[14] However, another factor that saw the demise of rental stores is the year-on-year rise of the

Figure C.1 Video Box Office membership card, c. early 2000s. Credit: Popular Film and Television Collection.

Figure C.2 Choices – one of Blockbuster's British rivals. Photographer unknown. Credit: Popular Film and Television Collection.

sell-through market, which continued to grow throughout the 1990s and, following the launch of DVD in 1997, into the new millennium. As discussed in Chapter 5, the Parkfield crash of 1990 led to the market being saturated with millions of sell-through cassettes, leading to a situation that some industry executives predicted the business would struggle to overcome. However, the buoyancy of sell-through enabled the market to level out much quicker than anticipated.

By 1992, in terms of national popularity, sell-through and rental were neck-and-neck. Within two years, the former overtook the latter for first time in video business history.[15] The reasons for this are the same as those that explained the overnight success of The Video Collection and its competitors in the mid-1980s: affordability and 'collectability'.[16] This was reflected by the operations of sell-through distributors, the majority of which had now created sublabels, which led to a broad array of different title groupings that harkened back to the catalogues of the first video companies. As discussed in Chapter 1, when Warner Bros launched into British video in 1980, its branding sought to unify its releases according to their statuses as Warner Bros films: the distribution company was the thread that bound them together and cause enough for consumers to choose its product over that of its competitors. A decade later, this strategy could no longer be relied on, and it became increasingly common for major distributors to do what independents such as Intervision, Fletcher, Mountain and others adopted in the beginning, and utilise sub-branding, employing sub-categorisations to speak to, for example, genre or other distinguishing qualifiers (see Chapter 3). Warner Bros thus had a Screen Classics label, a Maverick Directors label, a Family Entertainment label, a horror label ('Terror Vision') and so on.[17]

The major distributors did very well during this period because of their revenue sharing arrangements with chain stores and the popularity of their product in the sell-through market. However, whereas it was easy for the majors to straddle both rental and retail, independents tended to find greater success in sell-through. There were some exceptions to this rule: Guild and Medusa, for example, maintained both profitable rental and sell-through iterations, as did newer labels such as First Independent. However, as rental began to slump following the recession in the early 1990s, and to experience further peaks and troughs in the years that followed, sell-through continued to generate large turnovers, initially in non-filmic product. Indeed, in the mid-1990s, 75 per cent of the sell-through business was given over to the likes of television comedy, sports titles and children's cartoons – preferences apparent since the market's inception in the winter of 1985.[18] And, just as The Video Collection skyrocketed to become one of the most successful independent distributors of the era, by the following decade a flurry of independent rivals revelled in the fortuity of not being hamstrung by having to acquire the rights to expensive feature films to compete with the major players. The widespread popularity of children's entertainment was especially welcome. To keep costs down, and because VHS replication labs charged per the length of magnetic tape, such programmes would routinely run for an hour or less: a factor that did not appear to limit consumer interest.[19] And, as in the early 1980s, public domain cartoons from the 1950s and 1960s repeatedly found their way onto the market, repackaged to appear contemporary. Labels well-suited to this context included the likes of the aptly named Pocket Money Video, as were industry stalwarts such as Palace and newer generalist labels such as Missing in Action, whose early 1990s reissues of public domain Superman cartoons – the Max Fleischer serials of the 1940s issued onto cassette in the 1980s by Mountain and others – allowed the companies to trade in lucrative superhero properties in the wake of Tim Burton's blockbuster success *Batman* (1989), and new television shows, such as *Batman: The Animated Series* (1992–5) and *Lois & Clark: The New Adventures of Superman* (1993–7), without the big outlay typically required to license wares from the likes of Warner Bros and the characters' rightsholder DC Comics. Independent distributors could therefore quickly meet the demand for children's entertainment of a similar ilk, use little magnetic tape, sell cassettes at budget prices and profit handsomely.

The affordability of sell-through also opened collectors' markets in a host of niche areas that independent companies were well positioned to exploit.[20] Companies such as the British Film Institute, for instance, provided cineastes with access to art films that were otherwise difficult to obtain, such as Dudow and Brecht's *Kuhle Wampe* (1932). Softcore pornography also remained as popular as ever, following the ongoing success of 1980s stalwarts such as Electric Blue and a boom in direct-to-video erotic thrillers modelled on the success of the likes of *Basic Instinct* (Paul Verhoeven, 1992).[21] Realty-themed programmes made especially for video release, such as 1994's *Police Stop!* (a compilation of 'real life police pursuits'), led to the establishment of at least twelve new companies specialising in such fare, with some titles selling as many as ninety units per day from high street retailers.[22] Another growth area for independent companies was horror and exploitation films. This market, in part, gave way to affordable video nasty reissues which, as briefly discussed in Chapter 4, and which, as Kate Egan and Mark McKenna have explored at length, enabled independent companies to thrive on the controversy of the recent moral panic in spite of the fact that sell-through versions of previously banned titles such as *Zombie Flesh Eaters* (Lucio Fulci, 1979) and *Death Trap* (Tobe Hooper, 1976), were subjected to considerable cuts by the censor.[23] Success enjoyed by the relaunched VIPCO label inspired others to cash in on nostalgia for the nasties, such as horror and exploitation specialists Satanica, Crypt Keeper and Exploited, whereas other independent distributors, such as Redemption Films and Nouveau Pictures, drew less on the controversy of the nasties, instead looking to reclaim particular titles as misunderstood masterworks of the horror genre.[24]

There are countless other examples of sell-through success stories that collectively speak to the buoyancy of video retail and the threat it posed for the rental sector. Following the advent of DVD in 1997, consumer demand for sell-through product grew further, exacerbated by, among other reasons, the shortening of the respective 'windows' between a film's theatrical, video rental and sell-through release – the first *Harry Potter* film (Chris Columbus, 2001), for example, was released to rental and sell-through simultaneously – and the uptake of sell-through product by supermarket chains throughout the country.[25] The ubiquity of affordable titles in sell-through made the idea of paying a couple of pounds to rent a film once, when the same film could be acquired for £7 or less from Asda in the mid-2000s, a futile notion.[26] This, along with rise of internet piracy, and new means of formally accessing entertainment through Netflix and elsewhere meant that, in Britain, as elsewhere in the world, the days of video rental as a habitual practice were numbered.

## Nostalgia: a VideOdyssey

Numbered, yes. But did the practice of renting tangible video/DVDs/Blu-rays ever truly become 'extinct' in Britain? Not quite.

Daniel Herbert has shown in *Videoland* how the local video store continues to live on in regions throughout the US. The practice remains less apparent in the UK, where a mere handful of shops remain (though the definitive number is impossible to accurately determine). There are, however, a couple of high-profile shops renting DVDs and VHS that have, in recent years, generated national – and in some cases international – news coverage: 20th Century Flicks in Bristol and VideOdyssey in Liverpool, the appeal of which is, chiefly, nostalgic.

Stuart Tannock, in his oft-cited critique of nostalgia, defines the process as a 'structure of feeling' that 'invokes a positively evaluated past world in response to a deficient present world'.[27] He continues: 'The nostalgic subject turns to the past to find/construct sources of identity, agency or community, that are felt to be lacking, blocked, subverted, or threatened

Figure C.3  20th Century Flicks, Bristol, as it appears in *The Last Video Store*.

in the present.'[28] Past critiques of nostalgia, Tannock has it, are routinely 'hostile and dismissive, associating the phenomenon with dominant and conversative forces in society', and risk 'conflating nostalgia with its presence in, and use by, dominant and conservative groups'.[29] Such critiques fall short of seeing the progressive function that nostalgia may have, and indeed does have, in various contexts. For Tannock, nostalgia can function politically, and in resistance to ideological dispositions that critics argue the phenomenon of nostalgia upholds.

VideOdyssey and 20th Century Flicks are evidence of this truism in that both seek to champion an era of video lost to the late capitalism that Netflix and, for that matter, Blockbuster, symbolise for their owners. For the proprietors of Flicks, history is of huge importance to the shop's identity. In a short documentary made about the shop in 2020 – Arthur Cauty's *The Last Video Store* – one of its co-owners, Dave Taylor, describes it as 'the longest running video shop in the world'. The shop's 'strange idiosyncratic collection from trash to extremely highbrow', he claims, is one of the reasons for its survival, in addition to the fact that it houses 20,000 movies ('about five times more than Netflix'), and is home to small cinema. Flicks is, as Herbert theorises of certain stores in the US, a 'speciality store' in that it 'feature[s] a selection of movies that is historically deep, geographically expansive, and generically diverse'.[30] In the film, which is in part inspired by an op-ed written by Taylor, in which he lamented the surge of video-on-demand service providers and generated international news coverage, the shop is positioned as an alternative to the sanitisation of video rental because of the tangible experience it offers its customers.[31] It is an exercise in preserving, as store clerk Paul Green phrases it, 'that time and space' alien to the video-on-demand selection process, where staff, his colleague Daisy Steinhardt continues, are able to speak with their customers – fulfil the 'social role' of the store clerk, as Herbert argues – and offer them advice should they need it.[32] This nostalgia for 'human' interaction within the video store retail space is also what guides the proprietor of VideOdyssey, Andy Johnson, whose shop also doubles as a video game arcade and cinema, and appears strategically oppositional to the 'clean and bright' clinical spaces of Blockbuster's business model.[33] Both 20th Century Flicks and VideoOdyssey invest in their shops a cinephile's love for the art of cinema and a communal experience unsullied by the corporate sanitisation process. 'That's what people are really, essentially, coming in for', co-owner of Flicks, David White, adds. 'The movie is sometimes immaterial. It's the social interaction which, in today's world, there is less and less of.'[34]

Recently, the communal experience of video rental has developed into a form of street protest, thanks to the Free Blockbuster movement in the US. Free Blockbuster, through unofficial usage of the Blockbuster branding, is

Figure C.4 Street protest: Free Blockbuster.

reliant on volunteers to install blue and yellow boxes filled with physical media on street corners. Inspired by Little Free Library, 'the world's largest book-sharing movement',[35] the aim of Free Blockbuster is to create 'a place where people can leave movies so other people can borrow them'.[36] The movement's goal is implicitly political, appearing to kick against the control that Netflix and other streaming services wield over accessing particular titles, and the truism that, while the internet may create the illusion of infinite access, the presence of films on legal streaming sites is at the mercy of company executives. In this context, a film's physical DVD or VHS release might be the only means of accessing the title in question. Free Blockbuster plays on the corporation's iconic status, the idea that the lasting image of Blockbuster remains one of sanitisation and corporate stranglehold: a legacy that, it would appear, is ripe for subversion.

At the time of writing, Free Blockbuster is yet to make it to the UK, though British press interest in the US movement suggests this could soon change.[37] In one respect, it might appear ironic for a US movement, sporting US branding, to spring up in Britain to stake a claim in the nostalgic experience of video rental, when the likes of 20th Century Flicks offers an experience that extends back to Britain in the early 1980s (and one said to be far removed from that of Blockbuster). Nevertheless, in the event that Free Blockbuster does arrive, it will bring the British wave of nostalgia for renting physical copies of screen entertainment embodied by Flicks and VideOdyssey full circle.

Through an exploration of the first video distributors and video shops, through moral panic and legislation, to market rationalisation and corporatisation, *Rewind, Replay* has strived to provide a nuanced account of the beginnings of video distribution and rental/retail in Britain. I hope to have conveyed that the history of the British video boom is rich, that it has long warranted, like many of the videocassettes once adorning the shelves of shops throughout the country, being rewound and played back and, more than this, that it is worthy of many replays to come.

## Notes

1. Raiford Guins, *Edited Clean Version: Technology and the Culture of Control* (Minneapolis: Minnesota University Press, 2008), 100.
2. Louise Tutt, 'Counter Attack', UK96 Preview supplement, *Screen International* 1042 (26 January 1995), 43–4. Citation at 44.
3. For an account of Blockbuster's expansion from the perspective of an independent video shop owner, see Lyn J. Cobb, *More Than Just a Video Shop* (Hove: Eternal Sunshine, 2017), 103–8.

4. Martin Barker, 'The Newson Report: A Case Study in "Common Sense"', in Martin Barker and Julian Petley (eds), *Ill Effects: The Media Violence Debate* (2nd edition, London: Routledge, 2001), 27–46.
5. Peter Dean, 'Explosive Reaction Follows Link of Video to Toddler's Murder', *Billboard* (11 December 1993).
6. Chris Pharo, 'For the sake of ALL our kids ... BURN YOUR VIDEO NASTY', *The Sun* (26 November 1993), 1, 11.
7. Blockbuster representative quoted in Dean, 'Explosive Reaction'.
8. Greenberg, *From Betamax to Blockbuster*, 127–9.
9. On such controversies see, for example, Julian Petley, *Film and Video Censorship in Modern Britain* (Edinburgh: Edinburgh University Press, 2011), 109–28.
10. John Hazleton, 'Muspratt leaves Guild as company restructures', *Screen International* 488 (16 March 1985), 2.
11. Sam Andrews, 'UK is giving rental-by-mail a go', *The Hollywood Reporter* (13 January 2004).
12. On revenue sharing in the US see Daniel Herbert, *Videoland: Movie Culture at the American Video Store* (Berkeley: University of California Press, 2014), 164–8. On the UK context, at the beginnings of revenue sharing, see Ajax Scott, 'Cityvision shareholders to challenge Blockbuster bid', *Screen International* 840 (17 January 1992), 6.
13. Cobb, *More Than Just a Video Shop*, 165–7. Quotation at 165.
14. Kate Allen, 'Film rental: coming soon – but not to a video store near you', *Guardian Financial Pages* (10 May 2007), 29.
15. Anon., 'UK sell-through overtakes rental', *Screen International* 944 (11 February 1994), 22.
16. Charles Robinson, 'High class, low prices create retail boom', *Video Business* 6.43 (27 October 1986), 16.
17. Peter Dean, 'Sell-through shuffle', *Screen International* 828 (11 October 1991), 48.
18. Anon., 'UK sell-through overtakes rental', 22.
19. Graham Davidson (of Elevation Sales) quoted in Stuart Henderson, 'From Screen to Shelf: Perspectives on Independent Distribution', *Journal of British Cinema and Television* 6.3 (December 2009), 468–80. Quotation at 469.
20. Peter Dean, 'Niche Video Labels Thrive In UK', *Billboard* 106.11 (2 March 1994), 55, 59.
21. Anon., 'Electric sell through', *Video Business* 10.27 (2 July 1990), 4. On the erotic thriller boom, including films released direct-to-video, see Linda Ruth Williams, *The Erotic Thriller in Contemporary Cinema* (Edinburgh: Edinburgh University Press, 2005).
22. Dean, 'Niche Video Labels', 55.
23. See Kate Egan, *Trash or Treasure? Censorship and the Changing Meanings of the Video Nasties* (Manchester: Manchester University Press, 2007), and McKenna, *Nasty Business*.

24. As Mark McKenna argues of Redemption, 'Films that had traditionally been dismissed as having very little intrinsic value in the previous decade now had a chance to be repositioned and repackaged as "arty", "valuable" and "high end". Redemption's construction of itself as a company that was respectful of the films, recognising them as important canonical titles, is also revealing of a distinction between it and other companies such as VIPCO, a company that became the target of much criticism over the lack of attention to detail in the overall quality of its releases.' See McKenna, *Nasty Business*, 102–7. In the late 1990s, Nouveau Pictures, an arthouse label, distributed sell-through re-issues of several of Dario Argento's titles that were originally embroiled in the original nasties panic, including *Suspiria* (1977) and *Tenebrae* (1982).
25. On the shortening of theatrical windows in the context of British video retail, see Paul Crosbie, 'DEATH OF THE VIDEO SHOP', *The Sun* (13 July 2002). On supermarkets and video see Ritchie Paterson, 'SUPERMARKET SWEEP', *Screen International* 1029 (13 October 1995), 10; and Allen, 'Film rental: coming soon'.
26. Allen, 'Film rental: coming soon'.
27. Stuart Tannock, 'Nostalgia critique', *Cultural Studies* 9.3 (1995), 453–64. Quotation at 454.
28. Tannock, 'Nostalgia critique', 454.
29. Tannock, 'Nostalgia critique', 454. Trump's 'Make American Great Again', or Farage's 'We Want Our Country Back' are especially resonant examples in the twenty-first century.
30. Herbert, *Videoland*, 85.
31. See Owen Williams, 'The last video shop in Bristol makes an indie stand against the age of Netflix', available at: https://www.theguardian.com/cities/2014/oct/07/last-video-shop-bristol-20th-century-flicks-netflix-vhs.
32. Herbert, *Videoland*, 72.
33. See Alan Weston, 'VHS store which opened this year expands after being 'inundated with tapes', *Liverpool Echo* (31 December 2018), available at: https://www.liverpoolecho.co.uk/news/liverpool-news/vhs-store-opened-year-expands-15533109.
34. For a nuanced discussion of the social elements of video-store rental between clerks and customers, see Greenberg, *From Betamax to Blockbuster*, 104–9.
35. See http://littlefreelibrary.org.
36. See http://freeblockbuster.org.
37. Anon., 'Free Blockbuster: VHS tapes are back! But are they really worth the bother?' *The Guardian* (7 September 2021), available at: https://www.theguardian.com/technology/2021/sep/07/free-blockbuster-the-unlikely-return-of-the-vhs-tape.

# Select Bibliography

Most of the sources consulted in this book are primary sources, ranging from articles published in contemporaneous periodicals to video-related ephemera. Said references can be found in the Notes section of the book's respective chapters – there are simply too many to list here. The present list is one comprised of secondary sources, both academic and non-academic.

Aguilera Skvirsky, Salomé. *The Process Genre: Cinema and the Aesthetic of Labor* (Durham, NC: Duke University Press, 2020).
Alilunas, Peter. *Smutty Little Movies: The Creation and Regulation of Adult Video* (Berkeley: University of California Press, 2017).
Anderson, Otto. 'On the internationalization process of firms: a critical analysis', *Journal of International Business Studies* (Second Quarter, 1993), 209–31.
Baker, Stephen, and Paddy Hoey. 'The Picaro and the Prole, the Spiv and the Honest Tommy in Leon Griffiths's *Minder*', *Journal of British Cinema and Television* 15.4 (October 2018), available at: https://www.euppublishing.com/doi/abs/10.3366/jbctv.2018.0440.
Ballard, Roger. 'The South Asian presence in Britain and its transnational connections', in Bhikhu Parekh, Gurharpal Singh and Steven Vertovec (eds), *Culture and Economy in the Indian Diaspora* (London: Routledge, 2002), 197–222.
Barber, Sian. 'Power Struggles, Regulation and Responsibility: Reappraising the Video Recordings Act', *Media History* 24.1 (2016), 99–114.
Barker, Martin (ed.). *The Video Nasties: Freedom, Censorship and the Media* (London: Pluto, 1984).
Barker, Martin. 'Nasty politics or video nasties?' in Martin Barker (ed.), *The Video Nasties: Freedom, Censorship and the Media* (London: Pluto, 1984), 7–38.
Barker, Martin. 'The Newson Report: A Case Study in "Common Sense"', in Martin Barker and Julian Petley (eds), *Ill Effects: The Media Violence Debate* (2nd edition, London: Routledge, 2001), 27–46.
Barker, Martin, and Julian Petley (eds). *Ill Effects: The Media Violence Debate* (2nd edition, London: Routledge, 2001).
Barrett, Giles A., and David McEvoy. 'Temporal and geographical variations in ethnic minority business' in Leo-Paul Dana (ed.), *Handbook of Research on Ethnic Minority Entrepreneurship: A Co-evolutionary View on Resource Management* (Cheltenham: Edward Elgar, 2007), 337–59.

Benson-Allott, Caetlin. *Killer Tapes and Shattered Screens: Video Spectatorship from VHS to File Sharing* (Berkeley: University of California Press, 2013).

Berástegui Wood, Jorge. 'The Analysis of Hybridity in *My Beautiful Laundrette*', *Revista Canaria de Estudios Ingleses Año* 54 (2007), 137–47.

Billig, Michael. *Banal Nationalism* (London: Sage, 1995), 93.

Blanchlard, Simon. 'Cinema-going, going, gone?', *Screen* 24.4/5 (July 1983), 108–13.

Boettke, P. J. and C. J. Coyne. 'Entrepreneurship and development: cause or consequence?', *Austrian Economics and Entrepreneurial Studies* (2003), 67–87.

Bordwell, David, Kristin Thompson and Jeff Smith. *Film Art: An Introduction*, 11th edition (New York: McGraw Hill, 2017).

Buckingham, David. 'Electronic child abuse? Rethinking the media's effects on children', in Martin Barker and Julian Petley (eds), *Ill Effects: The Media/Violence Debate* (2nd edition, London: Routledge, 2001), 63–77.

Church, David. *Grindhouse Nostalgia: Memory, Home Video and Exploitation Film Fandom* (Edinburgh: Edinburgh University Press, 2014).

Cobb, Lyn J. *More Than Just a Video Shop* (Hove: Eternal Sunshine, 2017).

Corner John, and Sylvia Harvey. 'Introduction: Great Britain Limited', in John Corner and Sylvia Harvey (eds), *Enterprise and Heritage: Crosscurrents of National Culture* (London: Routledge, 1991), 1–20.

Corner, John, and Sylvia Harvey. 'Mediating tradition and modernity: the heritage/enterprise couplet', in John Corner and Sylvia Harvey (eds), *Enterprise and Heritage: Crosscurrents of National Culture* (London: Routledge, 1991), 45–73.

Cowling, Marc and Peter Mitchell. 'The evolution of UK self-employment: a study of government policy and the role of the macroeconomy', *The Manchester School LVX.4* (September 1997), 427–42.

Dellheim, Charles. *Inc.* (undated), available at: https://www.inc.com/magazine/19960701/1725.html (accessed 2 February 2021).

Dhaliwal, Spinder, and Peter Kangis. 'Asians in the UK: gender, generations and enterprise', *Equal Opportunities International* 25.2 (2006), 92–108.

Dudrah, Rajinder Kumar. 'Vilayati Bollywood: popular Hindi cinema-going and diasporic South Asian identity in Birmingham (UK)', *The Public* 9.1 (2002), 19–36.

Dyer, Richard. *White* (London: Routledge, 2002 [1997]).

Egan, Kate. *Trash or Treasure? Censorship and the Changing Meanings of the Video Nasties* (Manchester: Manchester University Press, 2007).

Elert, Niklas, and Magnus Henrekson. 'Evasive entrepreneurship', *Small Business Economics* 47.1 (June 2016), 95–113.

Ganti, Tejaswini. *Bollywood: A Guidebook to Popular Hindi Cinema* (London: Routledge, 2013).

Geraghty, Christine. *British Cinema in the Fifties: Gender, Genre and the 'New Look'* (London: Routledge, 2000).

Geraghty, Christine. *My Beautiful Laundrette* (London: I. B. Tauris, 2005).

Gidoomal, Ram. *The UK Maharajahs: Inside the South Asian Success Stories* (London: Nicholas Brealey Publishing, 1997).
Gillespie, Marie. 'Technology and tradition: audio-visual culture among South Asian families in West London', *Cultural Studies* 3.2 (1989), 226–39.
Gray, Ann. *Video Playtime: The Gendering of a Leisure Technology* (London: Routledge, 1992).
Greenberg, Joshua M. *From Betamax to Blockbuster: Video Stores and the Invention of Movies on Video* (Cambridge, MA: MIT Press, 2008).
Guins, Raiford. *Edited Clean Version: Technology and the Culture of Control* (Minneapolis: University of Minnesota Press, 2009).
Gunter, Barrie, and Malorie Wober. 'The uses and impact of home video in Great Britain', in Mark R. Levy (ed.), *The VCR Age: Home Video and Mass Communication* (London: Sage, 1989), 50–69.
Hall, Sheldon. 'Feature Films on British Television in the 1970s', *Viewfinder Online* (13 November 2015), available at: http://bufvc.ac.uk/articles/feature-films-on-british-television-in-the-1970s/fullpage (accessed 4 April 2018).
Hanson, Stuart. *Screening the World: Global Development of the Multiplex Cinema* (Cham: Palgrave Macmillan, 2019).
Hellman, Heikki, and Martti Soramäki. 'Economic concentration in the videocassette industry: a cultural comparison', *Journal of Communication* 35.3 (September 1985), 122–34.
Henderson, Stuart. 'From Screen to Shelf: Perspectives on Independent Distribution', *Journal of British Cinema and Television* 6.3 (December 2009), 468–80.
Herbert, Daniel. *Videoland: Movie Culture at the American Video Store* (Berkeley: University of California Press, 2014).
Hesmondhalgh, David. *The Cultural Industries* (3rd edition, London: Sage, 2021).
Hildebrand, Lucas. *Inherent Vice: Bootleg Histories of Videotape and Copyright* (Durham, NC: Duke University Press, 2009).
Hill, John. *British Cinema in the 1980s: Issues and Themes* (Oxford: Oxford University Press, 1999).
Hobson, Dorothy. *Channel 4: The Early Years and the Jeremy Isaacs Legacy* (London: I. B. Tauris, 2007).
Hunt, Leon. *British Low Culture: From Safari Suits to Sexploitation* (London: Routledge, 1998).
Hutchings, Peter. *Dracula* (London: I. B. Tauris, 2003).
Jain, Prakash C., and Ginu Zacharia Oommen. 'Introduction', in Prakash C. Jain and Ginu Zacharia Oommen (eds), *South Asian Migration to Gulf Countries: History, Policies, Development* (London: Routledge, 2016), 1–14.
Jones, Trevor. 'Small business development at the Asian community in Britain', *Journal of Ethnic and Migration Studies* 9.3 (1981), 467–77.
Kassaveti, Ursula-Helen. '"Sharp Sybaritic" Retrofuturistic Deco Realism: Some Preliminary Notes on the 1980s Airbrush Art', *Imaginations – Journal of Cross-Cultural Image Studies* 10.2 (December 2019), 89–117. Available at: http://dx.doi.org/10.17742/IMAGE.OI.10.2.4.

Kearns, Ade, Oliver Kearns and Louise Lawson. 'Notorious places: image, reputation, stigma. The role of newspapers in area reputations for social housing estates', *Housing Studies* 28.4 (2013), available at: https://www.tandfonline.com/doi/full/10.1080/02673037.2013.759546.

Kerekes, David. and David Slater. *See No Evil: Banned Films and Video Controversy* (Critical Vision/Headpress: Manchester, 2000).

Krämer, Lucia. *Bollywood in Britain: Cinema, Brand, Discursive Complex* (New York: Bloomsbury, 2016).

Lee, Jason. 'The devil you don't know? The rise and fall and rise of Linda Blair', in Jane O'Connor and John Mercer (eds), *Childhood and Celebrity* (London: Routledge, 2017), 122–32.

Levy, Mark, and Barrie Gunter. *Home Video and the Changing Nature of the Television Audience* (John Libbey: London, 1988).

Lobato, Ramon. *Shadow Economies of Cinema: Mapping Informal Film Distribution* (London: British Film Institute, 2012).

Lufferelli, Jonathan., Mudra Mukesh and Ammara Mahmood, 'Let the logo do the talking: the influence of logo descriptiveness of brand equity', *Journal of Marketing Research* 56.5 (2019), 862–78.

McDonald, Paul. *Video and DVD Industries* (London: British Film Institute, 2007).

MacDonald, Robert. 'Welfare dependency, the enterprise culture and self-employed survival', *Work, Employment & Society* 10.3 (September 1996), 431–47.

McKenna, Mark. 'A murder mystery in black and blue: the marketing, distribution, and cult mythology of *Snuff* in the UK', in Neil Jackson, Shaun Kimber, Johnny Walker and Thomas Joseph Watson (eds), *Snuff: Real Death and Screen Media* (London: Bloomsbury, 2016): 121–38.

McKenna, Mark. *Nasty Business: The Marketing and Distribution of the Video Nasties* (Edinburgh: Edinburgh University Press, 2020).

Magilow, Daniel H., Kristin T. Vander Lugt and Elizabeth Bridges (eds). *Nazisploitation! The Nazi Image in Low-brow Cinema and Culture* (New York: Continuum, 2011).

Maltby, Richard. *Hollywood Cinema: An Introduction* (2nd edition, Oxford: Wiley-Blackwell, 2002).

Martin, John. *Seduction of the Gullible: The Truth behind the Video Nasty Scandal* (Liskeard: Stray Cat publishing, 2007).

Mersey, Bob. 'What's happening to the GROCERY SYMBOL GROUPS?', *Retail and Distribution management* 1.2 (1 February 1973), 44–8.

Neves, Joshua, and Bhaskar Sarkar (eds). *Asian Video Cultures: In the Penumbra of the Global* (Durham, NC: Duke University Press, 2017).

Morris, Marc, and Nigel Wingrove. *The Art of the Nasty* (2nd edition, Godalming: FAB Press, 2009).

Newman, Michael Z. *Video Revolutions: On the History of a Medium* (New York: Columbia University Press, 2014).

Pearce, Harry. *Video Nasties: The True Story of Court Cases, Cock Ups & Collateral Damage* (Self Published, 2013).
Petley, Julian. 'Nazi Horrors: History, Myth, Sexploitation', in Ian Conrich (ed.), *Horror Zone* (London: I. B. Tauris, 2009), 205–26.
Petley, Julian. *Film and Video Censorship in Modern Britain* (Edinburgh: Edinburgh University Press, 2011).
Petley, Julian. '"Are We Insane?": The "Video Nasty" Moral Panic', *Recherches sociologiques et anthropologiques* 43.1 (2012), 35–57, available at: https://doi.org/10.4000/rsa.839.
Petley, Julian, Chas Critcher, Jason Hughes and Amanda Rohloff (eds). *Moral Panics in the Contemporary World* (London: Bloomsbury, 2013).
Petrie, Duncan J. *Creativity and Constraint in the British Film Industry* (New York: Palgrave Macmillan, 1991).
Pina, Joseph. *Running a Successful Video Club – Confidential Video Report* (3rd edition, London: Visionwell, 1983).
Ritzer, George. *The McDonaldization of Society: Into the Digital Age* (9th edition, Thousand Oaks: Sage, 2019).
Ritzer, George. *The McDonaldization Thesis* (London: Sage, 1998).
Sandu, Sukhdev. 'An introduction to *My Beautiful Laundrette*', British Library, available at: https://www.bl.uk/20th-century-literature/articles/an-introduction-to-my-beautiful-laundrette#.
Schaefer, Eric. *Bold! Daring! Shocking! True! A History of Exploitation Films, 1919–1959* (Durham, NC: Duke University Press, 1999).
Singh, Gurharpal. 'Introduction', in Bhikhu Parekh, Gurharpal Singh and Steven Vertovec (eds), *Culture and Economy in the Indian Diaspora* (London: Routledge, 2003), 1–12.
Speiser, Peter. *Soho: The Heart of Bohemian London* (London: British Library, 2017).
Tannock, Stuart. 'Nostalgia critique', *Cultural Studies* 9.3 (1995), 453–64.
Stanfield, Peter. *The Cool and the Crazy: Pop Fifties Cinema* (New Brunswick, NJ: Rutgers University Press, 2015).
Staszak, Jean-Francois. 'Other/otherness', in Rob Kitchin and Nigel Thrift (eds), *International Encyclopaedia of Human Geography* 8 (Oxford: Elsevier, 2009), 43–7.
Stringer, Julian (ed.). *Movie Blockbusters* (London: Routledge, 2003).
Struzan, Drew, and David J. Schow, *The Art of Drew Struzan* (London: Titan, 2010).
Tench, Ralph, and Liz Yeomans. *Exploring Public Relations: Global Strategic Communication*, 4th edition (Harlow: Pearson, 2017).
Uche, Chibuike. 'The British Government, Idi Amin and the Expulsion of British Asian Expulsion', *Interventions* 19.6 (2017), 818–36.
Upton, Julian. 'Electric Blues: The Rise and Fall of Britain's First Pre-recorded Videocassette Distributors', *Journal of British Cinema and Television* 13.1 (2016), 19–41.

Voss, Georgina. *Stigma and the Shaping of the Pornography Industry* (London: Routledge, 2015).

Wade, Graham. *Film, Video and Television: Market Forces, Fragmentation and Technological Advance* (London: Comedia, 1985).

Wagg, Stephen. '"At ease, corporal": social class and the situation comedy in British television, from the 1950s to the 1990s', in Stephen Wagg (ed.), *Because I Tell a Joke or Two: Comedy, Politics, and Social Difference* (London: Routledge, 1998), 1–31.

Walsh, Michael F., Karen Page Winterich and Vikas Mittal. 'Do logo redesigns help or hurt your brand? The role of brand commitment', *Journal of Product and Brand Management* 19.2 (2010), 76–84.

Warpole, Ken. 'The age of leisure', in John Corner and Sylvia Harvey (eds), *Enterprise and Heritage: Crosscurrents of National Culture* (London" Routledge, 1991), 133–45.

Wasser, Frederick. *Veni, Vidi, Video: The Hollywood Empire and the VCR* (Austin: University of Texas Press, 2011).

Welch, Lawrence S., and Reijo Luostarinen. 'Internationalization: Evolution of a Concept', *Journal of General Management* 14.2 (December 1988), 35–55.

Williams, Linda Ruth. *The Erotic Thriller in Contemporary Cinema* (Edinburgh: Edinburgh University Press, 2005).

Wyatt, Justin. *High Concept: Movies and Marketing in Hollywood* (Austin: University of Texas Press, 1994).

# Select Film/TV/Videography

*67 Days*, 1974, Yugoslavia, dir. Zivorad Mitrovic
*A Town Called Bastard*, 1971, Spain/UK, dir. Robert Parish
*Absurd*, 1981, US, dir. Joe D'Amato, 1981
*Adventures of Buster the Bear, The*, 1978, Japan, dir. Unknown
*Adventures of Choppy and the Princess, The*, 1967, Japan, dir. Osamu Tezuka
*Adventures of Reddy the Fox, The*, 1978, Japan, dir. Unknown
*Adventures of Ultraman, The*, 1979, Japan, dirs Various
*Aladdin's Lamp*, 1979, US, dir. Will Vinton
*Alaska Wilderness Adventure*, 1978, US, dir. Fred Meader
*Alice In Wonderland*, 1972, US, dirs Jules Bass and Arthur Rankin Jr
*Alison's Birthday*, 1979, Australia, dir. Ian Coughlan
*Alligator*, 1980, US, dir. Lewis Teague
*Amityville II: The Possession*, 1982, US, dir. Damiano Damiani
*Babyface*, 1977, US, dir. Alex de Renzy
*Beauty and the Beast*, 1976, US, dir. Fielder Cook
*Bed Hostesses*, 1972, Switzerland, dir. Michael Thomas
*Beyond the Living Dead*, 1973, Italy/Spain, dir. José Luis Merino
*Beyond, The*, 1981, Italy, dir. Lucio Fulci
*Bitch, The*, 1979, UK, dir. Gerry O'Hara
*Black Arrow, The*, 1973, Australia, dir. Leif Gram
*Black Pirate, The* (aka *Rage of the Buccaneers*), 1961, Italy, dir. Mario Costa
*Blazing Saddles*, 1974, US, dir. Mel Brooks
*Blood of Dr Jekyll, The*, 1981, France/West Germany, dir. Walerian Borowczyk
*Bogey Man, The*, 1980, US, dir. Ulli Lommel
*Born Innocent*, 1974, US, dir. Donald Wrye
*Caged Women*, 1975, Switzerland/West Germany, dir. Jess Franco
*Cannibal Ferox*, 1981, Italy, dir. Umberto Lenzi
*Cannibal Holocaust*, 1980, Italy, dir. Ruggero Deodato
*Cathy's Curse*, 1977, Canada, dir. Eddy Matalon
*Chariots of Fire*, 1981, UK, dir. Hugh Hudson
*Children of Ravensback, The*, 1980, US, dir. Max Kalmanowicz
*Christmas Carol, A*, 1970, Australia, dir. Leif Gram
*Cinderella*, 1970, US, dirs Jules Bass and Arthur Rankin Jr
*Clonus*, 1978, US, dir. Robert S. Fivesome
*Close Encounters of the Third Kind*, 1977, US, dir. Steven Spielberg

*Come Play with Me*, 1977, UK, dir. George Harrison Marks
*Conquest*, 1983, Italy/Spain/Mexico, dir. Lucio Fulci
*Cover Girl Models*, 1975, Philippines/US, dir. Cirio H. Santiago
*Crossbone Territory*, 1986, US/Philippines, dir. Danilo Cabreira
*Crypt of the Living Dead*, 1973, US/Spain, dir. Ray Danton and Julio Salvador
*Curtains*, 1982, Canada, dir. Jonathan Stryker
*Daily Fabel*, 1968, Netherlands, dir. Cocky Andreoli
*Dark Places*, 1973, UK, dir. Don Sharp 1973
*Dawn of the Mummy*, 1981, US/Italy/Egypt, dir. Farouk Agrama
*Day the Earth Caught Fire, The*, 1961, UK, dir. Val Guest
*Deadliest Season, The*, 1977, US, dir. Robert Markowitz
*Deadtime Stories*, 1986, US, dir. Jeffrey Delman
*Death Dimension*, 1978, US, dir. Al Adamson
*Death Threat*, 1976, US, dir. Jack Starrett
*Death Trap*, 1976, US, dir. Tobe Hooper
*Deep Throat*, 1972, US, dir. Gerard Damiano
*Deliverance*, 1972, US, dir. John Boorman
*Demons of Ludlow, The*, 1983, US, dir. Bill Rebane
*Devil in Miss Jones, The*, 1973, US, dir. Gerard Damiano
*Devil within Her, The*, 1974, Italy, dirs Sonia Assonitis and Roberto D'Ettorre Piazzoli
*Dirty Harry*, 1971, US, dir. Don Siegel
*Dogs to the Rescue*, 1972, Canada/Romania, dir. Paul Fritz-Nemeth
*Don't Go in the House*, 1979, US, dir. Joseph Ellison/
*Dracula*, 1973, US, dir. Dan Curtis
*Driller Killer, The*, 1979, US, dir. Abel Ferrara
*Elmer*, 1976, US, dir. Christopher Cain
*Emmanuelle*, 1974, France, dir. Just Jaekin
*Enter the Dragon*, 1973, Hong Kong/US, dir. Robert Clouse
*Entity, The*, 1982, US, dir. Sidney J. Furie
*Escape* (aka *The Woman Hunt*), 1972, Philippines/US, dir. Eddie Romero
*Evil Dead, The*, 1981, US, dir. Sam Raimi
*Evilspeak*, 1981, US, dir. Eric Weston
*Exit the Dragon . . . Enter the Tiger*, 1976, Taiwan/Hong Kong, dir. Tso Nam Lee
*Exorcist, The*, 1974, US, dir. William Friedkin
*Exterminator, The*, 1980, US, dir. James Glickenhaus
*Extra-Terrestrial Nastie, The*, see *Night Fright*
*Fables of the Green Forest*, 1978, Japan, dir. Unknown
*Fireback*, 1983, Philippines, dir. Teddy Page
*Flashdance*, 1983, US, dir. Adrian Lyne
*Fly Me*, 1973, Philippines/US, dirs Cirio H. Santiago, Jonathan Demme and Curtis Hanson
*Foolin' Around*, 1979, US, dir. Richard T. Heffron
*French Connection, The*, 1971, US, dir. William Friedkin

*Ghostkeeper*, 1980, Canada, dir. James Makichuk
*Grease*, 1978, US, dir. Randal Kleiser
*Happy Hooker, The*, 1975, US, dir. Nicholas Sgarro
*Hitter, The*, 1978, US, dir. Christopher Leitch
*Honey Baby*, 1974, US, dir. Michael Schultz
*Horror Star, The*, 1981, US, dir. Norman Thaddeus Vane
*Hot Sex in Bangkok*, 1974, Switzerland, dir. Michael Thomas
*House by the Cemetery, The*, 1981, Italy, dir. Lucio Fulci
*House of Evil* (aka *The House on Sorority Row*), 1982, US, dir. Mark Rosman
*I Spit on Your Grave*, 1978, US, dir. Meir Zarchi
*Impulse*, 1974, US, dir. William Grefé
*Ivanhoe*, 1975, Australia, dir. Leif Gram
*Jack and the Beanstalk*, 1979, Japan, dir. Gisaburo Sugii
*Jaws*, 1975, US, dir. Steven Spielberg
*Kingdom in the Clouds, The*, 1968, Romania, dir. Elizabeta Bostan
*Kingdom of the Spiders*, 1977, US, dir. John Cardos
*Knife for the Ladies*, 1972, US, dir. Larry G. Spangler
*Last Blockbuster, The*, 2020, US, dir. Taylor Mordern
*Last House on the Left, The*, 1972, US, dir. Wes Craven
*Last Video Store, The*, 2020, UK, dir. Arthur Cauty
*Live and Let Die*, 1973, UK, dir. Guy Hamilton
*Living Dead [at the Manchester Morgue], The*, 1974, Spain/UK, dir. Jorge Grau
*Long Days of Summer, The*, 1980, US, dir. Dan Curtis
*Love Camp*, 1977, Switzerland/West Germany, dir. Jess Franco
*Love Pill, The*, 1972, UK, dir. Ken Turner
*M\*A\*S\*H*, 1970, US, dir. Robert Altman
*Macbeth*, 1948, US, dir. Orson Welles
*Madman*, 1981, US, dir. Joe Giannone
*Madron*, 1970, US, dir. Jerry Hopper
*Magee*, 1978, Australia/US, dir. Gene Levitt
*Making of Michael Jackson's Thriller, The*, 1984, US, dir. John Landis
*Marriage of Maria Braun, The*, 1979, West Germany, dir. Rainer Werner Fassbinder
*Massacre at Central High*, 1976, US, dir. Rene Daalder
*Mausoleum*, 1982, US, dir. Michael Dugan
*Mean Streets*, 1973, US, dir. Martin Scorsese
*Men of Sherwood Forest*, 1954, UK, dir. Val Guest
*Metal Messiah*, 1978, Canada, dir. Tibor Takacs
*Minder* [TX], 1979–94, UK, dirs Various
*Moby Dick*, 1977, Australia, dir. Richard Slapczynski
*Mutiny in the Southseas*, 1965, West Germany/Italy/France, dir. Wolfgang Becker
*My Beautiful Laundrette*, 1984, UK, dir. Stephen Frears
*My Beautiful Video Shop*, 1989, UK, dir. Bonnie Molnar
*My Therapist*, 1983, US, dir. Gary Legon

*New Life in the Garden*, 1979, UK, dir. Nigel Houghton
*Night Fright*, 1967, US, dir. James A. Sullivan
*Nightmare on Alcatraz*, 1987, US, dir. Philip Marcus
*Nights of Terror*, 1980, Italy, dir. Andrea Bianchi
*Ninja Warrior* (aka Ninja Warriors), 1985, Philippines/US, dir. Teddy Page
*No Place to Hide*, 1973, US, dir. Robert Allen Schnitzer
*Nobody's Boy*, 1970, Japan, dirs Yugo Serikawa and Jim Flocker
*Noddy Goes to Toyland*, 1963, UK, dir. Arthur Humberstone
*Northville Cemetery Massacre, The*, 1974, US, dirs William Dear and Thomas L. Dyke
*One Flew over the Cuckoo's Nest*, 1975, US, dir. Miloš Forman
*Only Fools and Horses* [TX], 1981–96, UK, dirs Various
*Opening of Misty Beethoven, The*, 1976, US, dir. Radley Metzger
*Out of the Blue*, 1980, Canada, dir. Dennis Hopper
*Patrick*, 1978, Canada, dir. Richard Franklin
*Pieces*, 1981, Spain/US, dir. Juan Piquer Simón
*Pinocchio*, 1971, Italy, dir. Giuliano Cenci
*Pirates of the Mississippi, The*, 1963, West Germany/Italy/France, dir. Jürgen Roland
*Plague*, 1978, Canada, dir. Ed Hunt
*Playbirds*, 1978, UK, dir. Willy Roe
*Poltergeist*, 1982, US, dir. Tobe Hooper
*Popeye and Friends in Outer Space*, 1961, US, dirs Various
*Raiders of the Lost Ark*, 1982, US, dir. Steven Spielberg
*Rebel Rousers, The*, 1970, US, dir. Martin B. Cohen
*Rip Van Winkle*, 1978, US, dir. Will Vinton
*Robin Hood*, 1971, Australia, dir. Zoran Janjic
*Robin Hood*, 1972, US, dirs Jules Bass and Arthur Rankin Jr
*Rocky*, 1976, US, dir. Sylvester Stallone
*Rocky II*, 1979, US, dir. Sylvester Stallone
*Rocky III*, 1982, US, dir. Sylvester Stallone
*Run Like a Thief*, 1967, US/Spain, dir. Bernard Glasser
*Saturday Night Fever*, 1977, US, dir. John Badham
*Sentinel, The*, 1976, US, dir. Michael Winner
*Seven Against the Sun*, 1964, South Africa, dir. David Millin
*Sex at 7000ft*, 1977, West Germany, dir. F. J. Gottlieb
*Sex O'Clock News, The*, 1985, US, dir. Romano Vanderbes
*Sexual Desires*, 1983, Spain, dir. Alfonso Balcázar
*Sins within the Family*, 1975, Italy, dir. Bruno Gaburro
*Sleeping Beauty*, 1972, US, dirs Jules Bass and Arthur Rankin Jr
*Snow White*, 1955, West Germany, dir. Eric Kobler
*Snow White*, 1972, US, dirs Jules Bass and Arthur Rankin Jr
*Snuff*, 1976, Argentina/US, dir. Michael Findlay
*Someone Behind the Door*, 1971, France/Italy, dir. Nicolas Gessner

*Sound of Music, The*, 1965, United States, dir. Robert Wise
*Specters*, 1987, Italy, dir. Marcello Avallone
*SS Experiment Camp*, 1976, Italy, dir. Sergio Garrone
*Star Trek II: The Wrath of Khan*, 1982, US, dir. Nicholas Meyer
*Star Wars*, 1977, US, dir. George Lucas
*Sunday in the Country*, 1974, Canada/UK, dir. John Trent
*Superman II*, 1980, UK/US, dirs Richard Lester and Richard Donner
*Tales of La Manca*, 1980, Japan, dir. Kunihiko Yuyama, 1980
*Tales of Ordinary Madness*, 1981, Italy/France, dir. Marco Ferreri
*Tales of the Third Dimension*, 1984, US, dirs Todd Durham, Worth Keeter, Tom McIntyre and Earl Owensby.
*Techno Police*, 1982, Japan, dir. Masashi Matsumoto
*Texas Chain Saw Massacre, The*, 1974, US, dir. Tobe Hooper
*They Paid with Bullets*, 1969, Spain/Italy, dir. Julio Diamante
*Thing, The*, 1982, US, dir. John Carpenter
*Thor: The Conqueror*, 1982, Italy, dir. Tonino Ricci
*Tina Turner*, 1979, UK, dir. Steve Turner
*Tomorrow Man, The*, 1979, Canada, dir. Tibor Takacs
*Toolbox Murders, The*, 1978, US, dir. Dennis Donnelly
*Treasure Island*, 1976, US, dir. Will Vinton
*Treasures of the Snow*, 1980, UK, dir. Mike Pritchard
*Turn of the Screw, The*, 1974, US, dir. Dan Curtis, 1974
*Up Your Ladder* (aka *Up Yours*), 1979, US, dirs John Hayes and Eddie Eyder
*Video Nasties: Moral Panic, Censorship and Videotape*, 2010, UK, dirs Marc Morris and Jake West
*Video Play-Box 1*, 1980, UK, dir. Leslie Pitt
*Violators, The*, 1983, US, dir. Jeff Hathcock
*What Shall we Give Them to Eat?* 1980, UK, dir. Jan Martin
*When Every Day was the Fourth of July*, 1978, US, dir. Dan Curtis
*White Cargo from Hong Kong*, 1964, West Germany/Italy/France, dirs Giorgio Stegani and Helmut Ashley
*Who Killed Doc Robin?* 1948, US, dir. Bernard Carr
*Women in Cages*, 1971, Philippines/US, Gerardo de Leon
*Wonder Wall*, 1968, UK, dir. Joe Massot
*Zombie Creeping Flesh*, 1980, Italy, dir. Bruno Mattei
*Zombie Flesh Eaters*, 1979, Italy, dir. Lucio Fulci

# Select Periodicals

The following list comprises British magazines that are devoted to the video business or video consumption, or that feature extended sections addressing home video.

## Trade magazines

*Cinema TV Today*
*Home Entertainment Weekly*
*Network*
*Screen International*
*Television & Video Retailer*
*Variety*
*Video Business*
*Video Buyers Guide*
*Video News*
*Video Retailer*
*Video Trade Weekly*
*Video Week*
*VST – The Video Sell-through Magazine*

## Consumer magazines

*Adult Video*
*Cinema Blue*
*Cert X*
*Films and Filming*
*Late Nite Video*
*Movie Maker*
*Movie Star Video*
*Music & Video*
*Network Video*
*Popular Video*
*Practical Video*

*Screens*
*Sight & Sound*
*Stills*
*Television*
*Television & Home Video*
*Video*
*Video – The Magazine*
*Video Buyer*
*Video Home Entertainment*
*Video Index*
*Video Review*
*Video Today*
*Video World*
*Video X*

# Index

*Note:* **bold** indicates illustrations

Abbott, Norma, 86
ABC Video, 146
*Absurd* (1981), 139
Acadia, 203
ACE Europe, 98, 100, 104–5
action films, 23–5, 27, 28, 39, 43
Adam Corporation, 116, 117
Adams-Mercer, Fil, 133
Adamson, Al, 151
ADB Video, 99, 103
adult films, 4, 23, 25–7, 28–31, 33–8, 47, 49, 134–5, 137, 202; *see also* pornography
Adult Tape Centre, 34, **35**
Adult Video Company, 34
*Adventures of Buster the Bear* (1978), 102
*Adventures of Reddy the Fox* (1978), 102
*Adventures of Ultraman* (1979), 102
advertising, 19–21, 29, 31–4, 36–42, 45–9, 66, 83, 98–9, 102–3, 110, 116–17, 122, 141, 144–5, 153, 189–95
Advertising Standards Authority (ASA), 153
Aguilera Skvirsky, Salomé, 22
airbrush art, 150–2
*Aladdin's Lamp* (1979), 41
*Alaska Wilderness Adventure* (1978), 25
Algar, Niamh, 8, **10**
*Alice in Wonderland* (1972), 106
Alilunas, Peter, 4, 33–4
*Alligator* (1980), 44
Alvesson, Mario, 140
Amin, Idi, 73, 75, 77
*Amityville II: The Possession* (1982), 123
Anderson, Hans Christian, 105
Anglia Video, 176
'Angry Women' group, 119

*Animal Kingdom* (1981), 100
*Animals at Work and Play*, 104
animated films, 99, 104, 105–6
Apex Distribution, 147–52, 155, 156
Arcade Video, 110
Ariel, 146
Art Features, 25
ArTel, 98, 104
arthouse films, 23, 220
artwork, 6–7, 40–3, **41**, **43**, 108–9, **109**, 115–22, **118**, **120**, 150–6, **155**, **198**, 198–9
Asian video shops, 74–7, 81–5
Astra Video, 95, 98, 110, 119, 124, 142
Association of Cinematograph, Television and Allied Technicians, 119
Association of Video Film Dealers (AVFD), 122
Atlantis Video, 108, 115
audience measurement, 21
Audio and Visual Ltd, 21
audio-visual companies, 18–22, 64
Australia, 3, 45, 102, 117, 140, 141, 142, 143, 204
Austria, 204
avant-garde films, 25
Avatar Communications, 122, 146, 147, 154
Ayres, Steve, 159–62
Azad Video, 200, 203, 216

B movies, 136, 139–40, 146–56
B&Q, 177, 178, 180
*Babyface* (1977), 36–7
'back-to-back' piracy, 79–81
Bailey-Bond, Prano, 8–9
Baker, Stephen, 79

Ballard, Roger, 82
Barber, Sian, 135
Barker, Martin, 5, 135
Barratt, Michael, 22
Barrett, Giles, 82
*Basic Instinct* (1992), 220
*Batman* (1989), 220
*Batman: The Animated Series* (1992–5), 220
BBC 1, 47, 48, 49
BBC 2, 47, 48, 49
BBC Enterprises Film Sales, 21
BBC Video, 160
B.B. Star Video, 84
*Beauty and the Beast* (1976), 105
Bend, Oregon, 1–2, 217
benefits-based marketing, 98–103
Benson-Allott, Caetlin, 4
Betamax, 19, 20, 81, 105, 156
*Beyond, The* (1981), 154
*Beyond the Living Dead* (1973), 117, **118**
*Billboard*, 179
Billig, Michael, 195, 196
Birmingham, 74, 85
*Black Arrow, The* (1973), 102
black market, 155
Blair, Linda, 121
Blakemore, peter, 182–3
blaxploitation films, 115, 151
*Blazing Saddles* (1974), 32
Block, Richard, 177
Blockbuster Video, 1–4, **2**, 11, 13, 178–9, 191, 194, **201**, 201–5, 215–17, 222
*Blood of Dr Jekyll* (1981), 153–4, **155**
*Bloody Disgusting*, 9
*Blow Out* (1973), 23
Blu-Ray, 6, 215
Bogarts Video, 177, 180
*Bogey Man, The* (1980), 116, 117, **118**, 153
Bollywood, 74
Bond films, 28
Bookwise, 103
'borderline' nasties, 112–23, 155
Bordwell, David, 196
*Born Innocent* (1974), 121
box office charts, 27
branding, 40–3, **41**, **43**, 66, 116, 142–7, **145**, 178–82, **180**, **181**, 189, 192–4, 219

Branson, Richard, 145
Braveworld, 146–7, 155
Brent Walker, 26
Bright, Graham, 134
Bristol, 221
British Board of Film Classification (BBFC), 5, 8, 37, 95, 112–13, 117, 134–6, 138–9, 150, 153–6, 216
British Broadcasting Corporation (BBC), 7, 21, 22, 47, 48, 49, 86, 160
British Film Institute (BFI), 9, 220
British Video Association (BVA), 85–6, 112, 116, 135, 138–9, 142, 173, 175, 177–8, 185–6, 203, 216
*Broadcast*, 47
Brothers Grimm, 105
Brown, Maggie, 47–8
Brown, Percy, 78
budget labels, 26, 156–9
Bulger, James, 216
*Bumper Fun Video Annual Volume 1* (1982), 100
Burgess, Thomas W., 102
Burton, Tim, 220

cable television, 140, 161
Cal Vista International, 33–6, 28
Canada, 45
*Cannibal Ferox* (1981), 112, 153
*Cannibal Holocaust* (1980), **109**, 109–10, 151
Cannon Video, 147
capitalism, 2, 64, 69, 222
Capricorn, 139
*Captain Pugwash*, 105
Carnaby Video, 25, 46–7, 68–73, **69**, 74–5
Carshalton, 182–3
Cartoon Carousel label, 104
*Cartoon Festival* (1981), 105–6
*Cartoon Spectacular* (1982), 100
cartoons, 17, 19, 96, 97–8, 99–102, 104–6, 219, 220
catalogues, 12, 21–5, **24**, 29–31, 32, 34, 45, 98
*Cathy's Curse* (1977), 151
Cauty, Arthur, 222
CBS/Fox, 113–23, 136, 139, 152, 158, 174, 175, 178, 189, 190, 202

*Censor* (2021), 8–9, **10**
censorship, 5, 7, 8–9, 34–6, 78, 112–13, 116, 135, 152–6, 216, 221
Centre Video, 114
certification, 37, 95, 112–13, 117, 134–5, 136, 138, 150, 153–6, 216
Channel 4, 48, 119
Channel 5, 160, 162
Channel Video, 100
charts *see* box office charts; rental charts; sales charts
children's entertainment, 12, 19, 26, 96–108, 119, 122, 124, 162, 219–20; *see also* family entertainment
*Childrens Fun Show* (c.1982), 100
*Child's Play 3* (1991), 216
Chile, 204
Chippendale, Peter, 5
choice, 21, 44, 46–7, 124
Choices, 217, **218**
*Choppy and the Princess* (1967), 124
Christianshavn Video, 3
*Christmas Carol, A* (1970), 104
Christmas marketing campaigns, 100, 103–4, 160
*Cinderella* (1970), 106
Cinehollywood, 140
*Cinema Blue*, 34
Cinema Features label, 45
Cinema International Corporation (CIC), 26, 44, 95, 98, 104, 123, 136, 158, 159
*Cinema X*, 34
cinemas, 22–3, 27–8, 34, 45–6, 74, 105, 191–4
Cityvision, 178, 180–3, 186, 188–90, 200, 204
Clapham Junction, 203
Claridge, Maurice 'Mo', 115, 150, 152
class, 5, 11, 78–9, 84, 198–9
*Clonus* (1978), 115
*Close Encounters of the Third Kind* (1977), 28
closed-circuit television (CCTV), 19
*Club International*, 28–9
codes of practice, 138, 184, 185, 190
Cole, Mike, 139, 142
Coleman, Ronald, 29
collectors, 156, 219, 220–1

Colourbox, 147
colonialism, 73, 82
Columbia *see* RCA/Columbia
*Come Play With Me* (1977), 27–8
comedy, 27, 219
company logos, 40, 42, 43, 122, 143–4, **145**, 151, 179–81, **180**, **181**, 192
company slogans, 32–3, 42, 153
compendium videos, 100, 104–6
competition, 65, 70, 80, 124, 136–7, 140, 189
Conservative Party, 5, 64, 79, 134, 139
consumable identity, 40
*Continental Film Review*, 34
Cooper, Richard, 19, 21, 49, **63**
copyright, 20, 77–80, 83, 85–6, 105
Copyright Act, 85–6
Corkery, Liam, 187–8
Corkery, Rita, 187–8
Corner, John, 70
*Coronation Street* (1960–), 47
corporate identity, 105, 133, 140, 142–5, 178, 179, 189; *see also* branding
corporate videos, 19
*Crash* (1996), 216
Craven, Wes, 112
*Crossroads* (1964–88), 47
Crypt Keeper, 221
*Crypt of the Living Dead* (1973), 151–2
Curtis, Dan, 117
Custom Video, 184
Cyclo Video, 147

*Daily Fabel* (1968), 104
*Daily Mail*, 119, 138
Dapon Film Services, 26
*Dark Places* (1973), 119–21, **120**
Davis, George, 42
*Day the Earth Caught Fire, The* (1961), 23
DC Comics, 220
*Deadliest Season, The* (1977), 116
*Deadtime Stories* (1986), 155
'Dealer of the Month' column, 174–7, 184, 203, 204
*Death Dimension* (1978), 151
*Death Threat* (1976), 110
*Death Trap* (1976), 110, 116, 221
*Deep Throat* (1972), 34

# INDEX

*Deliverance* (1972), 32
Delta, 146
*Demented* (1980), 110
*Demons of Ludlow, The* (1983), 115
Denmark, 3
Derann Audio Visual, 25, 27, 32–3, 38–9, 98, 104
descriptive logos, 143–4
*Devil in Miss Jones, The* (1973), 34
*Dirty Harry* (1971), 32
'Disco Live' technology, 19, **20**
Disney, 98, 105–6, 113
diversification, 139, 140, 142, 161
Dixons, 33
documentaries, 1–2, 21–2, 161, 222
*Dogs to the Rescue* (1972), 41–2
Dolan, Des, 109, 147
Domestic Electric Rentals (DER), 65
Donovan, Paul, 147
*Don't Go in the House* (1979), 110
*Dracula* (1978), 39
*Driller Killer, The* (1979), 9, 95, 110, 116, 117, 151
Dubai, 141
Dudrah, Rajinder, 74
DVD, 6, 215, 217, 219, 221, 224
Dyer, Richard, 82

educational videos, 19, 96, 100–2
Egan, Kate, 5–6, 7, 64, 116–17, 124, 153, 220
*80s with Dominic Sandbrook, The* (2013), 7–8, **8**
Electric, 146
Electric Blue, 29, 49, 220
electronics rentals, 63
Elephant Video, 147, 154
*Elmer* (1976), 43
*Emmanuelle* (1974), 28
*Emmerdale Farm* (1972–), 47
*Enter the Dragon* (1973), 32
Entertainment in Video, 144–5, 146, 150, 151
Enterprise Allowance scheme, 64
*Entity, The* (1982), 123
entrepreneurship, 64–86, 177, 186–7, 196–7, 200
Esquire Video, 81–2, 83

ethnic minorities, 73–7, 81–5, 196, 198–9
European Creative Films, 154
*Evil Dead, The* (1981), 123
Exciting Lighting, 19
*Exorcist, The* (1974), 32, 121
exploitation films, 5, 7, 11, 25, 27–9, 45, 95, 108, 112–19, 146–56, 220–1; *see also* blaxploitation films; sexploitation films
Exploited, 221
*Exterminator, The* (1980), 27
*Extra-Terrestrial Nastie* see *Night Fright* (1967)

*Fables of the Green Forest* (1978), 99
fairy tales, 105–6
Family Code, 184, 185, 190
family entertainment, 11, 12, 25–8, 31, 41–3, 47, 99, 108, 123, 158, 187, 204; *see also* children's entertainment
Family Video label, 100
fan communities, 6–7
*Fawlty Towers* (1975–9), 86
*Fear Street* trilogy (2021), 9
feature films, 11, 17–19, 21–8, 31–2, 38–47, 49, 80, 96, 97, 99, 103, 105–6, 143, 156–60, 162, 220
Federation Against Copyright Theft (FACT), 85–6, 134
Feldmann, Paul, 188–9
feminism, 119
Ferman, James, 156
film critics, 36–7, 45
film reviews, 34, 36–7
film studios, 20, 25, 26, 27, 31–2, 39, 40, 42–3, 77, 95, 133, 158–9, 217
Films Galore, 139
Films International, 119–21
Finch, David, 147
First Independent, 219
*Flash Gordon*, 105
*Flashdance* (1983), 159
Fletcher Video, 45, 98, 104, 105–6, **107**, 124, 219
flexibility, 18, 31, 44, 46–7, 49, 104
*Forest, The* (1981), 115
format exclusivity, 44–5
France, 142
*Fred Bassett* cartoons, 104

Free Blockbuster movement, **223**, 223–4
*French Connection, The* (1971), 32
French Label, 36, 37–8, **38**
*Fun Time* (1982), 100
Futuristic Video, 147

*Games Radar*, 9
*Gentleman's Agreement?, A* (1983), 119
Geraghty, Christine, 191, 197
Germany, 142, 146
Gerstman, Richard, 42
Gibson, Hamish, 33
Gill, John, 36
Gillespie, Marie, 4, 83
Global Video, 200, 216, 217
Go Video, 95, 98, 100, 103, 108–10, 141, **141**, 147
Gold, Barrie, 137
Goldberg, Warren, 146–7
Golden Age of pornography, 34–7
Golders Green, 190–1
Granada, 65
Gray, Ann, 4
*Grease* (1978), 136
Green, Paul, 223
Greenberg, Joshua M., 2, 4, 75, 215
Gruber, Thomas, 179
*Guardian*, 180
Guild Home Video, 26, 98, 146, 150, 151, 217, 219
Guins, Raiford, 215
Gulf Video Centre (GVC), 83, 141
Gunter, Barrie, 4, 21

*Halloween 4: The Return of Michael Myers* (1988), 200
Hanson, Stuart, 191–2
Harding, Sandi, 1
*Harry Potter* films, 221
Harvey, Sylvia, 70
Hawkins, Peter, 105
Hellman, Heikki, 23, 123
Herbert, Daniel, 4, 10, 68, 204, 215, 221, 222
Heron Corporation, 145–6, 159, 160, 184
high concept marketing, 120–1
*High Society*, 36–7

high-street retailers, 11, 31–3, 63, 65, 103, 159–60, 162, 174, 177, 183, 188, 204
Hikon Video, 26
Hildebrand, Lucas, 4
Hindi films, 74–5, 81–2, 83–4
HMV, 160
HNP, 119–20
*Hobbit, The* (1977), 105
Hodder, Martin, 62
Hodgins, David, 139
Hoey, Paddy, 79
Hokushin, 25, 27–8, 39, **41**, 41, 45, 137
Hollywood, 4, 5, 26, 27, 28, 31–2, 40, 80, 85, 133, 136, 159, 191–2, 217
Hollywood Nites symbol group, 189–200, **193**, **195**, 204–5
Hollywood Video, 2, 191
home cinema, 18, 32, 191
Home Entertainment, 217
Home Video Holdings, 140
Home Video Productions (HVP), 98, 102, 103
Home Video Show, 73
Home Video Supplies (HVS), 26
Homerun Video, 200
*Honey Baby* (1974), 43
horror films, 6–12, 26–8, 43, 47, 85, 86, 95, 108–25, 146–56, 158, 186, 191, 200, 201, 216, 220–1
*Horror Star, The* (1981), 112
*House by the Cemetery, The* (1981), 154
Huizenga, Wayne, 2, 178
Hungerford shootings, 186
Hunt, Leon, 28
*Hustler*, 37

*I Spit on Your Grave* (1978), 119
illegal downloading, 217, 221
Independent Broadcasting Authority (IBA), 48
independent distributors, 4, 5, 9, 10, 17–50, 64, 95–113, 114–25, 133–63, 191, 219–21
independent video shops, 3, 13, 64–8, 71–86, 106, 113–14, 137–8, 162, 173–7, 182–200, 204–5, 216–19, 221–3
India, 73, 81, 82
instructional videos, 22

interactive videos, 100
Intercity Video, 26
Intercontinental Video, 26
International Publishing Corporation (IPC), 21, 49
internationalisation, 140–6
internet, 217, 221, 224
Inter-Ocean Video, 25
Intervision, 11–12, 19–27, **24**, 31, 39, 41–4, **43**, 47–50, 62, 65–7, 74–5, 98–9, **99**, 105, 108, 124, 137, 139, 140, 142, 151–2, 156, 174, 177–8, 219
Ireland, 3, 200, 203
Istead Audio Visual, 22
*IT: Chapter One* (2017), 9
Italy, 140
ITV, 47, 48, 177
*Ivanhoe* (1975), 102
Iver Film Services (IFS), 25, 42–3, 137, 143

*Jack and the Beanstalk* (1979), 99
Jackson, Michael, 161
Jacobs, Barry, 147
Jaekin, Just, 28
Jalhan, Bhupendra, 84
Japan, 17, 102, 204
*Jaws* (1975), 44, 95, 136
job creation, 64, 70
Johnson, Andy, 223
Judd, Alan, 142–3
Junior Video at Home, 98

Kenya, 73
Kenyatta, Jomo, 73
KIDEO, 98
Kidivid label, 100
KidVid label, 98, 104
kidvids *see* children's entertainment; family entertainment
*Kingdom in the Clouds, The* (1968), 41
Klinger, Barbara, 40, 46
*Knife for the Ladies* (1972), 43
*Knut Hamsun's Mysteries* (1978), 39
Kroc, Ray, 2
Kruger, Peter, 113
*Kuhle Wampe* (1932), 220
kung-fu films, 26, 28

Labato, Ramon, 4
Langham, John, 84
*Lassie*, 105
*Last Blockbuster, The* (2020), 1–2, **2**, 215
*Last House on the Left, The* (1972), 112
*Last Video Store, The* (2020), 222
Lawson, Maurice, 147
leasing, 80–1, 106, 113, 114
Lee, Peter, 177, 182–3
Leicester, 74, 75–7, 84–5
Leicester Video, 84
Levinson, Paul, 159–62
Levy, Mark, 4
Lightfoot, Chris, 42
Lightning, 114, 189
Little Free Library, 224
*Little Match Girl, The*, 105
*Little White Lies*, 9
*Live and Let Die* (1973), 28
Liverpool, 221
*Living Dead, The* (1974), 154
Loan Guarantee scheme, 64
Lobato, Ramon, 79–80
*Lois & Clark: The New Adventures of Superman* (1993–7), 220
London, 11, 18, 19, 27, 28–31, 34–6, 68, 82, 182–4, 190–1, 203
*London Programme, The*, 78
London Weekend Television (LWT), 78
*Lone Ranger, The*, 105
*Long Days of Summer, The* (1980), 39
Longman Video, 98, 102–3, 104
*Love Camp* (1977), 43
LoveFilm, 217
low-budget films, 9, 114, 115, 139–40, 146–56
low concept marketing, 120
Lufferelli, Jonathan, 143–4
Luton, 175–6

*Macbeth* (1948), 23
McDonald, Paul, 10
McDonaldisation, 3, 179
McDonald's, 2, 3, 179–80
McEvoy, David, 82
McKenna, Mark, 5–6, 7, 41, 135–6, 144, 220
*Madman* (1981), 112

*Madron* (1970), 45
Mafia, 78, 83
*Magee* (1978), 117
*Magic Well, The*, 105
Magnetic Video, 19, 25, 31–2, 33, 40–2, 136, 158
Mahmood, Ammara, 143–4
mail order, 12, 17, 62, 64, 66, 85
*Making of Michael Jackson's Thriller, The* (1984), 161
Maliphant, Chris, 147
Maltby, Richard, 191
Manchester, 182
Mandy, Steve, 114–15, 122, 190
Mann, Derek, 173
manufacturing, sales and distribution agreements (MSDAs), 114–22, 123, 136
market domination, 3, 13, 80–1, 136, 182, 183, 215
market penetration, 1–3, 62–3, 144, 182, 204
market rationalisation, 11–13, 44, 49–50, 69, 80, 96–8, 108, 113–15, 123, 136–7, 142, 146, 150, 224
market saturation, 44, 86, 96, 106, 114–15, 123–4, 133
Marks & Spencer, 160
*M\*A\*S\*H* (1970), 32
*Massacre at Central High* (1976), 110
Max Fleischer Studios, 104, 220
Maxirun, 184
*Mean Streets* (1973), 26
media, 5–12, 28, 31–4, 36, 50, 68–70, 78–9, 81–5, 86, 95–7, 108–13, 116, 119, 121–2, 124, 134, 138, 142–4, 152, 173–7, 180, 182–8, 191, 196, 200, 203, 216
*Media Fields Journal*, 4
Media Home Entertainment, 98, 110
Medusa Communications, 139, 146, 150, 151, 219
Mega Movies, 180
membership fees, 66, 67, 74, 176
*Men of Sherwood Forest* (1954), 41
*Men Only*, 28–9
Merlin Video, 110, **111**, 142, 145
*Mermaid Princess, The*, 105
*Metal Messiah* (1978), 45
MGM/UA, 98, 158, 159, 160

Michael Barratt Ltd, 21, 22
Middle East, 83
Milton Keynes, 191
*Minder* (1979–94), 78–9
Miracle Communications, 145
Miracle Films, 145
Missing in Action, 220
*Moby Dick* (1977), 104
Mogul Communications, 147
moral panic, 5, 11, 12, 86, 95–7, 220–1
Motion Picture Association of America (MPAA), 138
Motion Picture Export Association of America (MPEAA), 78, 85
Mountain Video, 25, **26**, 27, 39, 45, 49, 99–100, 104, 105, 108, 139, 219, 220
Movie Gallery, 2–3
Mukesh, Mudra, 143–4
Multibroadcast, 65
'Multiple Retailer of the Year' award, 203
multiplex cinemas, 191–4
*Music & Video*, 36
Music Television (MTV), 161
music videos, 17, 19, 21–2, 26, 47, 161–2
musicals, 27
Muspratt, Iain, 175, 217
*Mutiny in the Southseas* (1965), 39
*My Beautiful Laundrette* (1984), 196–9, **197, 198**
*My Beautiful Video Shop* (1989), 195–9, **197, 198**
*My Video Party* (1983), 100, **101**

NASA, 22
national chains, 3, 174, 177–84, 188, 200, 201–5
National Viewers and Listeners Association (NVLA), 97, 135
*Natural Born Killers* (1994), 216
Nell, Alex, 183
Neon label, 158
Netflix, 1, 215, 217, 221, 222, 224
Netherlands, 142
Neves, Joshua, 4
*New Life in the Garden* (1979), 22
New Right, 12, 62, 68–73
New World, 150
Newman, Michael Z., 4, 44–5, 46

*Newsnight*, 86
Nicholson, Jack, 39, 44
*Night Fright* (1967), 110
nightclubs, 19
*Nightmare on Alcatraz* (1987), 154
*No Place to Hide* (1973), 39, 44
*Nobody's Boy* (1970), 100
*Noddy Goes to Toyland* (1963), 103
non-English language films, 73–5, 81–2, 83–4
Normak Holdings, 21
Northern Ireland, 200, 203
Norwich, 176
nostalgia, 1, 7, 74, 192, 221–4
Nottingham, 187–8
Nouveau Pictures, 221
Nova Home Video Entertainment, 25

Obscene Publications Act (OPA), 34, 95, 137, 138
Obscene Publications Squad, 113
Odyssey, 121, 146, 147
off-air recording, 5, 20–1, 136
Oldfield, Fred, 183
*One Flew over the Cuckoo's Nest* (1975), 44
*Only Fools and Horses* (1981–96), 79
*Opening of Misty Beethoven, The* (1976), 34
organised crime, 18, 78–80, 83
Orson Video, 81–2, 83
outward growth, 139, 140–6

PACE, 147, 154
packaging, 40–3, **41**, **43**, 108–9, **109**, 115–22, **118**, **120**, 150–6, **155**
Palace, 123, 146, 220
Palace-Virgin-Gold label, 161
Paramount, 26, 32, 136, 158–9
Parkfield, 188–200, 219
*Party Laughs* (1982), 100
*Patrick* (1978), 45
Payne, Brian, 112
Peisinger, Jason, 161
Peters, Tony, 36
Petley, Julian, 5, 110, 135, 137, 138–9, 153
Petrie, Duncan, 198
Philips N1500, 19–20
*Pieces* (1981), 122
Pina, Joseph, 68–71, **72**

Pinewood Studios, 42, 143
*Pinocchio* (1971), 106
Pioneer Video Emporium, 75–7, **76**
piracy, 11, 12, 27, 64, 77–86, 105, 133–4, **134**, 221
*Pirates of the Mississippi* (1963), 39
*Plague* (1978), 115
Pleasure Tapes USA, 25
PMA Video, 39, 73
Pocket Money Video, 220
police raids, 110, 112–13, 122–3, 137–8
*Police Stop!* (1994), 220
*Poltergeist* (1982), 123
Polygram, 103–4, 160
popcorn, 45, 75
*Popeye and Friends in Outer Space* (1961), 105
*Popeye the Sailor Man* cartoons, 104
*Popular Video*, 36, 78, 79, 103–4
pornography, 5, 7, 11, 17, 18, 28–31, 33–8, 77–8, 85, 95, 134–5, 137, 178, 194, 216, 220; *see also* adult films
Portland Video, 158
posters, 9, 40, 43, 122, 150, 151, **198**, 198–9
Potters Video, 180
power selling, 36, 108–10, 115–16, 133, 150, 153, 155
Precision Video, 146
Premier Video, 115–16
price-based marketing, 98, 103–7
price reductions, 139–40, 147, 152, 158–60, 200
'princes of industry', 12, 64, 70, 86
privatisation, 64, 79
Probe Video, 26, 33–4
professionalism, 31, 40, 42, 83, 173, 175, 177, 201, 203
Psycho Video, 116–17
Pyramid Productions, 115, 146

Quayle, David, 177–8, 180–2, 202
Quick Video, 153–4

racism, 82–5, 199
racking, 139, 174–7, 178, 184, 217
Radio Rentals, 63, 65
*Radio Times*, 20

*Raiders of the Lost Ark* (1981), 159
Rank Audio Visual, 25, 98, 136
Rankin/Bass Productions, 105
RCA/Columbia, 113, 161
reality shows, 220
*Rebel Rousers, The* (1970), 39, 44
rebranding, 143, 145, 147, 178, 183; *see also* branding
recession, 7, 11, 12, 50, 62–73, 203–4, 219
Redemption Films, 221
Rediffusion, 65, 174
regional chains, 3, 177, 180, 183, 200
Relay, 114
'Rent British' campaign, 194
rental-by-mail, 215, 217
rental charts, 136
rental fees, 67, 74, 81, 103, 175–6, 200
re-releases, 100, 108, 116, 147–56, 220
revenue sharing, 217, 219
Rex, 158
Richard Price Television Associates (RPTA), 97–8, 105
*Rip Van Winkle* (1978), 42, 99
Ripley, Bev, 124
Rippledale, 34
Ritz Video Film Hire, 3, 11, 180–3, **181**, 188–90, 194, 200, 201–2, 203–5, 215
Ritzer, George, 3
*Robin Hood* (1971), 104
*Robin Hood* (1972), 106
*Rocky* (1976), 44
*Rocky II* (1979), 44
*Rocky III* (1982), 79
Rozella, David, 173
Rumbelows, 65
Ryan, Michael, 186

S. Gold and Son, 114, 137
Sachs, Andrew, 86
sales charts, 95, 123, 136, 162
Sandbrook, Dominic, 7–8, 8
Sarkar, Bhaskar, 4
Satanica, 221
satellite television, 140
*Saturday Night Fever* (1977), 136
school holidays, 98–102
science fiction, 23, 27, 28, 108, 115
Scotland, 200

Scott, Peter, 147
Screen Entertainment Ltd, 146
*Screen International*, 31–2, 124, 142–3, 173, 180
Scripglow, 137
Seaman, Tony, 78
Select Video, 105
self-regulation, 138
self-starters, 64, 70, 78, 85, 200
sell-through market, 12, 116, 125, 133, 140, 156–63, 177, 188–9, 196, 199, 219–21
sensationalism, 113, 115–16, 196
*Sentinel, The* (1976), 123
*Sex at 7000ft* (1977), 37
sex comedies, 27–8, 147
sex industry, 18, 28–31, 34–6
sexploitation films, 25, 34, 43
sexual violence, 116, 119–22, 154
Sheer Entertainment, 147
Sheffield, 183
*Sight and Sound*, 9
Silver Screen Video, 187–8
Simmonds, Derek, 32
Singh, Gurharpal, 76
*Sins within the Family* (1975), 37
16mm films, 18, 25, 32, 34, 156
*Sleeping Beauty* (1972), 106
Smith, Tim, 137–8
snack foods, 45, 75–7
*Snow White* (1955), 27
*Snow White* (1972), 106
*Snuff* (1976), 95, 119
soap operas, 47
Society for Film Distributors, 85
Soho, 28–31, 34–6
*Someone Behind the Door* (1971), 27
Something Special, 21
Sony, 19, 20, 81, 105, 161
Sony U-matic, 19
Soramäki, Martti, 23, 123
*Sound of Music, The* (1965), 32
South Africa, 141, 142
South Asian diaspora, 73–7, 81–5, 196, 198–9
space exploration, 22
Spain, 142
SPAR, 189, 217

# INDEX

*Spare Rib*, 119
*Specters* (1987), 154
Spectrum label, 103–4
Spielberg, Steven, 28
sports videos, 19, 21–2, 25, 219
spy films, 27, 158
*SS Experiment Camp* (1976), 95, 108–10, **109**
staff training, 179
Stallone, Sylvester, 39, 44, 79
star actors, 27, 31, 39, 44
*Star Trek II: The Wrath of Khan* (1982), 158
*Star Wars* (1977), 32, 39
Starcurve, 39
Steinhardt, Daisy, 223
stereotypes, 8, 38, 64, 78–9, 135, 173, 178–9
stigmatisation, 10, 12–13, 28–9, 34, 66, 84–5, 178–9, 186, 194
Stone, Elliot, 178–9, 180
*Stranger Things* (2016–), 9
streaming, 1, 224
*Street War* (1974), 115
Stringer, Julian, 40
Struzan, Drew, 150
sublabels, 158, 219
*Sun*, 216
Sundance Institute, 1, 8–9
*Sunday in the Country* (1974), 23
Super 8 films, 18, 25, 32, 33, 34, 39, 156
superheros, 23, 104, 220
*Superman* cartoons, 104, 220
*Superman II* (1980), 104
supermarkets, 221
'Superstore 88' campaign, 184–8, 204
'Superstore 89' campaign, 188, 204
Sweden, 140–1
symbol groups, 189–200, 204–5

Taboo Films International, 26
*Tales of La Manca* (1980), 99
*Tales of Magic*, 104
Tannock, Stuart, 221–2
Taylor, Dave, 222–3
Taylor, Kenneth, 182
TCR Video, 26
technicians' strike, 47

*Techno Police* (1982), 108
Tele-Cine X (TCX), 26, 34–7, 38
Telefusion, 65
*Television & Home Video*, 28, **30**, **48**, 48–9, 83
*Television & Video Retailer*, 32, 102–3
television channels, 18, 47–9, 140, 161
television listings magazines, 20–1
television movies, 39, 45, 102, 121
television schedules, 18, 46–7, 98
Tenner, Mike, 19, 21, 47, 49, **62**
Terry Blood, 114
Test Card, 49
Thatcher, Margaret, 11, 64, 68–73, 78–9, 186, 196, 197, 200
theatrical distribution, 18, 27–8, 34, 139, 145, 147
*They Paid with Bullets* (1969), 23–5
*Thing, The* (1982), 123
Thompson, Kristin, 196
Thorn EMI, 44, 46, 65, 95, 123, 146
thrillers, 26, 27, 158
*Thumbelina*, 105
time-shifting, 5, 20–1, 136
*Tin Tin* cartoons, 104
*Tiny Tots Fun Time* (c.1982), 100
Titles, 200
Toll, Mike, 201, 202
*Tom & Jerry* cartoons, 98
*Tomorrow Man, The* (1979), 45
*Town Called Bastard, A* (1971), 115–16
trade associations, 71–3, 85, 122, 138, 175, 184–5, 189–90
trade discounts, 136, 175, 189, 217
trade shows, 73, 123, 140, 142
*Treasure Island* (1976), 99
*Treasures of the Snow* (1980), 108
*Turn of the Screw, The* (1974), 117, **118**
*TV Times*, 20–1
20th Century Flicks, 221–3, **222**, 224
20th Century Fox, 25, 31, 39, 78, 136; *see also* CBS/Fox
21st Century Video, 26, 27, 156–8, **157**, 159

Uganda, 73, 75, 76–7
unemployment, 50, 62–3, 74
United Artists, 32, 39, 44, 98

United States, 1–4, 9, 17, 19, 27, 31–6, 40, 44–5, 62, 75, 78, 138, 141, 142, 158, 161, 178–83, 191, 194, 201, 221, 223–4
Universal Studios, 20, 26, 32
Upton, Julian, 5, 39, 63

*Variety*, 17, 21
VCL, 21, 22, 26, 45, **48**, 48–9, 98, 100–4, 139, 141–6, **145**, 156–8, 161, 162–3
VCR ownership, 17, 19, 21, 27, 34, 62–3, 160
Venezuela, 204
Vestron, 160, 161, 184
VHS, 19, 20, 81, 156, 220, 224
Vidcom, 140
Video at Home scheme, 65
Video Box Office, 175, 217, **218**
Video Brokers, 105
*Video Business*, 33, 70, 80–1, 84, 95, 98, 113, 115, 133, 136–7, 152, 174–7, 182–8, 191, 203
Video Club, The, 65, 66, **67**
video clubs, 12, 17, 46, 62, 64–6, 85, 98, 156
Video Collection, The, 159–63, 219–20
*Video Comic* (1980), 100, **101**
Video Exchange Club, 66
Video Film Organisation (VFO), 112
Video Flicks, 3
video games, 217, 223
Video House, The, 183
Video Instant Picture Company (VIPCO), 25, 45, 95, 110, 116–17, 152, 221
video libraries, 12, 19, 62, 65–6
Video Magic, 200, 203
video nasties, 5–12, 86, 95–7, 108–25, 133–7, 139, 142, 153–5, 173, 191, 194, 200, 216, 220–1
Video on Demand, 215, 222–3
Video Packaging Review Committee (VPRC), 152–3, 156
*Video Play-box 1* (1980), 97–8
Video Programme Distributors (VPD), 112, 141, 146
Video Recordings Act (VRA), 5, 10, 12, 95, 112, 124, 133–40, 142, 146, 150, 152–6, 162, 173, 186

video rental shops, 1–4, 11, 13, 63–86, 96, 106, 113–14, 137–8, 173–205, 215–19, 221–3
*Video Retailer*, 44, 109, 122, 139
*Video Review*, 37, 62, 66
video rights, 22, 38–9, 81, 139–41, 147, 156, 220
Video Shuttle, 183
Video Software Show, 123
Video Standards Council (VSC), 190
Video Store, The, 200, 203
Video Tape Centre (VTC), 98, 139, 140
Video Trade Association (VTA), 71–3, 138, 162, 173, 175, 176, 184–5, 189–90, 200
*Video Trade Weekly*, 155
Video Unlimited, 65, 66–7, **67**, 73, 137
*Video Viewer*, 110
Video Warehouse International, 25
*Video World*, 22, 32, 46, 66, 79, 83, 84, 86
VideOdyssey, 221–3, 224
Videoform, 145–6, 159, 174, 189
Videomedia, 26, 98, 137
Videorama label, 25
Videoserve, 174–5, 178
VideoSpace, 139
Vidi Vidio, 175–6
*Violators, The* (1983), 122
Virgin Records, 160
Virgin Vision, 145–6
Vision on Video, 25–6, 27
voluntary censorship scheme, 112–13, 138

Wade, Graham, 17
Walton Video, 32, 33, 38, 124
Warner Bros, 26, 31, 33, 219, 220
Warner Communications, 32, 39, 79, 143
Warner Home Video (WHV), 26, 32, 39, 40–2, 95, 98, 113, 123, 136, 156, 158
Wasser, Fredrick, 4, 10, 62, 161
Welles, Orson, 23
West Coast Video, 2, 178–83, **180**, 191, 194
westerns, 23, 27, 45, 115–16, 119, 158
W. H. Smith, 65, 160, 162
*What Shall We Give Them to Eat?* (1980), 22
Whelan, John, 70
*When Every Day was the Fourth of July* (1978), 39
White, David, 223

*White Cargo from Hong Kong* (1964), 39
Whitehouse, Mary, 97, 116
*Who Killed Doc Robin?* (1948)
wholesalers, 44, 68–70, 73, 75, 106, 114, 137, 156, 174–5, 189–90
Wober, Mallory, 4, 21
*Wonder Wall* (1968), 25
Woodstock Video, 25
*Woody Woodpecker and his Friends*, 104
Woolworths, 11, 65, 159–60, 162, 163, 177, 188

World of Video 2000, 110, 124
World Video Incorporated, 25
Wyatt, Justin, 120
Wynd-Up, 69, 114

Xtra-Vision, 3, 200, 203

*Zombie Creeping Flesh* (1980), 142
*Zombie Flesh Eaters* (1980), 9, 116, 117, **118**, 221
*Zorro*, 105